Lockheed's SR-71 'Blackbird' Family

A-12, F-12, M-21, D-21, SR-71

Lockheed Martin

James Goodall and Jay Miller

An imprint of
Ian Allan Publishing

Lockheed's SR-71 'Blackbird' Family
© 2002 Jim Goodall and Jay Miller
ISBN 1 85780 138 5

Published by Midland Publishing
4 Watling Drive, Hinckley, LE10 3EY, England
Tel: 01455 254 490 Fax: 01455 254 495
E-mail: midlandbooks@compuserve.com

Midland Publishing and Aerofax are imprints of
Ian Allan Publishing Ltd

Worldwide distribution (except North America):
Midland Counties Publications
4 Watling Drive, Hinckley, LE10 3EY, England
Telephone: 01455 254 450 Fax: 01455 233 737
E-mail: midlandbooks@compuserve.com
www.midlandcountiessuperstore.com

North American trade distribution:
Specialty Press Publishers & Wholesalers Inc.
39966 Grand Avenue, North Branch, MN 55056
Tel: 651 277 1400 Fax: 651 277 1203
Toll free telephone: 800 895 4585
www.specialtypress.com

Printed in England by
Ian Allan Printing Ltd
Riverdene Business Park, Molesey Road,
Hersham, Surrey, KT12 4RG

This book is dedicated to Lou Schalk,
the first A-12 pilot and the first "BlackBird" 3.0
Mach pilot. May 29, 1926-August 16, 2002

Photograph on the title page:
**Perhaps the most remarkable aeronautical engineer
of all time...the late Clarence L. "Kelly" Johnson is
seen standing in front of his career zenith, the inimitable Lockheed SR-71A.** Jim Goodall collection

Contents

Introduction 3

Chapters
  1 CL-400 and *Suntan* 5
  2 *Cygnus, Fish, Gusto, Kingfish,
     Oxcart,* A-12 11
  3 AF-12/YF-12A Long-Range
     Interceptor 35
  4 *Tagboard,* D-21, M-21 45
  5 *Senior Crown,* SR-71 57
  6 Pratt & Whitney JT11D/J58
     Bleed Bypass Turbojet Engine 91

Aircraft Histories, Chronologies,
  Dispositions, Personnel, etc. 99

Three-View Drawings 110

In Colour:
  A-12, F-12, D-21, M-21, SR-71 113

Photograph below:
**The first Lockheed A-12, Article 121, inside the
Skunk Works Building 82 manufacturing facility
at the airport in Burbank, California.**
Jim Goodall collection

Introduction

The post-World War II border closures of Soviet Russia-dominated eastern European countries that resulted in a rapid deterioration in diplomatic relations and a rise in Cold War angst, quickly created an ever-widening gap in Western intelligence resources that had, historically, provided considerable insight into the growth and technological status of the Soviet military/industrial complex.

During an extended period beginning in the late 1940s and culminating in the first overflights of Russia by the U-2 during the mid-1950s, a variety of aerial platforms were utilized to make short-range penetrations into Soviet airspace in futile attempts to acquire usable intelligence. The limited data acquired by these aircraft, coupled with the narrow spectrum of human intelligence (humint) resources that were then available, provided only tantalizing glimpses into the Soviet military and its operational capabilities through early 1956.

In the interim, over 50 US military aircraft, including Boeing B-29s, Boeing B-47s, Boeing B-50s, Douglas C-47s, Lockheed C-121s, Lockheed P2Vs, Martin B-57s, Martin P4Ms, and a variety of other oftentimes obscure allied aircraft – both manned and unmanned – were lost as a result of these clandestine missions.

The toll was embarrassingly high. Over 200 US military and government personnel were killed or missing and the resulting data was rarely timely and almost always of mediocre quality or questionable accuracy. More pointedly, it was becoming ever more difficult for the US Government to keep from the public eye these failed overt acts of espionage and the loss of life that often accompanied them.

The initial response arising from these potentially volatile and always illicit incursions was the enormously successful Lockheed *Skunk Works*-developed U-2. A purpose-built aircraft specifically designed to overfly unfriendly countries and penetrate denied airspace, the U-2 was the hardware result of a government decision to proceed with a highly unorthodox sensor system platform optimized to fly higher than any jet-propelled aircraft had ever flown before. It was to fly so high, in fact, that it would effectively be invulnerable to all known air defense systems.

Following a gestation that was rushed along by an indefatigable Lockheed engineering team and the man who is arguably the greatest American aircraft designer of the twentieth century, Clarence L. "Kelly" Johnson, the first U-2 was delivered clandestinely by Douglas C-124 in early 1955 to a newly created flight-test facility at Groom Dry Lake, Nevada. With noted Lockheed company test pilot Tony LeVier at the controls, this aircraft, CIA Article 341, took to the air for the first time during the afternoon of August 4. Almost exactly one year later, the first U-2s were deployed to England and declared operational. A few months later, while operating from Wiesbaden, Germany, they embarked on their first flights over the Soviet Union.

Over the following four years, the U-2's success as a sensor system platform became the stuff of legends. Until the fateful day on May 1, 1960, when CIA pilot Francis Gary Powers was blown from the sky by a barrage of surface-to-air missiles near the heart of continental Russia, the U-2 had gone about its secret mission with relative impunity. No other aircraft in history had ever been so consistently successful in avoiding interception over such a heavily defended target.

The U-2's story has since been thoroughly documented in several excellent books by such noted authors as Chris Pocock and Norman Polmar, and it is likely there will be more to come. Suffice it to say that its accomplishments are without peer in world history, and that its undeniable successes laid the groundwork for the subject aircraft of this monograph.

Though the U-2's altitude performance unquestionably placed it outside the threat zones of any known fighter or surface-to-air missile system in the world at the time of its mid-1950s debut, Lockheed's "Kelly" Johnson, the CIA's Richard Bissell, and the US State Department's Allan Dulles, as well as President Dwight Eisenhower – all were aware that technological advances almost certainly would eliminate this advantage in a relatively short period of time.

In fact, Russian knowledge of the U-2's existence – as well as its purpose – almost certainly expedited the introduction of weapons capable of shooting it down. Perhaps most importantly, it was determined that the loss of a U-2 while overflying Russia proper would be an extremely serious and politically embarrassing event with potentially confrontational overtones, but that the risk was worth the intelligence that was to be gained.

With these issues in mind, it became readily apparent to all who were intimate with the U-2 that a follow-on sensor platform with considerably greater performance capabilities was desirable – if the addictive flow of intelligence that was being generated by the U-2 was to be continued.

Several studies now were undertaken by US intelligence community and other US government teams (in particular, the US Air Force) in an effort to ascertain the best of the many reconnaissance platform options that might be available. Concurrently, a number of aircraft manufacturers, including Bell Aircraft Corporation, Boeing, Goodyear, General Dynamics, and Lockheed attempted to generate "paper" aircraft that would meet the forthcoming requirement.

Lockheed's efforts, still under the auspices of the then little-known Advanced Development Projects office referred to in-house unofficially as the *Skunk Works*, had been ongoing unabated even while work on the U-2 continued. An interim series of subsonic designs, under the codename *Gusto*, resulted in several serious configuration studies, including the penultimate *Gusto 2*. This latter machine, an all-wing configuration reminiscent of the World War II-vintage German Horten Ho/Go 229, was a twin-engine aircraft optimized not only for high-altitude performance like its predecessor, but also for reduced radar cross-section (RCS). Materials and configuration technology were all oriented to lower the chances of the aircraft being located and tracked by ground and airborne radar systems, and considerable work was undertaken toward this end.

Gusto 2 eventually proved a dead-end, primarily because its altitude capability offered little improvement over extant U-2 models and its vulnerability was reduced only slightly as a result of its somewhat lower RCS, but its successor, which in fact had moved along in parallel, would eventually prove anything but.

This, then, is the story – as gleaned from Lockheed and various private sector files – of what is unquestionably the most heralded aircraft of the twentieth century. It is, in fact, arguably the most important aircraft story of all time, primarily because it is about an astonishing technological achievement accomplished during a time when computers were complex behemoths of limited capability and the digital era was still a quarter century from conception. It can be stated, with some degree of certainty, that there will never be another conventional manned aircraft family quite like it.

James Goodall and Jay Miller
September 2002

Acknowledgements

The authors would like to thank the following for their assistance in the gathering of information and photographs for this book: Dick Abrams, Ed Baldwin Family, Ben Bowles, Buddy Brown, Ron Bullard, Fred Carmody, Glenn Chapman, Ken Collins, Paul Crickmore, Roger Cripliver, Joe Daley, Vincent Dolson, Joe Donoghue, Jim Eastham, Evan Elliott, Bill Fox, Robert J. Gilliland, Nora Goodall, Arne Gunderson, Cargill Hall, Leland Haynes, Eric Hehs, Tom Holtus, Marty Isham, Tony Landis (special thanks), Jack Layton, Lockheed Martin, Tom Long, Denny Lombard (special thanks), Mike Machat, Charles Mayer, Peter Merlin, Jerry Miller, Susan Miller, Bob Murphy, Frank Murray, Steve Myatt, Bill Park, Dennis Parks, Chris Pocock, Tom Pugh, Ben Rich, Brian Rogers, Mick Roth, Hal Rupard, Lou Schalk, Paul Suhler, Dennis Sullivan, Mele Vojvodich, Jim Walborn, and Bob Widmer.

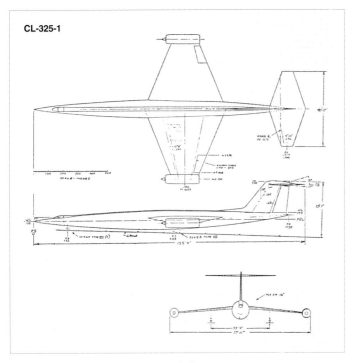

CL-325-1

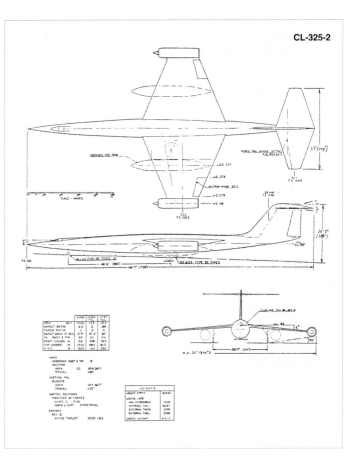

CL-325-2

Above left and right: The two predecessor designs leading up to the CL-400, the CL-325-1 and the CL-325-2. The former differed from the latter in being larger and in having a single liquid hydrogen tank. Noteworthy are the external liquid hydrogen tanks on the CL-325-2. Lockheed Martin/Miller Collection

Below: The CL-400 was the penultimate design giving birth to the legendary "Blackbird" 3.0 Mach-capable aircraft family. Hydrogen powered, it proved an exercise in futility for the *Skunk Works* when range and logistical problems proved insurmountable. Lockheed Martin/Miller Collection

Drawings not to scale.

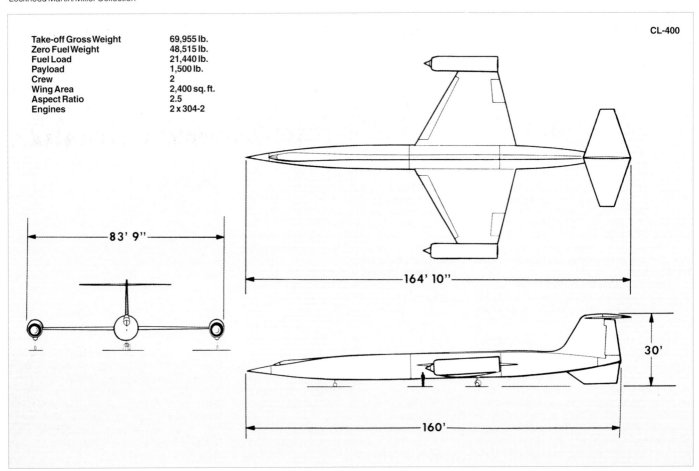

CL-400

Take-off Gross Weight	69,955 lb.
Zero Fuel Weight	48,515 lb.
Fuel Load	21,440 lb.
Payload	1,500 lb.
Crew	2
Wing Area	2,400 sq. ft.
Aspect Ratio	2.5
Engines	2 x 304-2

Chapter One

CL-400 and *Suntan*

Of the many aircraft whose origins can be traced back to Lockheed's renowned *Skunk Works*, none is more significant than the inimitable A-12. More than any other aircraft, this titanium masterpiece – the first in history capable of sustained flight at three times the speed of sound – represents the apex of aeronautical engineering in the twentieth century. This is true not only at Lockheed, but at every significant aircraft design bureau across the globe. Today, some four decades following its first flight, the A-12 remains the aircraft by which all others are judged.

The A-12 story began with the realization in the late 1940s that there was a US intelligence community shortfall that adversely impacted the country's decision-making abilities at all levels of government. Without fundamental knowledge of the status of foreign military services and their associated technology, it was all but impossible to assess what would be required indigenously to counter or offset any perceived threat. Additionally, and perhaps as importantly, critical issues impacting international diplomacy were similarly hindered by this intelligence gap.

Thus it was that during 1953, the seed was planted that eventually gave birth to the first *Skunk Works*-conceived strategic reconnaissance aircraft design, the CL-282. Arguably the progenitor of all the famous Lockheed machines to follow, this obscure F-104 derivative led eventually to the most successful subsonic reconnaissance platform in US history, the U-2. Overflying virtually every square inch of the globe during an operational career that now spans nearly half a century and continues unabated as these words are written, this aircraft remains without peer in the world.

As successful as the U-2 has become, it is somewhat ironic to note that, early in its operational career, it was predicted both by Lockheed engineers and members of the US intelligence community that it would have a relatively short service life. Though its extraordinary cruise altitude capability of 75,000 feet rendered it a difficult if not impossible to intercept target in light of late 1950s-vintage antiaircraft weaponry, many were acutely aware that such invulnerability almost certainly would be short-lived.

From 1956 to 1960, the initial photographic product of the overflights undertaken by the U-2 proved extraordinary. The aircraft's ability to penetrate unfriendly airspace while photographing critical strategic targets proved a windfall for US intelligence. For the first time since the end of World War II a window into military and domestic development in critical countries that included Russia, China, and North Korea, was finally open to those with a need to know. So many questions were answered in such a short period of time, it became difficult for then-President Dwight Eisenhower and others in his administration to keep in perspective the U-2's predicted short-term operational utility. The capabilities of the U-2's all-seeing cameras were highly addictive. It wasn't until the shootdown of Francis Gary Powers over central Russia on May 1, 1960, that the harsh reality of its ephemeral overflight career was brought home to roost.

Fortunately, work on a successor to the U-2 had been ongoing at Lockheed almost from the beginning of its design initiation. Clarence L. "Kelly" Johnson, the already-legendary engineer who presided over the hand-picked teams that created the P-38, the P-80, and the F-104, had also given birth to an enigmatic prototype development office hidden within the enormous confines of Lockheed's production facilities in Burbank, California, and eventually to become known worldwide as the *Skunk Works*. Created in 1943 to design, build, and flight test in extraordinary secrecy and in the shortest possible time the first truly successful US jet-powered fighter, the P-80, the *Skunk Works* would not resurface until some ten years later as the protective umbrella that kept from public scrutiny U-2 development and flight testing

Concurrent to the U-2 work, Johnson and his engineering team began exploring other avenues of opportunity. At least one of these eventually would come full circle as the point of origin for the world's first aircraft capable of cruising at 3.0 Mach. It is thus germane to the history of Lockheed's extraordinary "Blackbird" family – as these aircraft were much later nicknamed – to recount the development of a predecessor aircraft known as the CL-400.

Suntan:

The use of hydrogen as a fuel for aircraft powerplants first surfaced in the US as a viable option near the end of World War II. A most noteworthy study, undertaken by Alexis Lemmon, Jr. of the Office of Scientific Research and Development (OSRD) initiated during 1944 and released during May of 1945, concluded the combination of liquid hydrogen and liquid oxygen offered the highest specific impulse (thrust divided by total propellant flow rate; i.e., the amount of energy generated per quantity of propellant consumed) of any of the many fuels examined.

Lemmon's work became the primary postwar reference on the subject of unconventional fuels and proved particularly timely in light of the many propulsion options being explored during the immediate post-World War II period. German experiments with liquid oxygen and the subsequent evolutionary development of liquid hydrogen, led to the exploration of these fuels as a rocket oxidizer and propellant, respectively. The successes realized were significant, but they were achieved with considerable difficulty due to the severe logistical problems surrounding their production, containment, handling, and transport.

A variety of research programs, mostly under the auspices of Ohio State University working under the auspices of an Air Force contract, generated a considerable quantity of data related to the use of hydrogen fuel. Though the study concluded hydrogen was a viable option, nothing in the way of full-scale, flightworthy hardware to test these theories initially was built.

Concurrent with the Air Force effort, the Navy also pursued the use of hydrogen as a propellant, though specifically as it might be applied to a rocket for launching satellites into near-earth orbit. Retained to do the Navy's research were the Jet Propulsion Laboratory and Aerojet Engineering Corporation which presciently concluded that satellites were feasible and liquid hydrogen-based propulsion systems were practical powerplants.

Word of this effort eventually surfaced in Air Force circles. It was not long before similar studies, undertaken by the RAND Corporation and funded by the Air Force, reached similar conclusions. Aerojet Engineering, the Glenn L. Martin Company, and North American Aviation now contracted both with the Air Force and the Navy to build prototype liquid-hydrogen powerplants in order to study how they might be used in future satellite launch vehicles. By 1949, both Aerojet Engineering and the Jet Propulsion Laboratory had successfully tested rudimentary liquid hydrogen rockets.

Below: **A retouched photograph depicting the full-scale nose section mock-up of the CL-400 following completion at Lockheed's Burbank, California facility probably during 1958.** Lockheed Martin/Miller Collection

Sadly, these initial efforts proved somewhat premature, due in part to national economic difficulties and a short-sighted military bureaucracy. Regardless, the reference data the studies generated held the industry in good stead until the political climate was forced to change during 1950 as a result of military pressures in North and South Korea, China, Russia, and elsewhere. By now, the National Advisory Committee for Aeronautics (NACA) had initiated research into the use of hydrogen as a propulsion system fuel, and several national advisory groups, including the Scientific Advisory Board, had either directly or indirectly expressed an interest in further exploring hydrogen's unique properties.

On March 24, 1954, a British engineer by the name of Randolph Rae hand carried to the Air Force's New Developments offices at Wright Field a proposal he had drafted calling for the development of an aircraft powered by a unique liquid hydrogen-fueled engine. Rae held the patent on this engine, which he called *Rex I*. Basically a rocket-type gas generator driving a turbine (which in turn, through a geared transmission, drove a propeller), it required liquid hydrogen and liquid oxygen for fuel and oxidizer. The aircraft for which this engine was designed, described by Rae as "a lightly loaded low-speed plane having an exceptional L/D (lift over drag) characteristic," was optimized to cruise at an altitude in excess of 75,000 feet at a speed of about 500 mph.

Though the combined performance figures were stunning to say the least, the item of greatest interest to the Wright Field personnel responsible for reviewing the proposal was the *Rex I* engine itself. Over a period of time encompassing reviews by the Air Research and Development Command (ARDC) and many engineers at the Wright Air Development

Center, the Rae proposal, and in particular, the *Rex I* engine, became items of considerable controversy.

As it turned out, Rae's proposal could not have arrived at Wright Field at a more inopportune time. Its broad impact serendipitously touched upon sensitive issues in many Wright Field offices, not the least of which were those addressing the development of new powerplants, high-altitude airframes, the use of hydrogen fuel, and various subsystems that required high-altitude capability.

During the review of Rae's documents, Wright Field personnel voiced concerns over Rae's ability to bring the hardware to fruition, even in light of his formal association with the Summers Gyroscope Company. In the interim, a subdued but intense battle between the government, Rae, and the Garrett Corporation (which had quietly acquired Summers Gyroscope's interest in the Rae engine in order to obtain access to the *Rex I* patent) surfaced. This tug-of-war would continue throughout the rest of the *Rex* engine's tumultuous life.

Lockheed and the *Skunk Works* first entered this picture during mid-1954, when it was noted in the original Rae proposal that Lockheed would be provided $50,000 for airframe analysis. Concurrently, work was getting under way in the *Skunk Works* on the Model CL-282 which, as noted earlier, would lead to development of the definitive U-2 reconnaissance aircraft.

As this latter program progressed under the direction of the Central Intelligence Agency, Air Force analysts at Wright Field already had deduced that its ability to safely execute a mission over unfriendly territory would be time-limited because of expected advances in anti-aircraft technology and the unknown structural integrity issues of the air-

Above left and right: **The Pratt & Whitney Model 304 hydrogen expander engine was based on the company's standard J75 hydrocarbon-fueled engine.** Lockheed Martin via Goodall collection/Milier Collection

Below: **The Model 304 engine propulsion gas flow schematic.** Lockheed Martin/Miller Collection

frame. Additionally, concerns were expressed over the dependability of the powerplant, and the effectiveness of the experimental electronic countermeasures systems. Even before the U-2's first flight, the Central Intelligence Agency and the Air Force already were assessing replacement options.

During 1954, as work on the first U-2 progressed, "Kelly" Johnson expressed concern over the problem of fuel loss resulting from evaporation at high altitudes...and the adverse effect this would have on the aircraft's range. Consultations with Air Force engineers at Wright Field in Ohio, and Pratt & Whitney in Connecticut (builders of the U-2's J57-PW-37 turbojet engine), confirmed that conventional JP4 fuel would slowly evaporate as a result of "boiling" at the altitudes the U-2 was expected to achieve in cruising flight. A low-vapor-pressure fuel developed by Shell Oil Company eventually solved this problem, but perhaps more importantly, the meetings resulting in its development also served to expose Johnson to the attributes of hydrogen.

By mid-1955, Rae and the Garrett Corporation's problems with the Air Force had led to a stalemate resulting from the former's wish to execute both the airframe and powerplant development and the latter's desire to split the program into separate airframe and powerplant contracts (which was, in reality, the standard approach). Personal issues of patent infringement and division of work responsibility only added to the confusion, and it was not until October 1955 that contracts finally were let.

Though Rae and the Garrett Corporation assumed their initial differences with the Air Force now were resolved, the actual work statement from Wright Field, when it arrived several weeks later, quickly rekindled the original disagreement. Their belief that the proposed aircraft would be a high-altitude, long-range subsonic design had been mistaken; the Air Force contract called for a supersonic aircraft...with range of secondary importance. Lurking secretly in the background, as it turned out, was the Air Force's desire to create a replacement for the Central Intelligence Agency's still-untried Lockheed U-2.

Garrett, not wanting to forego the funding that had been allocated by the Air Force for the *Rex* engine (by now there were three jet

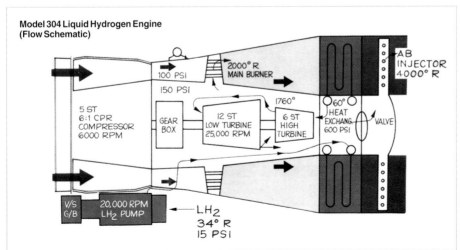

Model 304 Liquid Hydrogen Engine
(Flow Schematic)

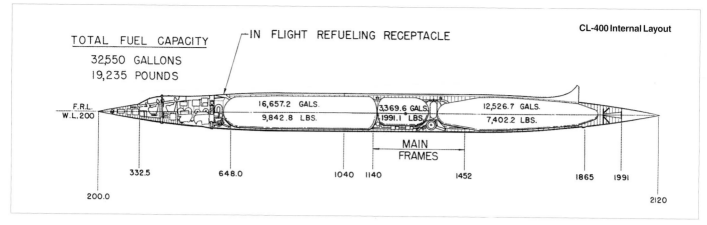

TOTAL FUEL CAPACITY
32,550 GALLONS
19,235 POUNDS

IN FLIGHT REFUELING RECEPTACLE

F.R.L.
W.L. 200

16,657.2 GALS.
9,842.8 LBS.

3,369.6 GALS.
1991.1 LBS.

12,526.7 GALS.
7,402.2 LBS.

MAIN FRAMES

200.0   332.5   648.0   1040 1140   1452   1865 1991   2120

versions being offered, including one for a supersonic cruise aircraft) elected to pursue an airframe study that had been given Rae during the negotiation process. A "Problem Statement for Aircraft Studies" dated November 7, 1955, resulted from this, and "Kelly" Johnson, because of the initial negotiations conducted during mid-1954, was invited to provide airframe input under a *Skunk Works* contract. Garret would provide size, weight, thrust, and specific fuel consumption figures to Lockheed, as well as engine pod dimension and technical data.

The *Skunk Works* engineering team, upon reviewing the Garrett data, concluded the proposed engines were not capable of providing the thrust levels required to meet the Air Force's performance specification. Agreements were then reached with Garrett on extrapolation of the data for engines of larger thrust, and specific fuel consumption as a function of Mach number. A cruise speed of 2.25 Mach was determined to be obtainable with engines providing 50 percent more thrust than those originally specified.

Above: **CL-400 fuselage cutaway provides detail of internal tank arrangement, camera bay location (with Type B camera installed), and tank capacities.** Lockheed Martin/Miller Collection

Below left: **CL-400 major component breakdown. Hydrogen tanks were independent units and not an integral part of the aircraft structure.** Lockheed Martin/Miller Collection

Below right: **A 4,000 gallon sump tank built for installation in the first CL-400, which was never completed.** Lockheed Martin/Miller Collection

The resulting size increase now forced the Air Force to re-evaluate the Garrett company's ability to build such an engine. Garrett had long been noted for small, auxiliary power unit-type turbine engines but had never built anything of the size now specified for the proposed hydrogen-fueled airplane.

Lockheed's *Skunk Works* study, released during January of 1956, contained two configurations for consideration. Both were powered by *Rex III* engines, which were optimized for supersonic flight. The first, referred to as the CL-325-1, had a straight, thin wing and a long, slender fuselage containing a single liquid hydrogen tank. The second, the CL-325-2, was smaller as a result of the use of jettisonable wing tanks to accommodate part of the liquid hydrogen load. Both were of conventional aluminum construction.

Information describing the two CL-325 configurations and the proposed *Rex III* engine was presented to the Air Force at Wright Field on February 15, 1956. The Air Force's reaction was unfavorable, not because of the quality of the presentation, but rather because the *Rex III*'s complexity was great and the ready availability of liquid hydrogen was decidedly questionable. Because of what now was perceived as an urgent requirement, Garrett's ability to design and produce an engine as complex as the *Rex III* in a "crash" program was considered highly unlikely. Though the company strongly contested these conclusions, on October 18, 1956, the Air Force issued a directive demanding that all *Rex* engine and all CL-325 work be stopped immediately except for completion of a final summary report.

Interest in hydrogen as an aircraft fuel did not die with the demise of the *Rex* engine program. Behind the scenes, other related programs had begun to gather momentum. A year before the *Rex*'s demise, following the completion of the various airframe design studies for Rae and the Garrett Corporation, "Kelly" Johnson and his *Skunk Works* team had begun hydrogen-fueled aircraft studies of their own in response to a continuing Air Force interest in developing a U-2 follow-on. During a Pentagon meeting with Lt. Gen. Donald Putt in early January of 1956 – even as the *Rex* program difficulties mounted – Johnson offered to build two prototype hydrogen-fueled aircraft powered by more conventional propulsion units. He guaranteed a first flight date within 18 months of contract signing. The proposed aircraft – based on the CL-325 – would be capable of cruising at an altitude of 99,384 feet and a speed of 2.50 Mach while having a range of 2,529 miles.

The Air Force – already somewhat frustrated at having to play a supporting role in the Central Intelligence Agency's U-2 operation – did not hesitate to confirm their strong interest in this latest *Skunk Works* offering...which potentially could serve as an Air Force-managed U-2 replacement. On January 18, 1956, Lt. Gen. Putt called a meeting to discuss the proposal with Lockheed representatives. In attendance were Lt. Gen. Clarence Irvine, then deputy chief of staff for materiel; Lt. Gen. Thomas Power, then head of the Air Research and Development Command; and Col. Norman Appold, then head of the Wright Air Development Center's powerplant laboratory.

During the meeting it was decided to fund Air Force studies to verify the feasibility of Johnson's proposal and to select a qualified manufacturer to design and develop a hydrogen-fueled engine. Appold, who was assigned the task of determining the latter, quickly

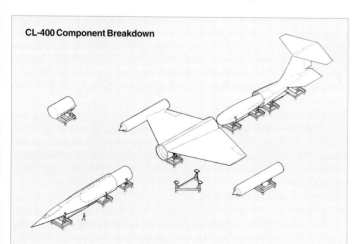

CL-400 Component Breakdown

CL-400-11 General Arrangement

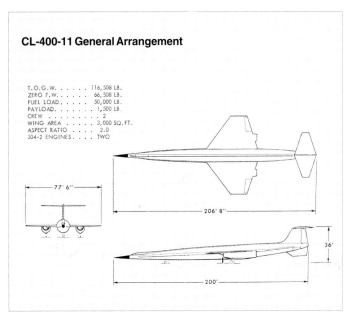

```
T.O.G.W. . . . . . 116,508 LB.
ZERO F.W. . . . . . 66,508 LB.
FUEL LOAD . . . . . 50,000 LB.
PAYLOAD . . . . . . 1,500 LB.
CREW . . . . . . . . 2
WING AREA . . . . . 3,000 SQ.FT.
ASPECT RATIO . . . . 2.0
304-2 ENGINES . . . TWO
```

77' 6"
206' 8"
36'
200'

CL-400-12 General Arrangement

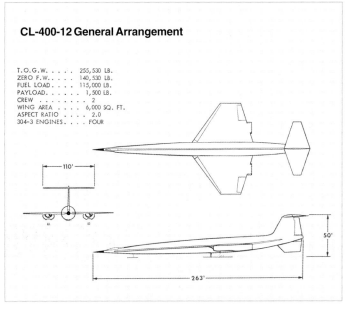

```
T.O.G.W. . . . . 255,530 LB.
ZERO F.W. . . . . 140,530 LB.
FUEL LOAD . . . . 115,000 LB.
PAYLOAD . . . . . 1,500 LB.
CREW . . . . . . . . 2
WING AREA . . . . 6,000 SQ. FT.
ASPECT RATIO . . . . 2.0
304-3 ENGINES. . . . FOUR
```

110'
263'
50'

CL-400-13 General Arrangement

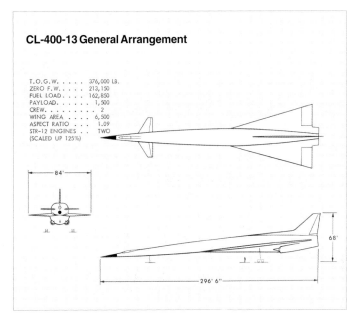

```
T.O.G.W. . . . . 376,000 LB.
ZERO F.W. . . . . 213,150
FUEL LOAD . . . . 162,850
PAYLOAD . . . . . 1,500
CREW . . . . . . . . 2
WING AREA . . . . 6,500
ASPECT RATIO . . . 1.09
STR-12 ENGINES . . TWO
(SCALED UP 125%)
```

84'
68'
296' 6"

CL-400-14 General Arrangement

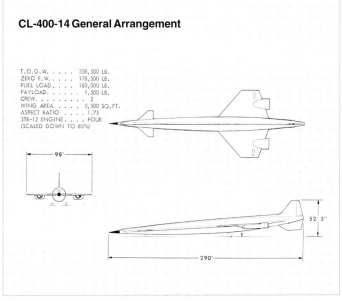

```
T.O.G.W. . . . . 358,500 LB.
ZERO F.W. . . . . 178,500 LB.
FUEL LOAD . . . . 180,000 LB.
PAYLOAD . . . . . 1,500 LB.
CREW . . . . . . . . 2
WING AREA . . . . 5,500 SQ.FT.
ASPECT RATIO . . . 1.75
STR-12 ENGINE . . . FOUR
(SCALED DOWN TO 85%)
```

98'
290'
52' 3"

CL-400-15JP General Arrangement

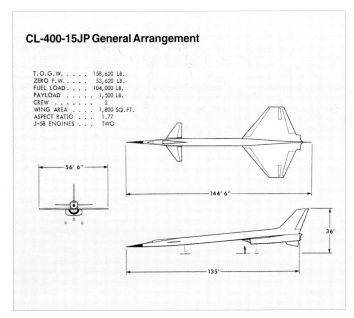

```
T.O.G.W. . . . . 158,620 LB.
ZERO F.W. . . . . 53,620 LB.
FUEL LOAD . . . 104,000 LB.
PAYLOAD . . . . 1,500 LB.
CREW . . . . . . 2
WING AREA . . . . 1,800 SQ.FT.
ASPECT RATIO . . . 1.77
J-58 ENGINES . . . TWO
```

56' 6"
144' 6"
36'
135'

Relative Size Comparison

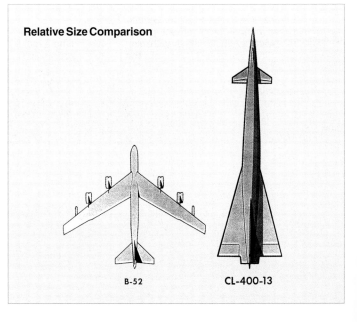

B-52   CL-400-13

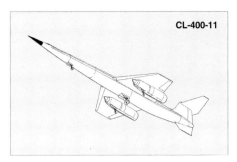

CL-400-11

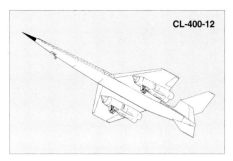

CL-400-12

narrowed the field to General Electric and Pratt & Whitney. Each company then was given two weeks to put together a proposal. By February 20, these had been received and reviewed and the Pratt & Whitney design had been chosen over General Electric's for further study. A six-month contract was signed on May 1, and on the same date, Lockheed was similarly given a study contract to pursue airframe configuration and materials options. As both companies already had initiated design work on their own, when the contracts were negotiated they were made retroactive to cover already incurred costs.

Lt. Col. John Seaberg, who by this time already had made his mark as a key figure in the birth of the U-2 program, now became involved in the new hydrogen-fueled aircraft project, directly under Appold. Seaberg would be responsible for airframe development and total program coordination. He would be assisted by Maj. Alfred Gardner, who would manage engine development, and Capt. Jay Brill, who would manage logistics. This team worked initially at Wright Field before moving to ARDC headquarters in Baltimore, Maryland, during mid-1956.

Only twenty-five people were given special access to the new program. With a top-secret classification, *Suntan* – as the new aircraft was codenamed – was considered militarily and politically sensitive primarily because its mission objectives required covert overflights of "unfriendly" territory.

Additionally, in order for Lockheed's *Skunk Works* to design and build the proposed prototypes in the shortest possible time, it was considered necessary for a "no-constraints" environment to be created and assiduously maintained. Too much access to the program invited scrutiny, and scrutiny implied committees, changes, and consequently, lost time and increased cost. In essence, and as per previous *Skunk Works* practice, it was reiterated that "too many cooks would spoil the broth." Authorizations allowing the *Suntan* team to waive normal procurement procedures and to award contracts directly with minimal review thus became part of the mechanism for success. It later was estimated that many months and thousands of dollars were saved as a result.

Extraordinary measures were taken to conceal *Suntan* from unauthorized personnel. The ARDC's *Suntan* team periodically changed project numbers, contracts were writ-

ten through other Air Force offices, and in Burbank, *Suntan* workers in the *Skunk Works* were isolated from their peers and cleared to operate independently of the normal design and manufacturing process. Special measures also were taken to prevent identification of *Suntan* visitors from the Air Force and other government agencies. All documentation and related paperwork were kept to a minimum or dispensed with altogether.

During 1956, Air Force enthusiasm for what Lockheed now was calling the CL-400 resulted in a contract for four production aircraft in addition to the original two prototypes and a single static test article. Paralleling this, Pratt & Whitney pursued development of their Model 304-2 engine that weighed 6,270 pounds and provided 9,450 pounds thrust at sea level (5,940 pounds of thrust at 2.50 Mach and 100,000 feet altitude). It utilized conventional intake air for the combustion process and liquid hydrogen for fuel. Relatively inefficient, it gave the CL-400 a range of only 2,500 miles...an Achilles heel from which the program would never recover.

Pratt & Whitney's design and development work on the Model 304 engine was accommodated at the company's facility in East Hartford, Connecticut. The first engine was completed on August 18, 1957, and shortly afterwards was shipped to the company's newly completed factory in West Palm Beach, Florida, for static testing. Model 304 ground runs were initiated there on September 11, 1957, using nitrogen to check the fuel system and rotating machinery such as bearings and seals. Gaseous hydrogen and liquid hydrogen shortly afterwards were used as fuels. The first run series lasted through October resulting in 4½ hours of running time including 38 minutes on liquid hydrogen. A second run series was started on December 20 following inspection.

Additional runs were continued into July at which time a major bearing, turbine, and heat exchanger failure effectively destroyed the engine. A second Model 304-1 had been placed on the static test stand several months after the first, with a first run being undertaken on January 16, 1958. Work with this engine continued into April, at which time it was disassembled for inspection. An improved engine, the Model 304-2 was run for the first time on

June 24, 1958, followed by another Model 304-1 test series and the delivery of several additional test engines in various configurations. In all cases, the tests went exceptionally well and the Air Force and Pratt & Whitney began to have considerable confidence in hydrogen-fueled powerplants.

While airframe and powerplant work continued at Lockheed and Pratt & Whitney, the logistical problems associated with the production and transport of liquid hydrogen were confronted by the Air Force's *Suntan* team and Lockheed's *Skunk Works* operation. Special liquid hydrogen transportation trailers, designated U-1 and U-2, were designed and built by the Cambridge Corporation and a special hydrogen liquefaction plant was placed in operation near Pratt & Whitney's Florida facility during the fall of 1957 (the latter was operated under contract by the Air Products Corporation). Two years later, during January of 1959, a larger liquefaction plant was built next to the old and placed in operation (ironically, by that date *Suntan* already had come to an untimely end).

Following the initial phase of study and experimentation, *Suntan* proceeded on schedule. About $95 million had been allocated by the Air Force, and construction of miscellaneous components had been initiated by the *Skunk Works*. Lockheed in fact had ordered no less than 2½ miles of aluminum extrusion; Pratt & Whitney was moving ahead with construction and static testing of various Model 304 engines; the Massachusetts Institute of Technology was working on an inertial guidance system; and Air Products Corporation was moving ahead with construction of the aforementioned large hydrogen liquefaction plant.

By early 1957, the technological problems lurking in *Suntan*'s background had begun to haunt it. Within six months of its formal approval by the Air Force, a difference of technical opinion over achievable range had surfaced as an item of considerable contention between the service and "Kelly" Johnson. Surprisingly, Johnson – the man who had sold the aircraft to the Air Force in the first place – after careful analysis of the airframe, the powerplant, the fuel, and the proposed mission requirements, had determined that severe range limitations could not be overcome with

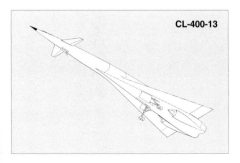

CL-400-13

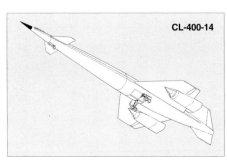

CL-400-14

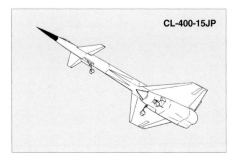

CL-400-15JP

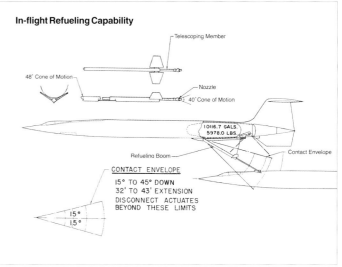

In-flight Refueling Capability

CONTACT ENVELOPE
15° TO 45° DOWN
32' TO 43' EXTENSION
DISCONNECT ACTUATES
BEYOND THESE LIMITS

extant technology. He concluded that the program should be terminated in favor of a more conventional hydrocarbon-fueled aircraft. During a March 1957 meeting with James Douglas, Jr., then Secretary of the Air Force, and Lt. Gen. Irvine, Johnson told them bluntly, "We have crammed the maximum amount of hydrogen in the fuselage that it can hold. You do not carry hydrogen in the flat surfaces of the wing..." and he noted that the range growth potential by adding more fuel was only 3%.

Air Force reaction to the meeting was mixed. *Suntan* proponents, particularly Appold and Seaberg, continued to support the project even in light of Johnson's negative assessment. By late 1958, however, it was apparent the program was in deep trouble.

Johnson apparently had held strong reservations concerning liquid hydrogen almost from the beginning. During *Suntan's* first six months of development, he had concluded a range of 2,500 miles was the maximum that could be expected of a hydrogen-fueled aircraft of this type. Air Force engineers at Wright Field had generated considerably more optimistic figures and had concluded 3,500 miles, if not greater, to be a more realistic range limit. Because of his intimacy with the actual hardware, however, Johnson became increasingly convinced the CL-400 would not be able to achieve the Air Force's optimistic projections. By mid-1958, others involved in the aircraft's development had reached similar conclusions. During February of 1959, upon Johnson's insistence, the program was terminated...even though national security issues, such as a U-2

successor, remained unresolved.

Approximately a year prior to the actual demise of the CL-400, the Air Force approved a series of follow-on studies to explore potential performance improvements. Boeing, Convair, and North American were invited to participate and the resulting design exercises gave some credibility to Air Force claims. Fourteen configurations were created by the *Skunk Works* team in response to the study initiative, but they generated little in the way of strong support, other than to verify Johnson's contention that hydrocarbon fuels were considerably more practical.

In the end, *Suntan* and the CL-400 died because of a combination of factors, not the least of which were Johnson's concerns about range; the logistics of processing, transporting and handling liquid hydrogen; excessive program costs (estimated by some to have required expenditures in excess of $250 million); and the advent of other, more practical intelligence-gathering options.

Although *Suntan* technology and equipment found no immediate use in the aircraft industry, in 1959, according to retired *Skunk Works* President Ben Rich – who worked on the CL-400 liquid-hydrogen systems and powerplant requirements – "the development data on handling, tank construction, and materials was turned over to Convair who had just won the *Centaur* rocket program. This was the first US liquid hydrogen-fueled space vehicle using a Pratt & Whitney rocket engine, developed on the technology acquired developing the Model 304 engine."

Rich, upon concluding, also noted that the program "showed that a large supersonic airplane and engine could be developed on a *Skunk Works* program basis. In addition, concurrent studies showed that the same mission range could be almost doubled (though with some altitude being sacrificed) using a hydrocarbon fuel which does not have the logistics and handling problems of liquid hydrogen. This subsequently led to the *Skunk Works* Blackbird development program."

Top left: **A one third scale wing panel was manufactured by Lockheed to test the thermoelastic effects of heating at high cruising speeds. The CL-400's wing was a dry wing without internal fuel tanks.** Lockheed Martin/Miller Collection

Top right: **Studies were conducted calling for the CL-400 to be in-flight refuelable from a CL-400 tanker. This would have been a first for liquid hydrogen.** Lockheed Martin/Miller Collection

Below left: **Lockheed built this dedicated hydrogen fuel test facility at the company's Burbank plant.** Lockheed Martin/Miller Collection

Below right: **Typical CL-400 mission included a cruise to target speed of 2.50 Mach at an altitude of 90,000 feet. Impressive figures for the 1950s.** Lockheed Martin/Miller Collection

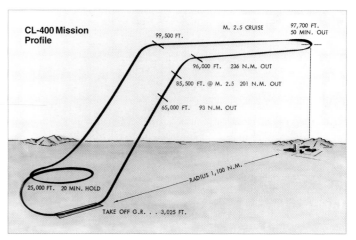

CL-400 Mission Profile

Cygnus, Fish, Gusto, Kingfish, Oxcart, A-12

As noted in the preceding chapter, *Project Suntan* had given "Kelly" Johnson and the Lockheed advanced development projects team a significant opportunity to explore the attributes of hydrogen propulsion for aircraft. Equally important, however, *Suntan* also permitted the exploration of advanced airframes optimized for the first time to cruise at speeds well in excess of 3.0 Mach. Though only paper exercises, the data generated by these studies later held the company in good stead until an opportunity to move ahead with a serious hardware contract (more likely with the demise of *Suntan*) presented itself.

Soon after the U-2's first flight during August of 1955, Richard Bissell (Allen Dulles' Special Assistant for Planning and Coordination – so named during 1954) moved quickly to organize the research and undertake the development of follow-on systems, including what was to become the A-12. Bissell, Johnson, and various members of the Killian Committee (formed under President Eisenhower to review and pass judgement on a broad spectrum of national security issues) had concluded the U-2 would have a period of invulnerability lasting no more than two years from the beginning of the Russian espionage effort (codenamed *Operation Overflight*).

One of the first surprises of the U-2 overflight program was the ease with which Soviet ground-based radar systems found and tracked the aircraft before, during, and after it penetrated Russian airspace. As a result, considerable effort was placed on reducing the aircraft's radar cross-section (RCS), but with only limited results. Several aircraft were consciously modified to incorporate radar energy absorbing coatings and a radar-attenuating web of wires, but neither of these then-highly-classified projects resulted in a noticeable lowering of detectability. In the end, it was concluded the effort and cost far outweighed any advantages. The aircraft's high operating altitude remained its best defense.

Consequent to this conclusion, new studies, conducted under the codename *Gusto*, were initiated at Lockheed exploring the design and possible development of a totally new subsonic reconnaissance platform that would be designed from scratch to incorporate the lowest RCS obtainable. By the advent of the U-2 in early 1955, it was realized by various government offices and "Kelly" Johnson's engineering team that little was really known or understood about techniques and materials that would lower an aircraft's RCS. Only a nominal amount of research had been undertaken to determine the most optimal designs and materials for reducing or reconfiguring

reflected radar energy, and the arcane art and science of electronic warfare – most specifically electronic countermeasures – was still in its infancy.

During the fall of 1957, Bissell, still convinced the U-2 would have a short service life, contacted Johnson and asked if the *Skunk Works* team would conduct an operations

Above left: **A stainless steel wind tunnel model of *Fish*.** Miller Collection via Roger Cripliver

Above right: **Wind tunnel model of *Fish* attached to B-58B carrier aircraft.** Miller Collection via Roger Cripliver

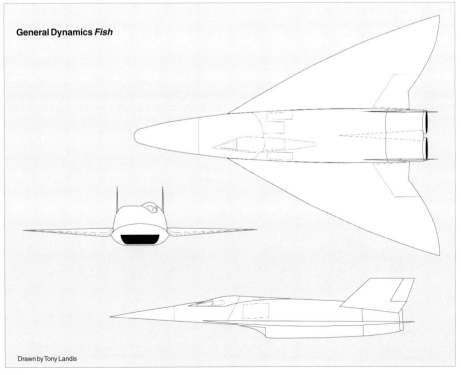

General Dynamics *Fish*

Drawn by Tony Landis

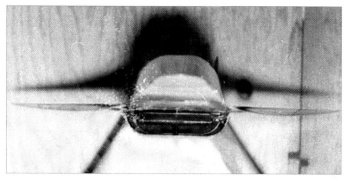

analysis to determine how far the probability of shooting down an aircraft varied respectively with its speed, altitude, and RCS. Johnson, already immersed in related studies for several other programs, including *Gusto*, agreed to accommodate the request. The resulting analysis concluded that supersonic speed coupled with the use of radar-attenuating materials and radar-attenuating design considerations greatly reduced the chances of radar detection...though it did not reduce it to zero. Bissell and Johnson both were intrigued by the study's findings and agreed that further exploratory work should be undertaken.

Attention in the Central Intelligence Agency, under the auspices of John Parangosky, now focused on the possibility of building a vehicle that could fly at extremely high speeds and extremely high altitudes while incorporating the most advanced radar-attenuating capabilities then available. During the fall of 1957, Lockheed Aircraft Corporation and the Convair Division of General Dynamics were invited by Parangosky's office to respond to a highly classified general operational requirement calling for a high-speed, high-altitude reconnaissance aircraft specifically to replace the increasingly vulnerable U-2. Security constraints prevented a formal contract or overt government funding, but it was understood that both companies, if the project was funded, would be compensated for the study expense when the time proved appropriate. Accordingly, General Dynamics, represented by Robert Whidmer, and Lockheed, represented by "Kelly" Johnson, agreed to participate. Over the course of the following year, configuration options were created and laboriously refined...all at no expense to the CIA.

In the interim, Bissell had realized that the development and production of the proposed advanced aircraft would be exceedingly expensive. He also realized there was considerable risk involved because the performance parameters selected had never previously been attainable with extant technology. Not surprisingly, General Dynamics and Lockheed were not in a position to guarantee success, and it would therefore be necessary for the government to assume most, if not all liability.

Bissell decided that in order to secure the necessary program funding, various high-ranking government officials would have to be cleared for access. Consequently, they would have to be given the best and most authoritative presentations on program advances as they occurred. In order to accommodate this, he moved to assemble a panel consisting of people he had identified as some of the most talented and brilliant in their respective fields. Among these was Edwin Land, father of the then-famous Polaroid camera, who was asked to serve as panel chairman.

Between 1957 and 1959, this panel met approximately six times, usually in Land's Cambridge, Massachusetts office. Johnson and General Dynamics' Bob Whidmer were sporadically in attendance and served to address the issues that had caused the panel to come into existence in the first place. The Assistant Secretaries of the Air Force and Navy and select technical advisors usually were on hand as well, these later all but eliminating bureaucratic and jurisdictional feuds that historically had stemmed from decision-making procedures that had excluded their participation. As it turned out, Air Force and Navy participation also resulted in valuable assistance and cooperation.

Johnson spent virtually every available minute working on the advanced aircraft program – which he referred to initially as the "U-3". As early as April 21, 1958, he noted in the first entry for what was to become his A-12 log/diary, "I drew up the first *Archangel* proposal for a Mach 3 cruise airplane having a 4,000 nautical mile range at 90,000 to 95,000 feet." Entitled "Proposal for a High-Speed Reconnaissance Aircraft", he noted, "After a substantial amount of studying the basic problem of advanced aerial reconnaissance an aircraft design has been developed which in the opinion of this writer, warrants development by the USA. Over several years, aircraft powered by advanced engines utilizing liquid hydrogen fuel, boron, water plus petroleum – and petroleum fuels have been evaluated for the basic mission by LAC."

Johnson outlined the aircraft requirements as follows: "High Altitude Cruise – 90,000'; Design Cruise Mach No. – 3.0; Engines – Two; Crew – Basic-one (Two in future); L/D req'd – 7 to 8; Range – 2,000 k.mi. Radius; Payload – 500#. Cruise fuel req'd for 4,000 k. miles, 43,400 lbs." Two engine types were examined, including the Pratt & Whitney J58 and the General Electric J93. The former offered 4,000 lb. thrust and the latter 2,000 lb. thrust at altitude. Though little additional effort was given to studying J93 configurations following this initial assessment, exploratory studies calling for the use of a variety of Marquardt ramjets would continue for many months and through a number of different *Archangel* configurations.

By June, more refined J58 studies had been undertaken with the conclusion that the afterburner-equipped engine would provide superior performance to the non-afterburner/dry version...even in consideration of the much greater weight and higher fuel consumption rate. Altitude capability of the aircraft, for instance, was 68,000 ft. using the dry engine compared with 86,000 ft. for the afterburner-equipped engine.

Eventually, Johnson concluded that their only chance of success in building a 3.0 Mach cruise capable aircraft would be to have a 41,000 lb. empty weight; a 100,000 lb. gross weight; 59,000 lb. of fuel; 2,000 lb. of fuel reserve; and 14,000 lb. of thrust. The radius of action would be 2,000 nautical miles using 43,000 lb. of available fuel.

Two months later, on July 23, he noted in the log, "I presented this airplane, along with the *Gusto* Model G2A, to the Program Office.

Top left: **Front view of *Fish* wind tunnel model illustrates heavily cambered wing leading edge and ventral intake design. Note up-ramping of nose undersurface.** Lockheed Martin via Roger Cripliver

Top right: **Full-scale pole model of *Kingfish* under construction (inverted) on August 20, 1959 at General Dynamics' Ft. Worth, Texas facility. Noteworthy is flat undersurface reminiscent of Lockheed F-117 approach to RCS reduction.** Vincent Dolson via Miller Collection

Bottom left: **Front view of *Kingfish* pole model (inverted) being installed on radar range at Groom Lake/Area 51 during 1959 tests.** Lockheed Martin via Roger Cripliver

Next page, top: **Side-view of *Kingfish* pole model (inverted). Serrated wing leading edge is sans pyroceramic inserts.** Lockheed Martin via Roger Cripliver

Next page, bottom left: **Rear view of *Kingfish* pole model showing rectangular exhaust nozzles for Pratt & Whitney J58s.** Lockheed Martin via Roger Cripliver

Next page, bottom right: **Front view of *Kingfish* pole model provides view of flat fuselage undersurface.** Lockheed Martin via Roger Cripliver

It was well received. The Navy mentioned a study they had been making on a slower, higher altitude airplane, on which the Program Office wanted my comments."

Another meeting with the Land panel took place on August 14 and Johnson would note, "They gave me a description of an inflatable airplane which they stated to be capable of 150,000 foot cruise altitude. It was ramjet powered and carried to altitude by a balloon. I made some rapid notes and found the balloon would have to be over a mile in diameter."

Work continued at a feverish pace at the *Skunk Works* on the new project. On August 25 Johnson would write, "Have contacted Marquardt and Pratt & Whitney and gotten some ramjet data. Have reconfigured the *Archangel* to include wingtip ramjets as per our proposal on the F-104 to the Air Force in 1954. This appears to give us an airplane which would cruise at Mach 3.2 at 95,000 to 110,000 feet for the full distance. As of today, it looks like the rubber blimp would have a radius of operation of 52 miles."

It is interesting to note that among the ramjet configurations studied for the Navy rubber aircraft was one calling for an engine with a length of 128 ft., a diameter of 15 ft., and an operating altitude of 150,000 ft. It is unclear as to exactly how this engine would have been utilized, but there is little question the aircraft it was to have propelled would have been considerably larger than the A-12 as eventually built.

Johnson also studied various means for launching the Navy aircraft, concluding that, "The most flexible launching system seems to be a combination of towing by a subsonic tow aircraft to an altitude of about 60,000 ft. and then rocket boosting the vehicle to 114,000 ft. and Mach 2.5 for ramjet ignition. Towing vehicles were designed for meeting these requirements." Included in the study were balloons capable of lifting the aircraft to launch altitude and at least one "four-engine tug aircraft". At least one study called for a U-2 tug which would have had two auxiliary Pratt & Whitney J57 engines mounted under the wings for additional thrust. It was to be capable of towing 29,000 lb. at 135 kts.

There were three basic aircraft designs being studied at this point. These were referred to as the "Inflatable Long Engine", "Inflatable Short Engine", and "Metal Long Engine". Respectively, these aircraft had empty weights of 22,090 lb., 20,335 lb., and 20,350 lb. Johnson determined that, "The inflatable structure will be exceedingly difficult to build. It will require very unusual tooling and long development spans to get and hold proper contours...vitally important to high performance. Flutter-criteria are completely unknown. Providing control surfaces with means for their operation requires great ingenuity." He went on to note that, "The vulnerability of the inflatable aircraft is self-evident. No practical pumps can be provided to furnish make-up air at the operating altitudes considered for this aircraft."

Johnson also was concerned about the proposed aircraft's radar cross-section, "While the inflatable aircraft does have certain characteristics favorable for reducing radar reflection in certain frequency bands, a careful examination of actual construction does not necessarily substantiate this. The large 15 ft. diameter metal ramjet is just as bad or worse than a comparable fuselage. Metal or thick fiberglass control rods, links, and hinges on the wing and tail will partially nullify the good basic wing design from a reflectivity point of view. Overall, the aircraft will probably still have a rather large return at search frequencies."

He concluded his study by noting:

"1. Inflatable wing and tail surfaces for the proposed design cannot be built for one pound of weight per square foot for the speeds and altitudes proposed."

"2. A metal surface can be built for 80% of the weight of the inflatable surface for the same speeds, altitudes, planform, and thickness. It would, however, still be 20% over the desired unit weight."

"3. Ramjet power plants will operate at the speeds and altitudes proposed when run on Borane fuels."

"4. Even using the most optimistic design criteria in terms of speeds, gust loads, structure, drag and propulsion, no aircraft system having any reasonable degree of feasibility

could be designed to fly the desired mission previously outlined."

"5. The best launching means for the aircraft studied was a combination of towing by another aircraft and then boosting to speed and altitude by rockets."

"6. The great technical risks involving high cost, great vulnerability, and overall lack of feasibility for the aircraft as proposed would indicate that other approaches to the problem should be considered more fruitful."

Obviously not impressed with the Navy's balloon-based proposal, Johnson continued to work with considerable intensity on what he already was viewing as the *Skunk Works'* most important aircraft. With Presidential approval of an advanced feasibility study under the new codename *Oxcart* on September 4, "Kelly's" team began to move ahead at a considerably more rapid pace.

Summarizing the period from September 17 through 24, he would write, "Spent considerable time in Washington and ended up in Boston on September 22nd and 23rd to review *Archangel* project. I presented a report on evaluation of Navy inflatable airplane design and also a revised version of the *Archangel* design for higher altitude performance. The inflatable airplane concept appears to have been dropped for our particular mission. Convair proposed a *Super Hustler*, which apparently was a Mach 4 ramjet, piloted, turbojet-assisted on landing, to be launched from the B-58 to do the mission. I presented *Gusto* 2A, which was very well received and also *Archangel II*. This airplane was 135,000 pound gross weight, powered by two J58 turbojets and two 75 inch ramjets. It could do 100,000 foot mission and 4,000 mile range. This airplane was not accepted, because of its dependence on penta-borane for the ramjet and the overall cost of the system. We left Cambridge rather discouraged with everything."

In the meantime, the Land Panel had approved the *Gusto* effort on September 1, 1958, essentially as a back-up to *Oxcart*. A contract was let the following June, but by then, the new 3.0 Mach reconnaissance aircraft program had reached the point of no return, and *Gusto* was no longer justified. It survived, though only with minimal support.

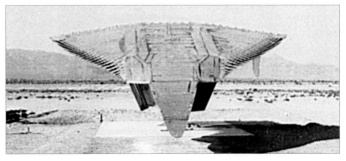

General Dynamics *Kingfish*

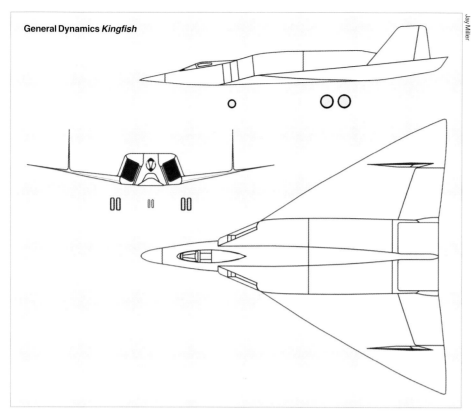

Original Johnson Sketch for 3.0 Mach Aircraft

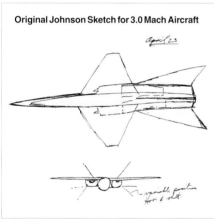

april 23

Above: ***Kingfish*** represented the last of a long line of General Dynamics design studies exploring the possibility of building a 3.0 Mach-capable aircraft. ***Kingfish*** was to cruise at 3.20 Mach. Its predecessor, ***Fish***, was to cruise at 4.0 Mach.

Left: Reproduction of "Kelly" Johnson's original hand-drawn sketch leading up to the first ***Archangel*** study, referred to as the A-1. Miller Collection

Below: One of earliest A-1 studies undertaken by the Lockheed *Skunk Works* team headed by "Kelly" Johnson. Ed Baldwin, "Kelly's" chief designer, accommodated virtually all of the early A-1 thru A-12 design studies. Evan Elliott collection

Archangel I (A-1) Early

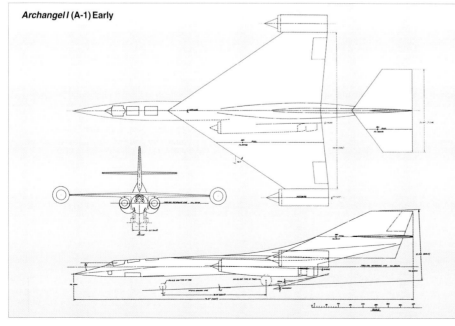

Johnson was now deep into *Archangel II*. This proposal was, in fact, only slightly larger than its predecessor design and offered few advantages other than an increase in altitude capability by 10,000 ft. Weight had increased from 41,000 lb. to 50,180 lb. and maximum speed remained in the 3.0 Mach range. During a flight back to California, following a meeting with the Land Panel, Johnson would note, "I thought it would be worth a try to break one existing ground rule...namely, that we should use engines in being. It was this factor which made the *Archangel II* so large, as we started out with some 15,000 to 18,000 pounds of installed powerplant weight on the J58s alone. Because the JT11A (J58) is a low-pressure-ratio engine, it seemed to me to be well-suited to high Mach number operation. I made a few numbers trying to scale down *Archangel II* to the 17,000 to 20,000 pound gross weight, and it appears feasible."

The General Dynamics team, headed by Bob Widmer and Vincent "Vinko" Dolson, had devoted no less time and energy to their proposal during the preceeding year. Developed from a proposed B-58 parasite known early-on as *Super Hustler*, it continued to evolve during the twelve-month study period. In its later stages, it was given the strange name of *Fish*, and then in a totally redesigned and enlarged version, *Kingfish*. In the latter configuration, it was an extraordinary vehicle. Carrying a crew of two (seated in tandem) and a large sensor package, it was optimized to cruise at 3.25 Mach and an altitude of 125,000 feet. Interestingly, the primarily ramjet-powered *Fish* would have been faster, at 4.25 Mach, and flown just as high, but as a result of its air-launch requirement, it lacked the logistical common sense of its slower successor.

In response to Richard Bissell's desire to have an aircraft with the lowest practical RCS, the original *Fish* study was to have been built primarily of pyro-ceram and other related heat-resistant, radar-attenuating materials. Following launch at 2.0 Mach from a specially modified B-58B (with lengthened fuselage, uprated J79 engines, a dedicated crew station, etc.) two Marquardt ramjets were to propel it throughout the cruise portion of its mission. Two retractable General Electric J85 turbojets were to provide propulsion during final approach and landing.

As *Fish* progressed under the watchful eyes of Widmer and Dolson, it was concluded that its size, propulsion system, and operational logistics were impractical and that it would be difficult to support in an operational environment. A major redesign effort ensued, resulting in *Kingfish*, which did away with the ramjet propulsion system and consequently the B-58 requirement. Instead of the ramjets, two Pratt & Whitney J58s were specified as the engines of choice, thus making the aircraft an autonomous unit capable of operation without an abnormal amount of logistical support.

On November 25, 1958, a crucial meeting was held in Washington, DC. The miscellaneous studies conducted by General Dynamics and Lockheed were reviewed by Land and his committee members and it was decided that each company would be given a year to refine its initial proposal and to essentially generate a definitive aircraft. This information was relayed to President Eisenhower for consideration. He and Killian now met with the Killian panel and reviewed the various design options and the *Gusto* program in general. At the end of the meeting, Eisenhower agreed that funding – once again from the CIA's special Contingency Reserve Fund – be allocated for the development of either the General Dynamics or the Lockheed 3.0 Mach reconnaissance platform.

Interestingly, Johnson had received word, apparently from Killian, that their initial efforts, which included the A-3 proposal at this point, had come up second best to the Convair aircraft, primarily because of its radar cross-section numbers. With this in mind, Johnson and the various other *Skunk Works* team members redoubled their efforts. From December of 1958 through July of 1959, they went through nine more major design studies. According to Ben Rich, who eventually would play a key role in the A-12's development, "Initially it was a small cadre composed of Dave Campbell, Dick Fuller, Don Nelson, Dick Cantrell, Ray McHenry, Bob Batista, Henry Combs, Merv Heal, Lorne Cass, Ed Baldwin, and Ed Martin...and we all worked for Dick Boehme, the program manager. Dick Bissell and John Parangosky from the CIA worked closely with Johnson, and Brig. Gen. Leo Geary was the Air Force's liaison with the CIA. We calculated everything with a slide rule and a Friden calculator." This was a difficult and laborious process, as computer technology was rudimentary at best, and capabilities were extremely limited. Complicating things was the extraordinary security blanket that had been thrown over the project. Rich would note, "The A-12 inhabited the black world for many years. The CIA knew about development of the A-12 as did a few people in the Air Force, a few Congressmen, and of course, President Eisenhower. Security rivaled the *Manhattan Project*. Those of us on the project never used

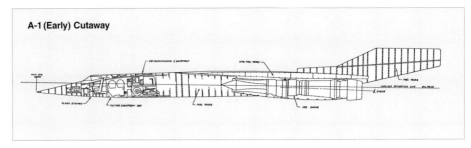

A-1 (Early) Cutaway

the name Lockheed, no drawings were stamped, and (later) parts were sent to C&J Engineering ("Kelly's" initials) and we had things mailed to post office boxes all over the city. We maintained perimeter security and even swept out our own offices."

"During this period we studied models from A-3 to A-12," Johnson would write. "Gradually it became evident that we could not obtain radar invisibility and all the other conditions desired for the airplane. In April 1959 I proposed the concept of a single-base operation with air-to-air refueling, operating out of Muroc. The A-11 resulted, as an airplane which we made no compromises for radar but which had very good performance, and was a straightforward twin J58 Mach 3.2 airplane."

"I gave the A-11 pitch and reported on about six months of radar studies which we made, in which we proved, at least to ourselves, that improvements available to radars at the present time would enable detection of any conceivable airplane which would fly in the next three to five years. We specifically computed that the probability of detection of the A-11 was practically 100%."

"I think I made some kind of impression with the radar people, because the ground rules changed shortly after this and it was agreed that the A-11 would make such a strong target that it might be taken for a bomber."

"Nevertheless, on July 3, when the Director of the Program Office visited me

Right: **Wind tunnel model of an early four-engined (two turbojets and two ramjets) A-2 study.** Miller Collection

Below left: **A late A-1 study incorporating many revisions dictated by studies undertaken by the *Skunk Works* engineering team, most notably "Kelly" Johnson and Ed Baldwin.** Evan Elliott collection

Below right: **One of earliest A-3 studies.** Miller collection

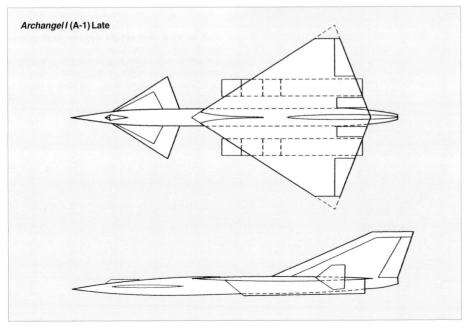

Archangel I (A-1) Late

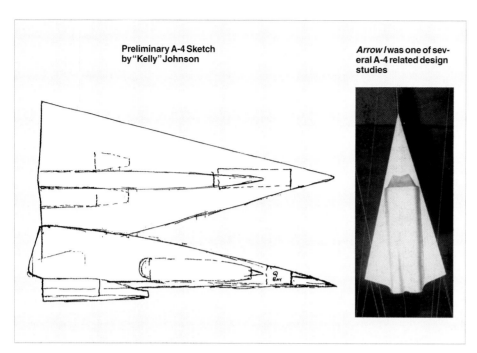

Preliminary A-4 Sketch by "Kelly" Johnson

Arrow I was one of several A-4 related design studies

again, just at about the time when I thought we were ruled out, they extended our program and agreed to take lower cruising altitudes which we could obtain with a version of the A-11 adapted in shape and treatment to reduce the cross-section. I proposed the A-12 with the J58 engines in a mid-wing arrangement, the use of chines on the fuselage and serrations on the leading edge incorporating radar treatment. This airplane weighs about 110,000 to 115,000 pounds and, by being optimistic on fuel consumption and drag, can do a pretty good mission. As of July 8, it seems there is a good chance that, if an airplane will be built for the mission, it will be ours."

Thus the definitive A-12 configuration was the last of twelve major configuration studies that had started with the original *Archangel* calculations of nearly a year earlier. Within each "A" study series, a large number of variations had been explored, most of which were assigned sub designators such as A-6-9, etc.

The various "A" series studies can be broken down as follows:

A-1: Conventional fuselage, sharply pointed nose, with truncated shoulder-mounted wing and cruciform tail. Engines mounted in various positions and some studies included canard surfaces on the forward fuselage.

A-2: A tailless, triangle-wing configuration that had a podded fuselage reminiscent of Johnson's P-38 of nearly a quarter-century earlier; with ramjets on the trailing edge of the wing at mid-span, it was an attempt to maximize fuel capacity while reducing weight.

A-3: Optimized for reduced radar cross-section, this was a tailless, swept-wing configuration with a single large vertical tail powered by two JT-12A turbojet engines and two 30-in. dia. wingtip-mounted ramjets. Wing area was 500 sq. ft.; gross weight was 17,000 lb.; est. weight at cruise altitude was 13,200 lb.; payload weight was 300 lb.; cruise was 3.0 Mach at 100,000 ft. Other A-3 studies referred to "an airplane 50% larger" using three JT-12s. Gross weight of this configuration was estimated to be 25,400 lb.; wing area was 750 sq. ft.; empty weight was 10,400 lb.; aspect ratio was 3.0; and wingspan was 47.5 ft.

A-4: Also referred to as the *Arrow*, this was an attempt to minimize radar cross-section while improving range and speed performance. In its initial form, the JP-150 fuel specified for the two 58-in. dia. ramjets offered considerably increased energy per pound of weight. Two Pratt & Whitney J57-43A "water injection" engines, rather than the previously specified JT-12s, were to be used to accelerate the aircraft to ramjet ignition speeds. Cruise altitude was reduced to 91,000 ft., and "rocket assist" was approved to assist during take-off and acceleration for ramjet operation. Wing area was 1,860 sq. ft. In profile, the A-4 was a

wedge-shape design with an extreme leading edge sweep angle and a single, tapering vertical fin that began at the aircraft's nose. The two J57s were mounted in the forward part of the fuselage and the two ramjets were mounted ventrally at the rear of the fuselage. Empty weight was estimated to be 35,200 lb. Take-off weight was estimated to be 72,100 lb. Range was estimated to be 3,000 miles. Johnson also proposed a single, large (63-in. dia.) ramjet for this proposal when he determined it "might layout better". In this configuration, he also showed the aircraft with a centrally mounted ramjet with two JT-12s mounted on either side. Additionally, an Aerojet Super Performance Rocket engine was mounted in the tail to assist during take-off. Drop tanks would be provided for the rocket fuel (H202). In a final series of A-4 studies, he proposed the use of a single J58 in place of the JT-12s and calculated this would offer an improved thrust-to-weight ratio, better overall performance, and overall lower weight.

A-5: No information.

A-6: This was the first of the studies to essentially blend the wing and fuselage into one large lifting surface. Much shorter and more compact than the definitive A-12, it was a truncated chined delta powered by ramjet engines mounted ventrally to each side of the fuselage centerline. Twin vertical tails and ramp-type intakes.

A-7: A much-developed derivative of the original A-1 study. At least three different versions were explored by Ed Baldwin, these being designated A-7-1, A-7-2, and A-7-3. The A-7-1 and A-7-3 were both high-wing designs whereas the A-7-2 was a low wing configuration. The designs varied dimensionally, with the A-7-1 having an overall length of 72.08 ft. and a wingspan of 33.33 ft. The A-7-2 had an overall length of 72.08 ft. and a wingspan of 33.33 ft. And the A-7-3 had a length of 93.75 ft. and a wingspan of 41.67 ft. All three designs had ramjets mounted on each wingtip and a single J58 mounted in the fuselage. The A-7-1 and the A-7-3 had a single ventral intake feeding the J58, and the A-7-2 had a bifurcated intake with inlets on each side of the fuselage.

A-8: No information.

A-9: No information.

A-10: The stretched and all-jet powered version of the A-9 optimized for reduced radar cross-section. Single vertical tail centrally mounted on empennage. Engines podded under shoulder-mounted wing with ramp-type intakes. No intake spikes.

A-11: Near definitive configuration. Single vertical tail, ventral engines under wings, and no chines to improve lift at cruise and concur-

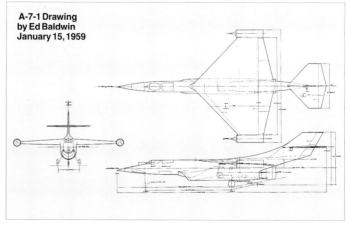

A-7-1 Drawing by Ed Baldwin January 15, 1959

rently to reduce radar cross-section. Vertical tail had aft-swept trailing edge and rudder. Tubular fuselage with shoulder-mounted delta wing and tandem cockpit.

A-12: Definitive configuration. Originally conceived with conventional rudders, pointed wingtips, minimal inward cant for vertical tail surfaces, and some area ruling on central fuselage tube. Initial design had vertical tails with aft-swept trailing edges.

Official approval to proceed with the program had finally been granted the CIA by President Eisenhower's office on July 20. During a meeting with the President, it was agreed that either the General Dynamics or the Lockheed proposal should be chosen for construction and flight test. It also was agreed that a final proposal review should be undertaken and that the winning design should be cleared for prototyping as quickly as possible.

On August 20, 1959, the final design submissions from General Dynamics and Lockheed were delivered to a joint Department of Defense/Air Force/CIA selection panel. The two aircraft, though strikingly different, compared favorably in terms of performance:

	Lockheed	General Dynamics
Length (feet)	102	79.5
Wingspan (feet)	57	56
Gross weight (pounds)	110,000	101,700
Fuel weight (pounds)	64,600	62,000
Speed	3.20 Mach	3.20 Mach
Range (n. miles total)	4,120	3,400
Range (n. miles @ altitude)	3,800	3,400
Cruise altitude (feet @ start)	84,500	85,000
Cruise altitude (feet @ middle)	91,000	88,000
Cruise altitude (feet @ end)	97,600	94,000
Expected First Flight Date	22 months	22 months

On August 28, Johnson noted in the log, "Saw the director of the program office alone. He told me that we had the project and that Convair is out of the picture. They accept our conditions (1) of the basic arrangement of the A-12 and (2) that our method of doing business will be identical to that of the U-2. He agreed very firmly to this latter condition and said that unless it was done this way, he wanted nothing to do with the project either. The conditions that he gave me were these:

(1) We must exercise the greatest possible ingenuity and honest effort in the field of radar.

(2) The degree of security on this project is, if possible, tighter than on the U-2.

(3) We should make no large material commitments, large meaning in terms of millions of dollars.

"We talked throughout the day on problems on security, location, manpower, and aircraft factors. At noon I took nine of the project people out for lunch, in celebration of our new project."

On August 29, 1959, Lockheed was given an official go-ahead on the A-12. This was followed, on September 4, with an advanced feasibility contract. Initial funding, for $4.5 million was approved to cover the period from September 1 to January 1, 1960. Project *Gusto* now was given considerably reduced priority and shifted to the status of A-12 backup. Concurrently, a new codename, *Oxcart*, was assigned to Lockheed's top secret project.

On August 31, Johnson noted in the log, "Started immediate action in Building 82A to build full-scale mock-up and 1/8 scale mock-up, an elevation post, and engineering reorganization and expansion, and plans for a complete rearrangement of offices and shop. I reported results of the trip to Robert Gross, Courtlandt Gross, Cyril Chappellet, Charlie Barker, and Hall Hibbard." On the next day, Johnson noted, "I consider this to be the first day on our new project, with a flight date set 20 months from today. The original 18-month program will be delayed to allow Pratt & Whitney to make a bypass version of the J58 engine." On February 8, 1960, the first production contract was let on *Oxcart*.

Not surprisingly, the design of the A-12 was clearly dominated by the aircraft's propulsion system. Underscoring this were the engine nacelles, which in fact were larger in diameter than the basic fuselage. The propulsion system consisted of three major elements: the inlet and inlet control; the Pratt & Whitney J58 (civil designation was JT11D-20) and its control; and the self-actuating, airframe mounted ejector nozzle. In the actual aircraft, engine access was provided by hinging the outer wing about the upper outboard nacelle split line.

Above left: Modified A-10 model in a Lockheed anechoic chamber and being utilized to explore its RCS envelope. Radar-absorbent panels and material have been added without regard to aerodynamic issues. Lockheed Martin/Miller Collection

Above right: *Gusto II* was one of several U-2 follow-on studies that continued the theme of subsonic, high-altitude performance and low RCS. Lockheed Martin/Miller Collection.

Below left: A-11 drawing underscores long-standing claims that the identity of the F-12 was purposefully misrepresented during President Johnson's unveiling of the aircraft during 1964. Lockheed Martin via Miller collection

Below right: Early A-12 study without chines. The latter were a relatively late add-on primarily to meet RCS requirements. Museum of Flight collection

Preceding page, bottom left: Near-definitive A-12 and ninth A-6 configuration studies. Lockheed Martin/ Miller Collection

A-11

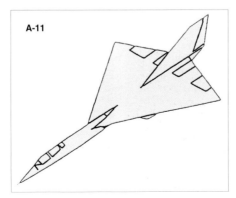

A-12 Early

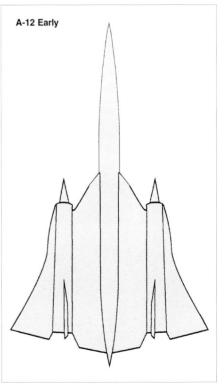

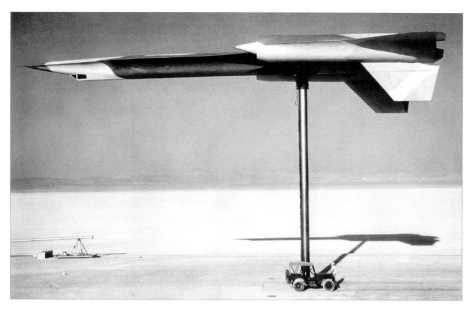

On September 3, the CIA authorized Lockheed to proceed with "anti-radar studies", aerodynamic, structural tests, and engineering designs. One week later, Johnson would write, "We will go forward with greater confidence, having in 18 months completed the circle and come back to an airplane very similar to the A1, which was our first proposal but considered to be too large, inadequate in the anti-radar concept, and to have too low performance. It was actually smaller than the A-12 and had better performance. All of this is now behind us and we have nothing to do but work."

The engineering team remained purposefully small. By now, under the supervision of Ed Martin, Dan Zuck had been assigned cockpit design, Dave Robertson had been brought onboard to handle the fuel system requirements, and Henry Combs and Dick Boehme had been assigned to head-up structures development. Dick Fuller, Burt McMaster, and Ben Rich also were intimately involved, though their time was being spent working at night at the NASA Ames high-speed wind tunnel facility south of San Francisco at Moffett Field, California.

By mid-October the radar cross-section model was nearing completion and low-speed wind tunnel testing was already under way with a small-scale model. "I had Dick Fuller and Bert O'Laughlin go up to Ames to make arrangements for high-speed tunnel tests ... (these) indicated the expected problems in regard to longitudinal stability with chines. We are extending the wing after the afterburner and believe we have usable solutions coming up. The overall problem of weight, balance, and stability is extremely high."

Work on the wind tunnel models, full-scale mock-up, and initial pieces of full-scale hardware progressed rapidly. By December 7, the RCS model – which had been loaded aboard a special trailer and trucked to Groom Lake/Area 51 during November – had permitted refinement of the design to establish the optimum external configuration for radar attenuation, and Johnson appeared to feel confident the aircraft would meet the promised RCS specification, "We are beginning to get the anti-radar return of the model down remarkably. Inlets are the problem in the forward aspect and the exhaust in the rear, as expected."

The powerplant issue had not been treated lightly, either by the *Skunk Works*' A-12 propulsion system manager, Ben Rich, or the CIA. Not only was the engine nacelle's RCS an issue of considerable concern and complexity, but also its highly advanced supersonic intake, its ejector nozzle configuration, and its basic aerodynamics. As Johnson, concerning these issues, would note, "This thing is fantastically hard to build, but we must take on the job because it involves so much of the airplane structure."

Pratt & Whitney, almost from the very beginning, had been involved in *Gusto* and its successor, *Oxcart*. Their J58, which was to be used in the new *Skunk Works* aircraft, had been sponsored originally by the Navy as a conventional, but very advanced turbojet engine providing extraordinarily high thrust with the ability to operate routinely at speeds up to 3.0 Mach.

The advances represented by the J58 had become increasingly difficult to justify by the Navy. Costs were mounting rapidly, there were technological difficulties that had yet to be overcome, and there was considerable doubt as to whether the engine would generate the thrust-to-weight and fuel consumption numbers Pratt & Whitney had promised.

Additionally, several of the aircraft for which the J58 was intended, including the Vought F8U-3, had ceased to exist. As a result, the Navy had begun to lose interest. In short, at the beginning of 1959, the engine was without a purpose or airframe.

As originally conceived, the J58 was to have been a large, conventional, moderate-pressure-ratio turbojet equipped with a large afterburner and designed to operate routinely in the high-Mach range of 2.5 to 3.0. It was designed to use conventional ram compression at supersonic speeds to augment the multi-stage compressor. With its conventional afterburner and a convergent-divergent exhaust nozzle, the J58 was expected to be capable of producing up to 45,000 pounds static sea level thrust.

The more radical approach to the A-12's required 3.0 Mach cruise speed led to a major J58 redesign. The resulting engine utilized bypass intake air from the fourth stage of the high-pressure compressor section and dumped it into the afterburner. This created a highly efficient ramjet effect and thus augmented the more conventional thrust being generated by the core engine.

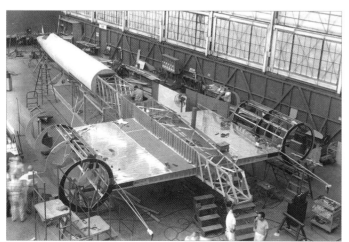

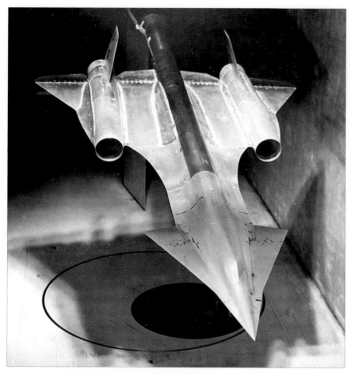

Above left and right: **Wind tunnel model of A-12, probably at NASA Langley. In configuration on the left, the model has been configured with canards. Aircraft as actually built is depicted on right.** Lockheed Martin via Miller Collection

Bottom left: **Instrument panel of the first A-12, No. 121, photographed on January 2, 1962...just three months prior to the aircraft's first flight on April 30.** Lockheed Martin via Miller Collection

Bottom right: **The first A-12 during the course of non-destructive structural testing at the Skunk Works' Burbank, California facility.** Lockheed Martin via Tony Landis collection

Funding allocated for *Oxcart* by the CIA also included developmental funding for the advanced J58. When, on January 30, 1960, Lockheed received official word that funding for twelve A-12s had been approved, Pratt & Whitney also was informed they were cleared to move ahead with the construction of three "advanced, experimental engines for durability and reliability testing." Additionally, three engines were to be made available for initiation of flight testing during early 1961.

Work on the A-12's sensors also had been started. Perkin-Elmer had been chose as the primary camera manufacturer. Because of the extreme complexity of its design a decision was quickly made to fund Kodak's proposed back-up system in case Perkin-Elmer ran into difficulty. At the same time, Minneapolis-Honeywell Corporation was selected to provide both the inertial navigation and automatic flight control systems. The Firewell Corporation and the David Clark Corporation became the prime sources of pilot equipment and associated life support hardware.

During early February of 1960 the CIA proposed to Lockheed that it serve to screen a minimum of 60 pilots in an attempt to assemble an initial group of 24. These men would be "sheep dipped" – as had those associated with the CIA's U-2 effort – and they also would be put through a physical review comparable to that created for the *Project Mercury* astronaut selection process. Johnson did not react to this with great favor, as he felt it would be some time yet before pilots, other than those already in the employ of Lockheed, would be needed. The following April, he picked Lou Schalk to accommodate the A-12's first flight.

The basic pilot candidate requirements were that they be between 25 and 40 years of age, be under six feet tall, and weigh no more than 175 pounds. Air Force files were screened for potential candidates and a pilot list was assembled. During the psychological

assessments, physical examinations, and refinement of criteria that followed many were quickly eliminated. Sixteen pilots were picked out of the first group following the pre-evaluation process. These sixteen underwent further intensive security and medical scrutiny by the CIA. Those who remained were then approached to take employment with the CIA on a highly classified project involving a very advanced aircraft. During November of 1961, commitments were obtained from five of the remaining pilots.

Because so few pilots had passed the rigorous screening process, a second search for pilots was undertaken shortly after the first was completed. When the second group of recruits was winnowed down, the confirmed pilots, other than Lou Schalk, included William Skliar, Kenneth Collins, Walter Ray, Lon Walter, Mele Vojvodich, Jr., Jack Weeks, Ronald "Jack" Layton, Dennis Sullivan, David Young, Francis Murray, and Russell Scott. Arrangements now were made with the Air Force to effect appropriate transfers and assignments to cover their training and to lay the basis for their transition from military to civilian status. Compensation and insurance packages were similar to those given the CIA's U-2 pilots.

While work on the A-12 at Lockheed's Burbank facilities progressed at a steady pace,

Though strong, relatively light, and capable of retaining its exceptional strength characteristics at very high temperatures, it also suffered from scarcity, high cost, and a reputation for being extremely difficult to work. Initially, over 80% of the titanium delivered to Lockheed had to be rejected due to metalurgical contamination. It was not until 1961 that the problem – attributed to embrittlement caused by impurities in the public water supply – was brought fully under control.

Learning to work with titanium proved a major undertaking for Lockheed. The myriad breakthroughs pioneered by the *Skunk Works* manufacturing team in conquering this metal remain one of the great and unheralded success stories of this most incredible program.

Among the many other manufacturing challenges was the need to develop high-temperature fuels that could be safely stored at the A-12's ambient fuel tank cruising speed temperature of 350° F; the need for nitrogen inerting of the fuel tanks as fuel was depleted; development of a special lubricating oil that could be used effectively on parts that had cruising speed stabilized temperatures of 600° F or more while remaining suitably viscous at temperatures of less than 40° F; development of a hydraulic seal material capable of maintaining its integrity at high temperatures; and a quartz glass windscreen pane that could retain its optical qualities while being exposed to the extreme temperatures of the A-12's operating environment (the pane, in fact, eventually took three years and $2 million to develop; it pioneered a unique process for metal-to-glass fusion using high-frequency sound waves).

Another major problem was the aircraft's radar cross-section (RCS). Initial studies had concluded that reducing the aircraft's radar reflectivity factor would significantly enhance its survival chances in a hostile environment.

ongoing studies of the basic configuration and its long-term potential continued in the *Skunk Works'* engineering department. On March 16, after several weeks of design and engineering effort, Johnson went to Washington in order to present an A-12 configuration study calling for an interceptor version optimized for air defense work. Specifically targeted was North American's ill-fated F-108 *Rapier*. A one third-scale extrapolation of the forthcoming 3.0 Mach-capable North American B-70 *Valkyrie* intercontinental heavy bomber, the F-108 would eventually fail to reach fruition. Prototype construction would be terminated in 1964, several years prior to the planned roll-out and first flight.

"I was given information on the Hughes AN/ASG-18 radar and the latest information on the Hughes GAR-9 rocket. Before leaving, the Air Force program office clearly explained that they wanted to know whether we could make use of this equipment in the A-12 and that, if we could, they would propose it as a standby air defense fighter. They said there

would not be any immediate order, but they were interested in getting development aspects of the fighter system carried along. I told them we could get them an air defense airplane in a couple of years under our present commitments. This would be A-12 number 6 or 7."

As jig assembly began inside Burbank's Plant 6 where the aircraft were to be assembled, the manifold difficulties entailed in the A-12's construction began to surface in ever-increasing numbers. The early decision to build the aircraft of titanium in order to cope with the high temperatures at the 3.0 Mach-plus cruise speeds was a first for the industry. Though miscellaneous aircraft parts had been manufactured from this material on a select few occasions, an entire airframe had never previously been attempted. As Ben Rich would note, the A-12 "was composed of 85% titanium and 15% composite materials." No other aircraft had ever utilized titanium for anything other than high-temperature exhaust fairings and related specific protection in high heat-sink areas.

Top: **The first A-12 during final assembly at the *Skunk Works* Burbank, California, facility on January 2, 1962. Lacking only its nose, it would soon be partially disassembled and trucked to Groom Lake/Area 51 for the start of its flight-test program.** Lockheed Martin via Jim Goodall collection

Below left: **A special, fully-enclosed trailer was built to transport the first A-12's components from Burbank, California to Groom Lake/Area 51 in Nevada by highway.** Lockheed Martin via Jim Goodall collection

Below right: **Production was well along on the first six aircraft by the time this photo was taken on August 23, 1963, inside Plant B-6 at Lockheed's Burbank facility.** Lockheed Martin via Jim Goodall collection

As a result, considerable emphasis was placed on studying the problem and creating innovative ways to reduce the total and incidental RCS. This requirement, emphasized by the DoD and CIA, became the basis in the US for virtually all low-observables studies and hardware to follow.

Areas causing the most RCS difficulty included the vertical stabilizers and the forward section of the engine nacelles. Lockheed, under the auspices of "Kelly" Johnson's *Skunk Works* team, spent an enormous amount of money and time exploring the use of ferrites, high-temperature radar-absorbing materials, and high-temperature plastic and first-generation composite structures to find methods for reducing the A-12's RCS. Eventually, the vertical tails, originally of titanium, were replaced by high-temperature composite surfaces. This almost certainly represented the first time such materials had been used in a major part of an aircraft's structure. Consequently they also represented the first use of such structures in extremely high-temperature environments.

The old U-2 test facility at Groom Lake/Area 51, Nevada, about 70 miles northeast of Nellis AFB, now was prepared to accept the first aircraft, which originally had been promised for delivery during May of 1961. Considerable work was required to bring the facility up to the standard needed for A-12 operations, and this had been initiated during September of 1960. Though a double-shift schedule was instigated for employees, the actual facility upgrade was not completed until mid-1964. In the interim, the runway was lengthened to 8,500 feet from the original 5,000; the highway leading to the location was resurfaced; three surplus Navy hangars were obtained, dismantled, and erected at the location's north side; and an additional 100 surplus Navy buildings were moved to the base and rebuilt.

While work at Groom Lake/Area 51 moved ahead at a rapid pace, the prototype aircraft were being assembled with considerable difficulty at Burbank. A review of Johnson's A-12 log underscores some of the problems:

August 30, 1960 – "The stress and flutter boys presented a study on aeroelasticity which was woefully in error. If it had been correct, the airplane couldn't fly at all."

September 14, 1960 – "Start design of the bomber version of the A-12."

September 30, 1960 – "We are in desperate trouble trying to get extrusions for the wing beams. The material is not acceptable."

October 3/24, 1960 – "Continuing to have many shop problems. Can't get material, and it appears that the schedule is slipping some more."

December 20, 1960 – "Have a very strong suspicion that Pratt & Whitney are not going to meet their schedule. They have run into trouble on the compressor with tip shrouds. Of course

they didn't mention this as being a major problem."

March 6, 1961 – "Having trouble with wing load distribution and have to put twist in outboard leading edge."

March 1 5/April 1, 1961 – "Just a great deal of work with the many problems we have trying to get this airplane built. Everywhere you turn there are tremendous problems requiring invention, new systems, and money."

Johnson, during March, informed the CIA that, "Schedules are in jeopardy on two fronts. One is the assembly of the wing and the other is in satisfactory development of the engine. Our evaluation shows that each of these programs is from three to four months behind the current schedule."

To this, the CIA's Bissell replied, "I have learned of your expected additional delay in first flight from 30 August to 1 December 1961. This news is extremely shocking on top of our previous slippage from May to August and my understanding as of our meeting 19 December that the titanium extrusion problems were essentially overcome. I trust this is the last of such disappointments short of a severe earthquake in Burbank."

But it wasn't. Johnson's frustrations continued without let-up:

April 12, 1961 – "Fighting a whole host of problems on powerplant, ejectors, plumbing, material shortages, lack of space."

July 10, 1961 – "Having a horrible time building the first airplane and we are stopped on the second by a change in the design of the radar configuration of the chines. Have shop

meetings often – about three times a week but it's hard to drive a willing horse. Everyone on edge connected with the production of the A-12 airplane, and we still have a long, long way to go. I told Courtlandt Gross and Dan Haughton how tough our problems are, with no under-estimation on my part of the extreme danger we will encounter in flying this revolutionary airplane. And told them some of the steps we are taking to minimize these dangers."

Concurrently, engine development also was proving a difficult task for Pratt & Whitney. Johnson would note in the log, "Pratt & Whitney told us the story on the engine, and said that the best delivery date we could get for two engines was March 1962 (they admitted this meant April...or March 31)." Realizing the engine problems could push the first flight date back even further, Johnson, on September 29, made a decision... "after a sleepless night, decided that we should have to try to fly with a J75 engine, doing everything possible to raise the take-off power, such as using water injection, and higher take-off temperature and rpm's."

With the delays now causing the cost of the program to soar, the CIA decided to place a top level engineer from the Air Force in residence at the *Skunk Works* to oversee progress. Norman Nelson, as Johnson noted, "brought in Lt. Col. Richmond Miller," on October 3, 1961, "...who had been on the program two weeks. Miller said he was supposed to be their man 'in charge of the airframe,' which neither he nor I understood. We know Miller from work on the U-2 at Edwards AFB. He is competent in

the flight-test area, but he follows the book religiously. He asked me for an A-12 flight manual, which I told him would be ready in about a year..."

The completion date of the first A-12 now had slipped to December 22, 1961, and the expected first flight date to February 27, 1962. Construction pressures were intense at Burbank and work went on around the clock in three shifts. Engine problems continued as well. Johnson, following a meeting with Pratt & Whitney in Florida, would note in his log, "Their troubles are desperate. It is almost unbelievable that they could have gotten this far with the engine without uncovering basic problems which have been normal in every jet engine I have ever worked with. Prospect of an early flight engine is dismal, and I feel our program is greatly jeopardized. It's a good thing we went to the J75, although these engines, too, have troubles and require new compressor discs."

At Groom Lake/Area 51, support aircraft began to arrive during the spring of 1962. Included were eight McDonnell F-101s for chase and training, two Lockheed T-33s for proficiency training, a Lockheed C-130 for cargo transport, a Cessna U-3A for administration purposes, a helicopter for search and rescue, and a Cessna 180 for liaison use. In addition, an F-104 was assigned for use as a chase plane.

During January of 1962 a secret agreement was reached with the Federal Aviation Administration permitting expansion of the restricted airspace surrounding Groom Lake/Area 51. Select FAA air traffic controllers were cleared for *Oxcart* operations. Additionally, select military radar facility personnel were briefed and told not to report radar sightings of high-performance aircraft.

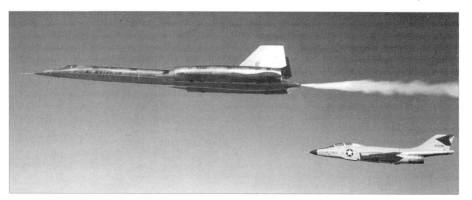

Above: **Powered by two Pratt & Whitney J75s, the first A-12, Article 121 departs Groom Lake/Area 51 on its first official flight for CIA and Lockheed patrons on April 30, 1962. Lockheed test pilot Lou Schalk was at the controls.** Lockheed Martin via Jim Goodall collection

Left: **The first A-12, Article 121, during initial fuel emergency dump trials with F-101B chase.** Lockheed Martin via Tony Landis collection

During mid-February of 1962 the first A-12 was at last ready for final assembly. Johnson and the CIA had decided that, in light of the secrecy surrounding the project, the aircraft would not be flown from Burbank to Groom Lake/Area 51. A special trailer, evolved from a unit constructed specifically to transport the RCS test specimen, was therefore designed and built to haul the aircraft to Groom Lake/Area 51 by road. A thorough survey of the route during June of 1961 ascertained the hazards and problems of moving the actual aircraft and showed that a package measuring 35 feet wide by 103 feet long could be moved over the road without major difficulty...though some obstructing road signs would have to be displaced and select trees would have to be trimmed.

During the third week in February, the entire fuselage of the first A-12 – referred to by the Agency as Article 121 – minus wings, was crated, covered with canvas, and loaded on the special $100,000 trailer. On February 26, Johnson noted, "The convoy left at 2:30 a.m. to go to Groom Lake/Area 51. Everything went smoothly and it arrived at 1:00 p.m. on February 28. Dorsey Kammerer did his usual splendid job of organizing the move."

Shortly after its arrival at the remote Nevada site, reassembly of the first aircraft and installation of the J75 engines was initiated. It was soon discovered, however, that fuel tank sealing compounds had failed to adhere to the titanium fuel tank walls. When the tanks were filled for the first time, the aircraft leaked like a sieve. Johnson counted a total of sixty-eight. He would note, "This is a cruel blow, as it will delay us a month or more." There was no choice, the tanks had to be laboriously stripped and resealed.

After the leak problem was, in part, solved, and following a fairly short but intense series of static tests that included initial J75 engine

runs, slow-speed taxi trials, and brake tests, the A-12 was cleared for its initial flight. On April 25, 1962, everything appeared ready. The *Skunk Works*' Lou Schalk, a competent, long-time company test pilot who had joined the A-12 program two years earlier, had been hand-picked by "Kelly" Johnson to handle the flight-test program. Schalk had spent many hours in a rudimentary A-12 simulator at the Burbank facility participating in the development of the cockpit layout and design. He later worked hands-on as the real cockpit went together inside the first aircraft. By the time of the first taxi and flight tests, he was as prepared as it was possible for a pilot to be under the circumstance of the many unknowns that lay ahead.

Johnson had flown to the location to witness the first flight and noted in his log, "Went to Groom Lake/Area 51 and stayed over night. Made our first flight under very difficult conditions. Flew about 1½ miles at an altitude of about 20 feet. Aircraft got off the ground with lots of right rudder on, and then required change of rudder angle to 24° immediately.

This set up lateral oscillations which were horrible to see. We were all concerned about the ability of Lou Schalk to stop, but he did this very nicely, without severe braking. The lake is soft enough so that we can roll onto it at fantastic speeds and stop readily. Actual trouble was later shown to be due to nose wheel steering problems."

Bill Fox, Honeywell's flight-test engineer assigned to Groom Lake/Area 51 and present for the first flight, recalled, "I walked out to the north side of the hangar where the bird was sitting with lots going on around it. I sat down against the hangar and Lou Schalk came over and sat beside me. We joshed a little and soon I noticed Lou had dozed off so I kept quiet. Soon Larry Bohannon came over and was about to talk to Lou and then noticed he was asleep. He said, "Gosh, I 'd like to talk to him about some things but I don't want to wake him up." After a few minutes Lou snapped to life and Larry came back and briefed him on a couple of last minute items. I thought, 'that is about as cool a test pilot as I have ever seen', and remember it vividly."

Above: **Article 121 during the course of a test flight on July 10, 1962. None of the firsts three A-12s was retrofitted with the distinctive RCS leading edge composite "pie slices".** Lockheed Martin via Tony Landis collection

Right: **Drawing illustrating the various equipment call-outs specific to the A-12.** Lockheed Martin via Jim Goodall collection

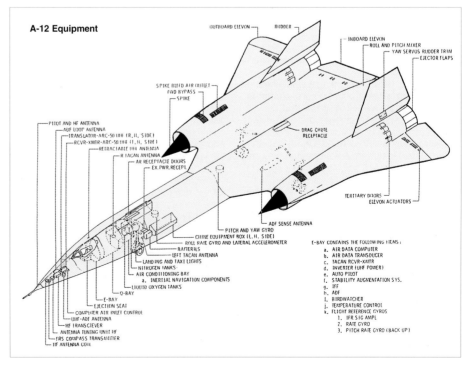

Left: **Article 121 during the course of the A-12's early flight-test program over Groom Lake/Area 51 in Nevada. The aircraft is jettisoning fuel from its dump pipe located on the extreme aft end of the empennage.** Lockheed Martin via Tony Landis collection

Schalk, in recounting the first flight during a 1993 interview, had a different perspective on what actually happened: "It had a very light load of fuel so it sort of accelerated really fast. Not many people really knew that we were going to lift the airplane off...some of the people in flight-test engineering didn't know this. I was probably three to four percent behind the aft limit center of gravity when I lifted off the airplane...so it was unstable...and we fought it longitudinally which translated into lateral and directional problems, too.

"The airplane wallowed through the sky until I finally felt I had it under control enough to put it back down on the ground ... which I did. By that time I was over the lakebed. This developed a big cloud of dust and the tower wanted to know if everything was ok. I said 'yes...but I'm going to have to roll out here on the lakebed and I'll turn around and come back'. But they couldn't hear me because the UHF transmitting antenna was on the bottom of the fuselage and that blanked out my transmission...so no one heard what I was saying. So they asked me again and I said there was no problem. I wasn't trying to stomp on the brakes or anything. Everyone was having a heart attack...I finally made the turn and came out of the cloud of dust and they saw I hadn't run into the mountains on the other side of the lake and blown up the airplane, so there was a big sigh of relief.

"I still didn't know what the devil was wrong with the airplane...why it handled so poorly – it didn't do that way on the simulator and 'Kelly' and I and Fuller – we were talking about what we should do if we fly the airplane the next day. I said I think we should turn on the dampers and fly with the dampers on...they were off when I was taxiing; they said fine. On the second first flight we were going to fly the airplane around with the gear down. The third official flight was the one we pulled up the gear.

"On the second flight with the gear down the airplane took off fairly smoothly...I couldn't wait to get up to about 10,000 feet. I'm flying along below gear speed and I turned one damper off, and then another damper off, and then another damper off – no problem. Then I got the clue as to what had gone wrong on the first flight. There were a sequence of fuel tanks in the fuselage of the airplane ... one through six and one through seven – they had all the fuel in the back end...there was nothing up front for the taxi tests. When we actually flew the airplane it was loaded properly and I was in a c.g. that was ahead of the aft limit and the airplane flew fine...I lifted the airplane off the runway for ten seconds...I never thought to check where all the fuel was. Probably had 12,000 pounds of fuel (all aft) during the taxi tests."

The day following the first flights, Johnson would write, "We decided to fly with the stability augmentor engaged on April 26, which is obviously a day for the A-12, in that 2 x 6 = 12. Everyone was awake just about through the night. We rolled out early and at 07:05 a.m. took off, making a beautiful take-off. However, due to failure of a forward fillet bracket, we shed almost all the left hand fillets and one on the right side, starting before we left the runway. Fortunately, I had spent the previous day with Lou Schalk, explaining that the fillets were non-structural and that we might have troubles. A beautiful landing was made and in flight we investigated the effect of the stability augmentors. We showed that the first flight troubles were not caused by basic aircraft stability."

An "official" first flight with appropriate government representatives on hand now was made on April 30. Nearly a year behind schedule, the aircraft became airborne for the first time. With Lou Schalk at the controls, the A-12, in bare metal and without markings of any kind, lifted off at 170 knots. The landing gear was retracted and an ascent was made to 30,000 feet. A top speed of 340 knots was reached during the flight which lasted for 59 minutes. Following an uneventful landing, Schalk expressed satisfaction with the aircraft's stability and the way it handled.

On the second flight, on May 4, the A-12 went supersonic, reaching 1.10 Mach. Problems were minimal. Johnson now began to feel confident that the flight-test program would progress rapidly...possibly recovering some of the time that had been lost in the drawn-out manufacturing process. Another company test pilot, Bill Park, also joined the *Skunk Works* team to share flight testing with Schalk.

Though static testing, by mid-June, had cleared the airframe for the initial flights, problems had remained with the integrity of the vertical fins. Static test failures had occurred on numerous occasions. The metal fins, in particular, had proven very susceptible to fatigue anomalies. Even more frustrating was the fact the low RCS composite Narmco fins also had been prone to failure with surprising regularity.

On June 26, the second A-12, Article 122, arrived at Groom Lake/Area 51 and was immediately consigned to a three-month RCS static test program, even before it was completed and its engines were installed. The third aircraft, Article 123, arrived during August and was flown for the first time during October, and the fourth aircraft, the single two-seat A-12 trainer, arrived by trailer during November. The fifth aircraft, minus engines, arrived on December 19.

The trainer, with an elevated second seat in the position behind the cockpit normally occupied by sensor gear, was equipped with J75 engines so that flight testing could be expedited. It was presumed that having this aircraft available in the shortest amount of time possible would permit training of Agency pilots in concert with the delivery and availability of operational aircraft. This aircraft, eventually nicknamed "Titanium Goose", flew for the first time during January of 1963.

Earlier, during mid-August of 1962, Johnson brought another test pilot onboard by the name of Jim Eastham who eventually would become the first pilot to fly the interceptor development of the A-12 known as the YF-12A. Consequent to that, he would also fly the heavily modied, sixth, Convair B-58 *Hustler*, 55-665, which became the testbed for the enormous Hughes AN/ASG-18 radar system and its special AIM-47 missile.

In a letter to the CIA dated September 18, 1962, Kelly writes, "We have now completed our studies on the use of the A-12 as a satellite launcher. Over the past several months I have shown some of the preliminary studies which are now finalized in the two attached reports. You will notice certain inconsistencies in the two reports due to the security problem between our ADP group working on the airplanes and the LMSC group working on the satellite section.

"We addressed our attention only to the configuration C satellite-booster combination, which makes use of a *Polaris* main booster and other gear as described in the report. I did not feel It desirable at this time to consider the development of a completely new booster system – for this reason. The payload that we launch into the single orbit mission is quite high, in the region of 900 to 1000 lbs., and the sheer size and bulk of the *Polaris* attached to the A-12 necessitates two refuelings to get to the launch area. The launching problems of this booster satellite combination from the A-12 poses some fairly substantial problems, particularly in the check out which must be done by the second man provided in the A-12. There is also the problem of stabilizing the booster after launch so that it does not become a nose-down attitude prior to firing.

On October 5, 1962, the first A-12, re-engined with the first flightworthy J58 mounted in its left engine nacelle (a J75 was retained in the right), took to the air for the first time. On October 11, Johnson met with Pratt & Whitney representatives to go over difficulties with the J58. "We are having a terrible time trying to fly the prototype J58. It is down in thrust; fuel control is inconsistent; there are thrust jumps at different throttle positions; and we have continual trouble with the afterburner lighting system and plugged spray bars." It wasn't until January 15, 1963, that the first flight with two J58s installed took place.

Many teething problems with the engines now surfaced. Among the more notable were:

(1) An inability to simply start the engines. Inlet air proved insufficient for initial engine ignition. Eventually, a pair of suck-in doors were added to the nacelle and Pratt & Whitney added an engine bleed from the bleed bypass ducts to the nacelle.

(2) Engine differences. One engine often ran faster than the other. Engine temperature

Top: **The first A-12, Article 121, over Nevada on July 10, 1962.** Lockheed Martin via Tony Landis collection

Center and bottom: **Two views of Groom Lake/Area 51 in Nevada. Top photo (rotated with north to left) shows the entire facility, including the nearly 17,000 feet of runway that cuts diagonally across the southwest side of the dry lake for which the facility is named. Largest buildings in lower photo (taken in the early 1960s) were constructed specifically to accommodate the A-12 program.** Both Jim Goodall collection

sensors were later modified to pull them out of a hot air reverse flow situation. The sensor locations were changed and the hydromechanical controls were upgraded from a single temperature sensor to redundant sensors.

(3) The aircraft burned too much fuel when going transonic. To help solve the problem, thrust measurements were taken in flight and movies were made of ejector operation in flight. Local Mach numbers also were measured. Two problems were uncovered. The back end of the nacelle went supersonic long before the rest of the aircraft, and it was discovered that wind tunnel drag data for the nacelle fairing was not accurate. The solution was more transonic thrust. This led to the development of a variable inlet guide vane. Coupled with a pilot-induced dive to achieve supersonic speed before climbing to cruise altitude, the fuel problem – at least in part – was solved.

Other problems included plumbing fatigue, engine mount failures, throttle creep, low thrust as a result of engine nacelle leaks, and inlet un-starts resulting from asymmetric flow anomalies.

Serendipitously, the Cuban missile crises now reinvigorated the program. The loss of Maj. Rudolph Anderson's U-2 over Cuba on October 27, underscored the increasing vulnerability of this subsonic platform when operating in denied airspace. This was not lost on intelligence community offices involved with the overflight program. Successful execution of *Oxcart* now became a matter of highest national priority.

On November 14, Johnson again met with Pratt & Whitney representatives, this time in Washington, DC. It appeared the ongoing engine problems were not going to be solved without considerable effort. "The thrust of the engines was down, specific fuel consumption was up. The initial engines would not run well above 75,000 feet. Pratt & Whitney showed their program for getting performance back, but this could not be accomplished until engine #19 ... due for delivery in April 1963."

Left: **Early production standard A-12 cockpit.**
Lockheed Martin via Miller Collection

Below: **Article 130, Air Force serial number 60-6933, at Groom Lake/Area 51 still in original delivery markings. Black paint covered radar-attenuating composite wing inserts.** Lockheed Martin via Jim Goodall collection

Next page top: **Article 125, bearing Air Force serial number 60-6928, at Groom Lake/Area 51, prior to departing on a test flight. This aircraft and its pilot, Walter Ray, later were lost on January 5, 1967.** Lockheed Martin via Jim Goodall collection

Next page bottom: **Article 132, Air Force serial number 60-6938, taxis to the departure runway at Groom Lake/Area 51 for the beginning of a test mission.** Jim Goodall collection

On January 5, Johnson noted in his log that Bob Gilliland had been hired as the program's fourth pilot. He was scheduled to arrive at Groom Lake/Area 51 on January 15.

By the end of 1962, two A-12s were in flight test (one powered by J75s and the other powered by one J75 and one J58). A speed of 2.16 Mach and an altitude of 60,000 feet had been achieved. Flight-test progress was still slow and the engine delays and thrust deficiencies remained a major concern. The engine problem had, in fact, led to CIA director John McCone writing Pratt & Whitney, "I have been advised that J58 engine deliveries have been delayed again due to engine control production problems ... By the end of the year it appears we will have barely enough J58 engines to support the flight-test program adequately ... furthermore, due to various engine difficulties we have not yet reached design speed and altitude. Engine thrust and fuel consumption deficiencies at present prevent sustained flight at design conditions which is so necessary to complete developments."

By the end of January 1963, ten J58s had been delivered to Groom Lake/Area 51. The first A-12 flight with two J58s was finally undertaken on January 13. The other aircraft now were retrofitted with J58s, and all forthcoming aircraft were flown with J58 propulsion. The only exception became the A-12 trainer, which though intended for conversion to J58s, was left equipped with J75s throughout its life.

On March 20, Johnson wrote in his log, "We have been to Mach 2.5 and as high as 70,000 feet, but we are in trouble from Mach 2.0 up." Problems with the propulsion system continued. On May 2, Johnson "went to Groom Lake/Area 51 to find out why we have not been able to get beyond Mach 2.0 during recent flights. It develops that Hamilton Standard had changed the gain of the spike control, and the main control contributed to the instability. Greatly displeased that the responsible engineers could not find this out on their own, and no one seemed to know which controls gave which performance, until I made a review of the ships' records, and then it became perfectly clear."

At approximately this same time, the CIA's Deputy Director for Research, Herbert Scoville, Jr., penned a memo, dated April 10, 1963, discussing the "Proposal for Surfacing an LRI (Long Range Interceptor – i.e., YF-12) Prototype as a Cover for the *Oxcart Program*". He wrote: "The *Oxcart* program initiated in 1959, has during the ensuing years and up to the present time progressed through the development and initial construction and, surprisingly, through an entire year of flight testing and flight training without a single exposure or significant security breach which resulted in attracting public attention to the program.

"This accomplishment becomes even more remarkable when it is appreciated that practical considerations have forced us to adhere to a pattern that is widely known and associated with the U-2 program and involving such elements as Lockheed, "Kelly" Johnson, Pratt & Whitney, etc.

"With the advent of the R-12 (i.e., SR-71) procurement, it should be recognized that the program cannot be contained in the same manner as in the past. More than 7,000 persons in industry already are either fully or partially cleared. In addition, the increased frequency of flights will almost inevitably result in an incident under circumstances that we may not be able to control. The magnitude of the program in itself negates any effort at complete concealment, and there is already awareness in the aviation industry that Lockheed is engaged in a highly classified project of a unique nature. It must be assumed that public exposure is only a matter of time and steps must be taken now to prepare to meet this contingency and protect the *Oxcart* phase of the program.

"In addition to concealing the true mission of the *Oxcart* vehicle and plausibility ascribing to it a different purpose, there is the more difficult and potentially explosive political problem of explaining and justifying the limited competition procurement of the aircraft and the secrecy which cloaked its development.

*Our success to date in protecting the *Oxcart*/AF-12 programs from public exposure is cited as an argument in favor of continuing our present policy without change. Under this concept we would not voluntarily surface any part of the program until forced to do so by some untoward incident of compromise.

"The cover story which will be employed in surfacing the AF-12 portion of the program must contain as many elements of the truth as possible, short of jeopardizing the *Oxcart* version. With this as a primary consideration, it becomes more and more obvious that the best solution is to surface the long-range interceptor prototype, the first one of which will be available by approximately mid-July 1963.

"It is proposed that the Defense Department announce that a prototype on a long range interceptor developed by Lockheed Aircraft Company for the USAF will commence flight tests at Edwards AFB on or about July 15, 1963. Whether the LRI, currently designated the X-22, will go into full production will depend on the decision of the Secretary of Defense which, in turn, will be based on the results of a major study and evaluation of further Air Force interceptor needs currently under way at the Pentagon and due on the desk of Secretary McNamara early June.

"The announcement will further state that the LRI prototype is the result of a limited design competition between Convair and Lockheed in 1959 which resulted in the selection of the LAC design using the Pratt & Whitney J58 engine. The stringent security measures applied to the development program from its inception resulted from a decision by the previous administration to deny the Soviets critical information on our future air defense systems which could vitally affect their decisions with regard to offensive weapon systems and countermeasures. The program was reviewed by the present administration in 1961, and the decision was made to continue development of the aircraft under the same rigid security policy then in effect."

By May 21, 1963, the Perkin-Elmer Type I camera was initially ordered in a quantity of six units; one flyable prototype and five production models. During the course of prototype development the efforts of the contractor to get the ultimate resolution from the system led to a degree of complexity that appeared undesirable. Accordingly, a second contract was let to Eastman Kodak for a flightworthy prototype, using the philosophy of simple mechanical design, and accommodating the camera to the environment rather than changing the environment to suit the camera – as Perkin-Elmer had done. At the same time a modification of the "B" camera was supported as a backup system to insure that one of the three types would be available for use in the A-12. All three systems had met their design goals insofar as it had been possible to test them in a vehicle that would provide the "high, hot, and fast" environment for which they were designed. By the

middle of May there were three Perkin-Elmer cameras, three Eastman cameras, and one modified type "B" at the test site. During February of 1963, a contact was let to Hycon Manufacturing for three cameras of a design similar to the "B" cameras that were then being used successfully in the Idealist program.

The Perkin-Elmer Type I camera employed an optical system that delivered the same resolution across the full frame as it did at the optical axis, a distinct advantage since much of the photography of interest was on occasion at an 80 mile slant range from the aircraft and 10 degrees off-axis from the lens. The Eastman Kodak Type II camera was a simple and maintenance-free design but it could not provide the high resolution of the Perkin-Elmer Type I. Its shortcoming was partially overcome, however, by a slightly longer focal length and in some respects, better stereo coverage. The Type III, or "B" camera, was modified to operate in the *Oxcart* environment. Flight tests showed that the modifications were successful and that satisfactory performance could be expected when carried by an A-12.

The final camera type, the Hycon Type IV, in design and concept, followed the pattern of the "B" design used in the Idealist program. It took advantage of state-of-the-art developments in film, transport, optical technology, and vibration control. Ground resolution was better than the Type II or III cameras. It had a seven position lens mode consisting of 3 right obliques, one vertical, and 3 left obliques that provided 25 nautical miles of coverage on either side of the flight path. Although this was a new and untried system, the major components had been tested on previous programs. Further, the basic concept was the same as the "B" camera that the contractor had utilized for many years during the course of the U-2 program.

By May of 1963, the Type I camera had delivered the best resolution during flight test and had shown good reliability during its 19 flights to date. The Type II had demonstrated similar reliability but with a lower ground resolution. The Type III was only considered "a backup system" and was not tested. And finally, the Type IV appeared to have the greatest potential for a high-resolution system, but

to date, had not been flight tested and would not be until September.

On May 24, the third A-12, Article 123, involved in a subsonic engine test flight and piloted by Ken Collins, crashed 14 miles south of Wendover, Utah. Collins ejected successfully and was unhurt. The aircraft wreckage was recovered in two days and all persons at the scene were identified and requested to sign a secrecy agreement. A press cover story referred to the crashed aircraft as a Republic F-105. The A-12 fleet was temporarily grounded following the accident while an investigation was conducted. A pitot-static system failure due to icing was quickly determined to be the culprit.

By mid-1963 five A-12s were flying. This, coupled with the loss of a third aircraft, renewed Agency and Air Force concerns over how long the project could be kept secret. The program had gone through development, construction, and a year of flight testing without attracting public attention. But the Department of Defense was having difficulty in concealing its participation because of the increasing expenditure rate which had, until now, gone unexplained. There also was a realization that the technological data would be extremely valuable in connection with feasibility studies for the supersonic transport program...which was rapidly accelerating throughout the US aerospace industry. Finally, there was a growing awareness in the higher reaches of the aircraft industry that something new and remarkable was going on. Rumors were spreading.

The four-week period from September 12 to October 10 was summarized by Johnson with, "We have been to Mach 3.0 twice, now, the first time being on July 20. On the second flight, we blew an engine at design speed. It was very difficult to slow down and it rattled Lou Schalk around for three minutes. The aircraft stability augmentation system did precisely as I asked it to do three years ago and no high structural loads were obtained."

By November, the aforementioned intake problems were finally being brought under control. "Today we flew the mice installation (mice were small bump fairings that protruded into the intake airstream and served to smooth

the flow to the engine compressor section face; ed.), to change the subsonic diffusion angles in the duct. This change corrected the roughness encountered at Mach 2.4 and up, and it is the first major improvement in the duct. Collected 25 cents from Rich, Fuller, and Boehme ("Kelly" had bet the three engineers that the mice installation would solve the problem; ed.)."

Jim Eastham now took the first A-12 out to 3.30 Mach and then cruised at 3.20 Mach for fifteen minutes. "At about this same time, we flew the second aircraft for 53 minutes at Mach 2.65 or above." By the end of 1963, the CIA's A-12 flight-test program had resulted in 573 flights totaling 765 hours. Nine aircraft were on hand at Groom Lake/Area 51. As noted earlier, during July, 3.0 Mach had been reached for the first time and during November, design speed – 3.20 Mach – had been reached at an altitude of 78,000 feet. The following February 3, an A-12 had cruised at 3.20 Mach at an altitude of 83,000 feet for ten minutes. By the end of 1964 the A-12 fleet – now consisting of eleven aircraft – had logged over 1,214 flights and 1,669 hours of flying time. Only 6 hours and 23 minutes of this had been at 3.0 Mach. Only 33 minutes of the latter had been at 3.20 Mach.

These numbers changed drastically within the following year. By late 1965, some 33 hours had been logged at 2.60 Mach or above, and total 3.0 Mach time was now 9 hours. All 3.0 Mach time had been logged by test aircraft. The CIA's "operational" aircraft, because of extant propulsion system difficulties, were temporarily limited to maximum speeds of 2.90 Mach.

During mid-1964, difficulties with the A-12, also reflected in the YF-12 interceptor derivative (which had, by now, flown), had yet to be fully overcome. Transonic acceleration remained troublesome and miscellaneous subsystems still required major improvements

in dependability. On July 9, Lockheed test pilot Bill Park was forced to eject from A-12, Article 133, during final approach to landing at Groom Lake/Area 51. Bill was uninjured and the cause of the accident was quickly determined to be "a stuck outboard elevon servo valve."

It should be noted at this point that on July 24, 1964, President Johnson made the first official announcement concerning the forthcoming Lockheed SR-71. As part of the A-12's history, it is necessary to understand that from this point forward, there was a plan to replace the A-12 with Air Force's follow-on aircraft.

During mid-August, there were discussions on the status of *Oxcart* and its effect on the upcoming speed run attempt with the AF-12 (i.e., YF-12A) and the possibility of using the first two *Oxcart* aircraft to set the world speed record for class. The time when the speed test could be conducted was discussed and it became apparent that the whole idea was premature. The three YF-12As at Edwards had not been brought up-to-date from a modification standpoint and it was thought these would be necessary to meet the 3.20 Mach condition. Earlier emphasis had been placed on armament, missile adaptation and so on while upgrades had been placed on hold.

In a "Memorandum for the Record" dated August 18, 1964, John A. McCone, Director of Central Intelligence, sent the following communication to "Kelly" Johnson. "Speed Test. Johnson stated on orders received from McMillian on Wednesday, August 12, thirty-seven Lockheed personnel had been transferred from Area 51 to Edwards AFB. The engines on plane 122 had been removed and boxed for shipment and loaded on a C-130, but had not been moved The order received from McMillian called for placing the speed test on the highest priority, to be accomplished in September. It is recognized that this would delay further flights on 121 and 122 for two to

four weeks (probably the latter – would limit testing to flights of 129 during September. The speed test program would remove 2 *Oxcart* A-12s (121 and 122) from the test program until September 15th at the earliest."

Johnson was deeply concerned over the possibility of attaining the operational readiness by November 1. Certainly this could not be done unless, "Lockheed be instructed to place the operational readiness of the A-12 on the highest priority and that no one interfere. NRO must understand this and SAC, who are now becoming more active with their RS-71 program, must recognize this priority.

"NRO, CIA and the operational people at Area 51 recognize that we seek in project *Skylark* (Cuban overflight program) an operational readiness against Cuba and therefore we must be constrained to Introduce only such modifications, ECM equipment and other gadgets as are required for the mission. (This should include *Bird Watcher*.)"

In closing, the McCone memo stated, "With respect to the Lockheed organization, Johnson claims he has the 'bases covered'. I was of the impression that the organization is overloaded and believe it most important to get the A-12 fully checked out and off his mind so as to turn him loose to work on the AF-12 and the RS-71."

Attempts to make the A-12 operational had been short-circuited by the various technological difficulties that continued to surface. During August of 1964, it was determined that the CIA required four operational aircraft to overfly Cuba by November 5. Johnson noted this with, "We have been told by the Soviets that immediately after the election they intend to shoot down every U-2, which we are operating at a rate of 18 sorties per month. Should this be done, we would be unable to find out whether they put missiles back in; the A-12 is vital for this purpose."

Top: **Nicknamed "Titanium Goose", the single two-seat A-12 is seen during the course of an early test flight over Groom Lake/Area 51. This aircraft spent its entire career powered only by the original Pratt & Whitney J75s with which it was delivered. "Kelly" Johnson made his only A-12 flight in this aircraft.** Lockheed Martin via Tony Landis collection

Left: **The "Titanium Goose" departs Groom Lake/Area 51 on an early test flight.** Lockheed Martin via Tony Landis collection

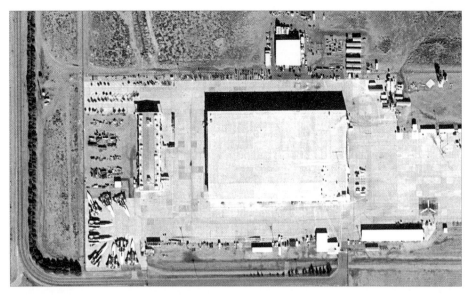

Though transition training was now taking place at Groom Lake/Area 51, by November of 1964 there still was not a single Agency pilot qualified to fly the extremely temperamental A-12 – which the CIA now was sometimes referring to under the codename *Cygnus* – on a reconnaissance mission. As a result, Johnson volunteered Lockheed test pilots to make the overflights of Cuba.

According to Johnson's log, under the then-classified project codename of *Skylark*, the CIA accepted his offer, and on November 10 the first A-12 operational mission and first penetration of denied airspace was successfully completed.

Unfortunately, the official CIA record disputes Johnson's recollection. It summarizes the first operational mission as follows: "By early 1964 Project Headquarters began planning for the contingency of flights over that island (Cuba) under a program designated *Skylark*. Bill Park's accident in early July held this program up for a time, but on 5 August, acting DCI Marshall S. Carter directed that *Skylark* achieve emergency operational readiness by November 5. This involved preparing a small detachment which should be able to do the job over Cuba though at something less than the full design capability of the *Oxcart*. The goal was to operate at Mach 2.80 and 80,000 feet altitude.

"In order to meet the deadline set by Gen. Carter, camera performance would have to be validated, pilots qualified for Mach 2.80 flight, and coordination with supporting elements arranged. Only one of several equipments for electronic countermeasures (ECM) would be

ready by November and a senior intra-governmental group, including representation from the President's Scientific Advisory Committee, examined the problem of operating over Cuba without the full complement of defensive systems. This panel decided that the first few overflights could safely be conducted without them, but the ECM would be necessary thereafter. The delivery schedule of ECM equipment was compatible with this course of action.

After considerable modifications to the aircraft, the detachment simulated Cuban missions on training flights, and a limited emergency *Skylark* capability was announced on the date Gen. Carter had set. With two weeks notice the *Oxcart* detachment could accomplish a Cuban overflight, though with fewer ready aircraft and pilots than planned.

During a briefing for the Director of Central Intelligence, on February 26, 1965, the status of *Skylark* was reviewed. The first upgrades, referred to as the *Phase II Skylark*, provided for modifications to improve the *Skylark* capabilities from the 2.90 Mach to 3.05 Mach level. The second modification served to provide the special ECM package, codenamed *Supermarket*, and for a three-refueling-mission capability.

The *Supermarket* defensive ECM package consisted of *Blue Dog*, *Big Blast*, *Pin Peg*, and *Mad Mouth*. *Blue Dog* consisted of a receiver and an antenna array optimized to

provide a visual indication to the pilot of where a surface-to-air missile system's tracking radar energy was relative to the nose of the aircraft. It served to tell the pilot that his aircraft was being tracked and from where. If the pilot had DF indicators simultaneously on both sides, the system (whatever it was) was dead ahead of the aircraft.

The pilot's visual indicators were located on top of the viewing periscope and enclosed in the cockpit glare shield. The outermost lights of the five indicators were the DF lights. The next set of lights on either side of the DF lights, were the LI or Launch Indicators. If these lights illuminated, it meant the SAM site had gone to high PRF (pulse repetition frequency) and most likely had launched. If the center light illuminated, it was a lock-on.

The *Supermarket* ECM (jamming) system, code named *Big Blast*, was a very powerful noise jammer that denied target range from SA-2 radar. This forced the missile into a three point guidance mode and early arming of its fuse. *Big Blast* normally was not employed if the other systems were in working order.

The *Pin Peg* system was a "confusion missile jamming system" that passively intercepted SA-2 radar signals and essentially recorded the command information to the missile and replayed it back. Command guidance information was repeated, thus confusing the

missile during its flight to target. Another system, *Mad Moth*, denied accurate angle-of-intercept information to the SA-2 tracking radar.

A redundancy existed between the recognition and jamming systems employed in the A-12. This gave it a lower degree of vulnerability and accounted for a high degree (100%) of total system reliability.

During the following weeks the detachment concentrated on developing *Skylark* into a sustained capability, with five ready pilots and five operational aircraft. The main tasks were to determine aircraft range and fuel consumption, attain repeatable reliable operation, finish pilot training, prepare a family of *Skylark* missions, and coordinate routes with North American Air Defense, Continental Air Defense, and the Federal Aviation Administration. All this was accomplished without substantially hindering the main task of working up *Oxcart* to full design capability. Regardless, according to the CIA document quoted, "*Oxcart* was never used over Cuba. U-2s proved adequate and the A-12 was reserved for more critical situations."

As of January 26, 1965, five Perkin-Elmer camera systems had been delivered to Groom Lake/Area 51 and were in flight-test status. Two Eastman Kodak and one Hycon system cameras also were on hand. The Hycon system was being readied for its initial test flights. All systems had performed satisfactorily within the constraints of flight-test operations. Approximately 105 payload flights had been made to date, these exploring the effects of altitude, speed, and course changes on the sensor payloads. The tests were far more demanding than expected operational missions, as the quantity of flight envelope variations was far greater than what was expected to actually occur.

Not surprisingly, the majority of the sensor system test flights were actually for pilot training. Aircraft functional check-out was the primary objective with photography being only incidental. No degradation of the photography due to thermal gradients or turbulence had yet been noted at speeds up to 2.96 Mach and pressure altitudes of 80,000 feet.

During 1965, the "critical situation" the Agency's A-12 Detachment had been waiting for finally emerged in Asia. On March 18, 1965, the CIA's John McCone discussed with Secretary of Defense Robert McNamara and Secretary Cyrus Vance the increasing hazards to U-2 and unmanned drone reconnaissance of China. "It was further agreed that we should proceed immediately with all preparatory steps necessary to operate the *Oxcart* over Communist China, flying out of Okinawa. It was agreed that we should proceed with all construction and related arrangements. However, this decision did not authorize all

preparatory steps and the expenditure of such funds as might be involved. No decision has been taken to fly the *Oxcart* operationally over Communist China. This decision can only be made by the President."

Four days later, Brig. Gen. Jack Ledford, Director of the Office of Special Activities, briefed Mr. Vance on the scheme which had been drawn up for operations in the Far East. The project was called *Black Shield*, and it required the A-12 to operate out of Kadena Air Force Base in Okinawa. In the first phase, three aircraft would stage to Okinawa for sixty-day periods twice a year, with about 225 personnel involved. Following this, *Black Shield* would advance to a point of maintaining a permanent detachment at Kadena. Secretary Vance made $3.7 million available to provide support facilities on the island, which were to be available by early fall of 1965.

The deployment of surface-to-air missiles around Hanoi also had caught US forces in the rapidly escalating Vietnam war off guard. Secretary McNamara, after being briefed, called this to the attention of the Under Secretary of the Air Force on June 3, 1965, and inquired about the practicability of substituting A-12s for U-2s. He was told that *Black Shield* could operate over Vietnam as soon as adequate aircraft performance was achieved.

Thus with deployment impending in the fall, the detachment went into the final stages of its program for validating the reliability of aircraft and aircraft systems. It set out to demonstrate complete systems reliability at 3.05 Mach and 2,300 nautical miles range, with a penetration altitude of 76,000 feet. A demonstrated capability of three aerial refuelings also was to be part of the validation requirement.

Concurrent with operational activities, work continued on the A-12's propulsion system throughout much of 1965. On January 4, Johnson noted, "it appears that our duct problems at high speed are stemming from excess leakage at the engine face and various bypass doors. Have concluded 10,764 wind tunnel tests on the inlet alone, and every one of them confirms our present design. The addition of mice not only solved the roughness problem but gained us 2% in ram. We will gradually work up to our basic performance, as close as we can expect to get it, considering the engine's overweight and added equipment in the airplane."

On January 27, 1965, an A-12 had embarked on the type's first long-range, high-speed flight. Airborne for an hour and forty minutes, it spent an hour and fifteen minutes at 3.1 Mach or above. The mission covered 2,580 nautical miles while at an altitude of between 75,600 and 80,000 feet.

On March 18, Johnson sent Hamilton Standard a letter saying Lockheed no longer could use the AIC-10 inlet control. "We have

Top: **A-12, 60-6924, Article 121, was the first airplane completed and the first to fly...and thus the prototype for the series. Following retirement and storage, it was restored for static display purposes and today can be seen at Blackbird Airpark west of the *Skunk Works* Palmdale, California facility.** Jim Goodall

Next page bottom: **Another A-12 following restoration, 60-6931, Article 128, is currently displayed at Minnesota Air Guard Facility, Minneapolis-St. Paul International Airport, Minnesota.** Jim Goodall

spent $17 million on the thing to this point, but it just will not do the job and is totally unpredictable."

Difficulties with the A-12's performance as a result of intake problems had become the aircraft's Achilles' heel, particularly in the flight regime between 2.40 and 2.48 Mach. Ongoing studies of the intake and its spike had failed to uncover a solution to airflow anomalies until a review of the Hamilton Standard actuator had determined it was not working. At that point, Ben Rich, who was responsible for the *Skunk Works'* side of the propulsion system package and, in particular, the intake design, concluded the Hamilton Standard hydro-mechanical spike control unit could not be made to work. Garrett Corporation then provided an electrically-powered actuator that, following installation, solved almost all the spike control problems virtually overnight.

The A-12 flight-test program had not gone without losses. At Groom Lake/Area 51, the number six aircraft, piloted by Mele Vojvodich, Jr., crashed on December 28, 1965. It had yawed violently shortly after taking off on a test flight. When additional corrective actions by the pilot had not stabilized the aircraft, Vojvodich ejected. He landed with only minor injuries, but the A-12 was a total loss. Johnson would note, "Coming down in the airplane with Bill Park and Burt McMaster, we analyzed the situation within a half hour. The SAS gyros were hooked up backwards. This is the first thing I told the accident board to look at. Prior to leaving Groom Lake/Area 51, Ed Martin cut the gyros out, keeping the wires connected. Lo and behold – the pitch and yaw gyro connections were interchanged in the rigging, which explained the accident completely."

Continuing concerns about various A-12 systems and their impact on the aircraft's performance were addressed during the fall of 1965 when four A-12s were selected for assignment to *Black Shield*. Johnson took personal responsibility for seeing to the solution of the various problems and assuring the CIA the aircraft would be ready for operational service on schedule. During the tests that ensued, an A-12 achieved a maximum speed of 3.29 Mach, an altitude of 90,000 feet, and a sustained flight time above 3.20 Mach of one hour and fourteen minutes. The longest flight lasted six hours and twenty minutes.

On November 20, 1965, Johnson wrote Gen. Ledford, "...overall, my considered opinion is that the aircraft can be successfully deployed for the *Black Shield* mission with what I would consider to be at least as low a degree of risk as in the early U-2 deployment days. Actually, considering our performance level of more than four times the U-2 speed and three miles more operating altitude, it is probably much less risky than our first U-2 deployment. I think the time has come when the bird should leave its nest."

Ten days later, the 303 Committee received a formal proposal calling for the A-12 to be deployed to the Far East. The proposal was rejected. The Committee did agree, however, that short of actually moving aircraft to Kadena, all steps should be taken to develop and maintain a quick reaction capability. The aircraft should be ready to deploy within a 21-day period at any time after January 1, 1966.

Throughout 1966, the A-12 program had continued to flounder. In effect, it had no legitimate mission. During the year, repeated requests to authorize flights over China and North Vietnam were refused. The CIA, the Joint Chiefs of Staff, and the President's Foreign Intelligence Advisory Board favored the overflights, while Alexis Johnson of the State Department, McNamara, and Vance of the Defense Department opposed them. Perhaps most importantly, the President sided with the opposition...agreeing that the political and technological risks were too great.

On May 12, 1966, Johnson wrote in the log, "As of this date, there is still no go-ahead for the deployment, although it seems fairly optimistic. The airplanes are ready to go. We do not yet have the range up to the design value, but two-thirds of the loss has been due to weight changes due to added equipment. One third of it is due to loss in range cruising. We can do about 3,000 nautical miles, but they, of course, do not get the range that we can."

On October 10, he noted, "Still no deployment. We are making 40 flights a month. The airplane is working quite well. It has not yet obtained its range. We are down to working on duct leakage and basic engine performance."

An impressive demonstration of the A-12's capability occurred on December 21, 1966, when the *Skunk Works'* Bill Park flew the aircraft 10,198 statute miles in six hours. Parks had departed Groom Lake/Area 51 and had flown northward over Yellowstone National Park, then east to Bismarck, North Dakota. and on to Duluth, Minnesota. He had then turned south and passed Atlanta, Georgia enroute to Tampa, Florida, then northwest to Portland, Oregon, and then back for a pass over Groom Lake/Area 51. From there, he had headed eastward passing over Denver, Colorado, and St. Louis, Missouri. Turning around at Knoxville, Tennessee, he had passed Memphis, Tennessee, for his return to Groom Lake/Area 51. It was a record unapproachable by any other aircraft in the world. Sadly, it would not become public knowledge until almost three decades after its occurrence.

On January 5, 1967, Walter Ray and the fourth A-12 were lost during the course of a routine training flight from Groom Lake/Area 51. The post-accident investigation led to the conclusion that a fuel gauge apparently failed and the aircraft's fuel supply had depleted without the pilot being fully aware of the problem. The engines flamed out shortly before the aircraft reached the runway. Ray ejected but was killed when he failed to separate from the ejection seat before impact.

The CIA's inability to justify using the A-12 operationally, by the end of 1966 had led to concerns the aircraft would soon be placed in storage. As late as January 26, 1967, Johnson made the following comments in the A-12 log, "We are still not clear on going about storing the airplanes. I spent some time yesterday with Larry Bohanan going over the personnel problems in our flight-test crew. It is inevitable that we lose half of our good people this year. And there is no flight-test activity in CALAC to use them. In spite of the plans to store the airplanes, Headquarters are going ahead with putting changes on the airplanes, because the word hasn't gotten around. I'm trying to get some direction to this program, to prevent further waste of money. I think back to 1959, before we started this airplane, to discussions with the Program Office where we seriously considered the problem of whether there would be one more round of aircraft before the satellites took over. We jointly agreed there would be just one round, and not two. That seems to have been a very accurate evaluation, as it seems that 30 SR-71s give us enough overflight reconnaissance capability and we don't need the additional ten A-12 aircraft."

The plan to place the A-12s in storage continued to accelerate during the first few months of 1967. On March 21, Johnson wrote, "The Air Force and the Program Office are having quite a time about storing the A-12s. It appears that half of them will be stored by the middle of this year and all of them by February of 1968. In the meantime, five airplanes will be kept on alert status for deployment."

With this bleak prognosis, it came as somewhat of a surprise during early May when prospects for operational deployment suddenly took a new turn. Concerns that surface-to-air missiles would be deployed in North Vietnam suddenly provided the small A-12 community with a raison d'etre during early 1967. The President now asked for a review of surface-to-air missile activity in North Vietnam and what might be done to monitor it.

The Agency, in response, briefed the 303 Committee and once again suggested the A-12 be used. It was noted that its Hycon camera was far superior to those then being used on the various Teledyne Ryan drones and operational SAC U-2s...and its vulnerability was considerably less. As a result, the State and Defense Department members of the Committee elected to re-examine the requirements and political risks. While this was taking place, the CIA's director, Richard Helms, submitted to the 303 Committee another formal proposal to deploy the A-12. President Johnson, concurrently, granted permission for use of the unique aircraft and on May 16, his assistant, Wait Rostow, formally conveyed the President's decision. *Black Shield* was put into effect immediately.

On May 17, the first support components of *Black Shield* were airlifted to Kadena AB in Okinawa. They were followed on May 22 by the first A-12, Article 131, piloted by Mele Vojvodich, which arrived six hours and six minutes after departing Groom Lake/Area 51. The flight required three aerial refuelings and attained 79,000 ft. during cruise at 2.90 Mach for two legs and 3.10 Mach for one. On May 24, Article 127, piloted by Dennis Sullivan, flew non-stop from Groom Lake/Area 51 to Kadena AB, Okinawa in six hours. The flight was similar to that of Article 131, except an altitude of 81,000 ft. was reached during the cruise portion of the flight. Ken Collins left Groom Lake/Area 51 on May 26 in Article 129 and headed for Kadena. As a result of inertial navigation system failure and communications system problems, Collins landed at Wake Island enroute before proceeding on to Kadena the next day.

On May 29, 1967, the unit was declared ready to fly its first operational mission. Under the command of Col. Hugh Slater, 260 personnel had been transferred to Kadena as part of the *Black Shield* team. Except for hangars, which were a month short of completion, everything was in shape for sustained operations. The next day, the detachment was alerted for a mission to be scheduled for May 31.

On May 31, Article 131 departed on the first operational A-12 mission – BSX-001 – albeit in the middle of a heavy rain (a first for the A-12). The flight followed a predetermined route over North Vietnam and the Demilitarized Zone. It lasted three hours and 39 minutes. Cruise legs were flown at 3.10 Mach at an altitude of 80,000 feet. Results

were satisfactory and seventy of the 190 surface-to-air missile sites in North Vietnam were photographed...along with nine other priority targets. There were no radar signals detected – implying the Chinese and North Vietnamese had not known about the aircraft's flyover.

Fifteen *Black Shield* missions were alerted during the period from May 31 to August 15, 1967 and seven were actually flown. Four of these resulted in detectable radar activity, but no hostile action was taken. By mid-July, the A-12 overflights had determined with a high degree of confidence that there were no surface-to-surface missiles in North Vietnam.

All operational missions were planned, directed, and controlled by Project Headquarters in Washington, DC. A constant watch was maintained on the weather in the various target areas, Each day, at a specified hour (1600 hours local), a mission alert briefing was given to appropriate *Black Shield* personnel. If the forecast weather appeared favorable, the Kadena base was alerted and provided a route to be flown. The alert preceded actual take-off by 28 to 30 hours. Twelve hours prior to take-off (H minus 12) a second review of the target area's weather was made. If it continued favorable, the mission generation sequence continued. At H minus 2 hours, a "go-no-go" decision was made and communicated to the field. The final decision depended not solely on weather in the target area but also on conditions in the refueling, launch, and recovery areas.

Operations and maintenance at Kadena began with the receipt of alert notification. Both a primary aircraft and pilot and a back-up aircraft and pilot were selected. The aircraft were given a thorough inspection and servicing, all systems were checked, and the cameras were loaded. Pilots received a detailed route briefing in the early evening prior to the day of flight. On the morning of the flight a final briefing occurred, at which time the condition of the aircraft and its systems was reported, last minute weather forecasts reviewed, and other relevant intelligence communicated together with any amendments or changes in the flight plan. Two hours prior to take-off the primary pilot had a medical examination, got into his full pressure suit, and was taken to the aircraft. If any malfunctions developed on the primary aircraft, the back-up could execute the mission one hour later.

A typical *Black Shield* mission route profile over North Vietnam included a refueling south of Okinawa shortly after take-off, the planned photographic pass or passes over the target(s), withdrawal to a second aerial refueling in the Thailand area, and return to Kadena. So great was the A-12's speed that it spent only twelve and a half minutes over North Vietnam in a typical "single pass" mission, or a total of twenty-one and a half minutes on two passes. Its turning radius of 86 miles was such, however, that on some mission profiles it might be forced during its turn to intrude into Chinese airspace.

Once landed at Kadena, the film was removed from the camera, boxed, and sent by special aircraft to a processing facility. Film from earlier missions was developed at the

Above: **A-12, 60-6931, Article 128, is part of the Minnesota Air Guard Museum exhibit at Minneapolis-St. Paul International Airport, Minnesota.** Jim Goodall

Next page top: **Fuselage internal details.** Lockheed Martin via Miller Collection

Next page bottom: **Desk model study of an A-12-optimized pod carrying a synthetic aperture radar (SAR) system.** Lockheed Martin via Tony Landis collection

Eastman Kodak plant in Rochester, New York. By late summer of 1967, an Air Force Center in Japan began processing it in order to place the photo intelligence in the hands of American commanders in Vietnam within twenty-four hours of a *Black Shield* mission's completion.

Johnson had been kept apprised of A-12 activity and successes. On July 18, 1967, he noted in the A-12's log, "The results of the deployment appear to have been very successful. In six flights, more data was obtained than had been gathered the prior year by all other reconnaissance methods. In spite of this favorable performance, I am shocked and amazed to find that the airplane will be returned in December and be stored at Palmdale. At that time, SAC will be deployed with the SR-71."

Between August 16, and December 31, 1967, twenty-six missions were alerted. Fifteen were flown. On September 17, one surface-to-air missile site tracked the vehicle with its acquisition radar but was unsuccessful with its *Fan Song* guidance radar. On October 23, a

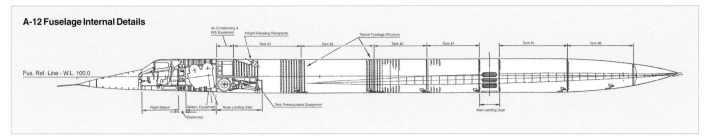

A-12 Fuselage Internal Details

Fus. Ref. Line - W.L. 100.0

North Vietnamese surface-to-air missile site for the first time launched a single, albeit unsuccessful missile at an A-12. Photography from this mission documented the event with photographs of missile smoke above the missile firing site and with pictures of the missile and its contrails. The A-12's electronic countermeasures system appeared to have performed well against the missile's systems.

During mission BX-6734 on October 30, 1967, pilot Dennis Sullivan detected radar tracking on his first pass over North Vietnam. Two sites prepared to launch missiles but neither did. During the second pass, at least six missiles were fired, each confirmed by vapor trails documented on mission photography. Sullivan saw these vapor trails and witnessed three missile detonations. Post-flight inspection of the aircraft revealed that a small piece of threaded metal had penetrated the lower right wing fillet area. The fragment was not a warhead pellet but was probably part of the debris from one of the missile detonations.

Between January 1 and March 31, 1968, six missions were flown out of fifteen alerted. Four of these were over North Vietnam and two were over North Korea. The first mission (flown by Agency pilot Frank Murray) over North Korea on January 26 occurred during a very tense period following seizure of the USS *Pueblo* on January 23. The objective was to discover whether the North Koreans were preparing any large scale hostile moves on the heels of this incident. Chinese tracking of the flight was detected, but no missiles were fired.

The Department of State was reluctant to endorse a second mission over North Korea for fear of the diplomatic repercussions which could be expected if the aircraft came down in hostile territory. Brig. Gen. Paul Bacals then briefed Secretary Rusk on the details and objectives of the mission and assured him the aircraft would transit North Korea in no more than seven minutes. He explained that even if some failure occurred during flight the aircraft would be highly unlikely to land either in North Korea or China. Secretary Rusk made suggestions to alter the flight plan, thus becoming the project's highest-ranking flight planner.

Between April 1, and June 9, 1968, two missions were alerted for North Korea. Only the mission which flew on May 8 was granted approval. Flown by Jack Layton, in Article 131, it would prove to be the last operational A-12 mission...ever.

During November of 1965, the very month when the A-12 finally was declared operational, the moves toward its retirement had commenced. Within the Bureau of the Budget a memorandum was circulated expressing concern at the costs of the A-12 and SR-71 programs, both past and projected. It questioned the requirement for the total number of aircraft represented in the combined fleets and expressed doubt about the necessity of a independent Agency program. Several alternatives were proposed to achieve a substantial reduc-

tion in the forecast spending, but the recommended course was to phase out the A-12 by September of 1966 and stop any further SR-71 procurement. Copies of this memorandum were sent to the Department of Defense and the CIA with the suggestion that those entities explore the alternatives proposed in the paper. The Secretary of Defense declined to consider the proposal, presumably because the SR-71 would not be operational by September of 1966.

The A-12 program remained suspended in this state until July of 1966 when the Bureau of the Budget proposed that a study group be established to look into the possibility of reducing expenses on the A-12 and SR-71 programs. The group was requested to consider the following alternatives:

(1) Retention of separate A-12 and SR-71 fleets, i.e., status quo.

(2) Co-location of the two fleets.

(3) Transfer of the A-12 mission and aircraft to the Strategic Air Command.

(4) Transfer of the A-12 mission to SAC and storage of the A-12s.

(5) Transfer of the A-12 mission to SAC and disposal of the A-1 2s.

The study group included C. W. Fisher, Bureau of the Budget; Herbert Bennington, Department of Defense; and John Parangosky, CIA. It concluded its review through the fall of 1966 and identified three principal alternatives of its own. These were:

(1) To maintain the status quo and continue both fleets at current approval levels.

(2) To mothball all A-12 aircraft, but maintain the capability by sharing SR-71 aircraft between SAC and the CIA.

(3) To terminate the A-12 fleet during January of 1968 (assuming an operational readiness date of September 1967 for the SR-71) and assign all missions to the SR-71 fleet.

On December 12, 1966, there was a meeting at the Bureau of the Budget attended by Richard Helms, George Schultze, Cyrus Vance, and Richard Hornig (scientific advisor to the President). Those present voted on the alternatives proposed in the Fischer/Bennington/Parangosky report. Vance, Schultze, and Hornig chose to terminate the A-12 fleet and Helms was in favor of eventually sharing the SR-71 fleet between the CIA and SAC. The Bureau of the Budget immediately prepared a letter to President Johnson setting forth the

course of action recommended by the majority. Helms, having dissented from the majority, requested his Deputy Director for Science and Technology to prepare a letter to the President stating the CIA's reasons for remaining in the reconnaissance business.

On December 16, Schultze handed Helms a draft memorandum to the President which requested a decision either to share the SR-71 fleet between the CIA and SAC or terminate the CIA's reconnaissance capability entirely. This time, Helms replied that new information of considerable significance had been brought to his attention concerning SR-71 performance. He requested another meeting after January 1, to review pertinent facts and also asked that the memorandum to the President be withheld pending the meeting's outcome. Specifically he cited indications the SR-71 program was having serious technical problems and that there was real doubt that it would achieve an operational capability by the time suggested for termination of the A-12 program. Helms therefore changed his position from sharing the SR-71 aircraft with SAC to a firm recommendation to retain the A-12 fleet under civilian sponsorship. The Budget Bureau's memorandum was nevertheless transmitted to the President who, on December 23, 1966 accepted the Vance, Hornig, and Schultze recommendation and directed the A-12 program be terminated by January 1, 1968.

This decision meant that a schedule had to be developed for orderly phase-out. After consultation with Project Headquarters, the Deputy Secretary of Defense was advised on January 10, 1967, that four A-12s would be placed in storage during July of 1967, two more by December, and the last four by the end of January 1968. During May, Vance directed that the SR-71 assume contingency responsibility to conduct Cuban overflights as of July 1, 1967, and take over the dual capability over Southeast Asia and Cuba by December 1. This provided for some overlap between A-12 withdrawal and SR-71 assumption of responsibility.

Meanwhile, until July 1, 1967, the A-12 Detachment was to maintain its capability to conduct operational missions both from a prepared location overseas and from the US. This included a 15-day quick reaction capability for deployment to the Far East and a seven-day

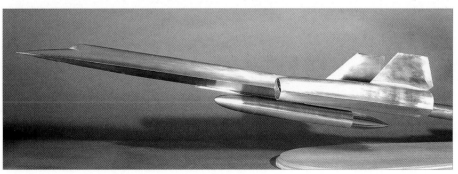

quick reaction for deployment over Cuba. Between July 1 and December 31, 1967, the fleet would remain able to conduct operational missions either from a prepared overseas base or from home base, but not from both simultaneously. A quick reaction capability for either Cuban overflights or deployment to the Far East would also be maintained.

All of these arrangements were made before the A-12 had conducted a single operational mission or even deployed to Kadena. As noted earlier, the first A-12 mission over North Vietnam took place on the last day of May 1967. In succeeding months it demonstrated both its exceptional technical capabilities and the competence with which its operations were managed. As word began to get around the A-12 was to be phased out, high officials began to feel some disquiet. Concern was shown by Walt Rostow, the President's Special Assistant; by key Congressional figures; members of the President's Foreign Intelligence Advisory Board; and the President's Scientific Advisory Committee. The phase-out lagged, and the decision was then re-examined.

Alternatives were reviewed once again and in a memorandum to Paul Nitze, Richard Hornig, and several others, dated April 18, 1966, Cyrus Vance questioned why, if eight SR-71s could be stored in one option, why could they not be stored in all options, with the resulting savings applied in each case. He questioned the lower cost figures of combining the A-12s with the SR-71s and disagreed, for security reasons, with co-locating the two fleets. Above all, however, he felt that the key point was the desirability of retaining a covert reconnaissance capability under civilian management. It was his judgment that such a requirement existed and he recommended that A-12s continue at their own base under CIA management.

In spite of all these belated efforts, Clark Clifford on May 16, 1968, reaffirmed the original decision to terminate the A-12 program and store the aircraft. At his weekly luncheon with his principal advisors on May 21, 1968, the President confirmed Secretary of Defense Clifford's decision.

During early March of 1968, SR-71s began arriving at Kadena to take over the Black Shield commitment, and by gradual stages the A-12 was placed on standby to back up the SR-71. During April of 1968, Johnson would note in the A-12 log, "The A-12 aircraft are operating with a 30-day overlap with three

SR-71s deployed from Beale. The photographic take of the A-12 is considerably better than that of the SR-71s because the Hycon camera in the latter airplane isn't doing its job."

As noted earlier, the last operational mission flown by the A-12 took place on May 8, 1968, over North Korea, following which the Kadena Detachment was advised to prepare to go home. On May 24, 1968, Johnson would write, "The decision was taken to phase out the A-12 by about mid-June." On May 29, 1968, he would note, "Plans were put into effect for storing the A-12 aircraft at Palmdale."

In fact, Project Headquarters had selected June 8, 1968, as the earliest possible date to begin redeployment, and in the meantime, A-12 flights were limited to those essential for maintaining pilot proficiency. After the Black Shield aircraft returned to the US they were placed in storage at Lockheed's Palmdale, California facility. Those already at the location were placed in storage beginning June 4...with the last going into storage three days later.

During its final days overseas the A-12 program suffered a final blow that was as inexplicable as it was tragic. On June 4, an aircraft piloted by Jack Weeks set out from Kadena on a check flight necessitated by an engine change. Weeks last was heard from when 520 miles east of Manila. At that point, he disappeared. Search and rescue operations found nothing. No cause for the accident was ever ascertained and the Weeks disappearance remains a mystery to this day.

The final A-12 flight took place on June 21, 1968, when the last remaining aircraft, Article 131, was ferried from Groom Lake/Area 51 to Palmdale by CIA pilot Frank Murray and placed in storage. It would remain there for the following two decades.

On June 24, Johnson wrote, "While the intelligence community in Washington wanted very much to keep the A-12 program going, the present financial situation cannot stand the strain. It's a bleak end for a program that has been overall as successful as this."

In summary, the A-12 program, from its inception during 1957 through its termination in 1968, lasted just over ten years. The Skunk Works produced fifteen A-12s and three YF-12As. Five A-12s and two YF-12As were lost in accidents. As a result of those accidents, two pilots were killed, and at least six had narrow escapes. In addition, two F-101 chase aircraft were lost with their Air Force pilots during the A-12 test program.

The main objective of the program – to create a reconnaissance aircraft of unprecedented speed, range, and altitude – was triumphantly achieved. It may well be, however, that the most important aspects of the effort lay in its by-products – the notable advances in aerodynamics, engine performance, cameras, electronic countermeasures, pilot life support systems, and the arcane art of milling, machining, and shaping titanium. Altogether, it was a pioneering accomplishment almost certainly never to be repeated in the history of aviation.

In a ceremony at Groom Lake/Area 51 on June 26, 1968, Vice Admiral Rufus Taylor, Deputy Director of Central Intelligence, presented the CIA Intelligence Star for Valor to pilots Kenneth Collins, Ronald Layton, Francis Murray, Dennis Sullivan, and Mele Vojvodich for participation in the Black Shield operation. The posthumous award to pilot Jack Weeks was accepted by his widow. The Air Force Legion of Merit was presented to Colonel Slater and his Deputy, Colonel Maynard Amundson. The Air Force Outstanding Unit Citation was presented to the members of the 1129th Special Activities Squadron, Detachment 1 (the A-12 Detachment) and the USAF supporting units. "Kelly" Johnson was a guest speaker at the ceremony. In moving words he lamented the end of an enterprise which had marked his most outstanding achievement in aircraft design. In retrospect, it's readily apparent that it also marked the apex of an era in aviation history that almost certainly will never again be seen again.

The following is a listing of all units to which the A-12s were assigned:

1129th Special Activities Squadron

Groom Lake/Area 51, Nevada – This was also known at one time or another as "Watertown Strip", "The Area", "The Ranch", "Paradise Ranch", "Dreamland" and "The Test Site". The unit's only operational deployment was to Det 1, Kadena AB, Okinawa. It was established during 1961/62 and operated by the Central Intelligence Agency.

On May, 17 1967, the first A-12 support components were airlifted to the island. As noted elsewhere in this chapter, the mission was called Black Shield and was formally sanctioned by President Johnson. The first A-12, Article 131/60-6937 arrived at Kadena on May 22, after a 6 hour, 6 minute flight from Groom Lake/Area 51, Nevada. A second A-12, Article 127/60-6930 arrived on May 24, and a third A-12, Article 129/60-6932, arrived on May 27 (following a delay due to INS problems during a stopover at Wake Island). The Oxcart Detachment unit, with 260 personnel and under the command of Col. Hugh Slater, was declared operationally ready on May 29, 1967. The Black Shield team received authorization for its first Operational Mission the following day.

The unit was deactivated during June of 1968, at the same time the A-12 was pulled from operational service.

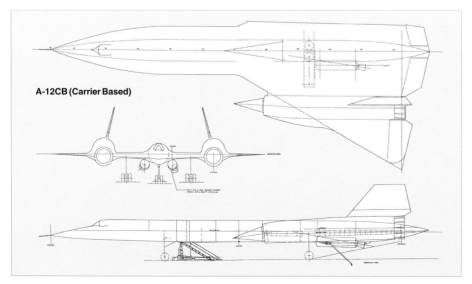

A-12CB (Carrier Based)

Chapter Three

AF-12/YF-12A Long-Range Interceptor

On September 30, 1964, Colonel Allen K. McDonald, YF-12A Program Manager for the Air Defense Command was quoted, "Interceptor development in the past has been characterized by a series of small, incremental improvements. The performance of each new interceptor exceeded that of its predecessors by tenths of a Mach number, a few hundred feet in altitude, and a small increase in combat radius. Radar detection ranges and air-to-air missile ranges likewise advanced in small steps, and each new interceptor continued to depend heavily upon the close control provided by the ground radar environment. By comparison, the YF-12A and its armament system represents a giant step forward in capability and independence of operation.

"In a September 30th statement regarding the YF-12A, General John K. Gerhart, CINC, North American Air Defense Command, stated 'I have been intimately familiar with the development of the Lockheed built YF-12A since its inception.'"

"I have seen it fly, and am abreast of its test program, including the Hughes fire control system and air-to-air missile with which it is equipped. All tests to date indicate to me that the aircraft qualified as an outstanding interceptor."

President Johnson was briefed on the A-12 program a week after taking office during November of 1963. He reacted by directing that a formal public announcement be prepared for release shortly after the first of the year. "Kelly" Johnson had been invited to participate in the unveiling process and on February 25 noted, "Plans going forward for surfacing of the AF-12 program. I worked on the draft to be used by President Johnson and

proposed the terminology 'A-11' as it was the non-anti-radar version."

In fact, a decision had been made to unveil the YF-12A long-range interceptor version rather than the actual A-12. The YF-12A, referred to initially by Johnson as the AF-12, had come into being during the fall of 1960 as the end product of a proposal to the Air Force for a long-range, high-speed interceptor to counter newly perceived Soviet airborne threats. During late October, a letter of intent for $1 million was delivered to Lockheed to "go forward with Plan 3A". As a result, the seventh A-12 was marked to become the AF-12 prototype. Late in the year, Rus Daniell was assigned as AF-12 project engineer by "Kelly" Johnson.

Above: **Full-scale forward fuselage mock-up of the AF-12 during July of 1964. A direct offshoot of the chine-equipped A-12, the AF-12 eventually would metamorphose into the YF-12A. Note suspended AIM-47 mock-up left rear.** Lockheed Martin via Tony Landis collection and (insert) Lockheed Martin via Jim Goodall collection

Right: **One twelfth-scale supersonic wind tunnel model being tested at NASA Ames, California.** Lockheed Martin via Jim Goodall collection

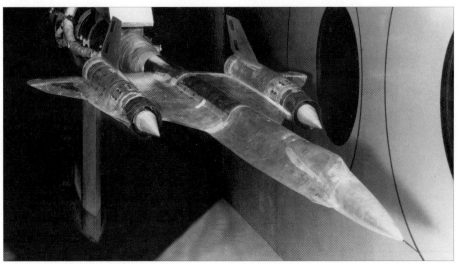

Left: The second YF-12A (aka AF-12), 60-6935, under construction in Building 309/310 of the *Skunk Works* in Burbank, California. The YF-12A project was segregated from the rest of the production line primarily because A-12s were still in production and it was required by the CIA that Air Force personnel privileged to the YF-12A would not be able to see the A-12. Lockheed Martin via Jim Goodall collection

Center and Bottom: The second YF-12A, 60-6935, on the ramp at Groom Lake/Area 51, Nevada. The aircraft is still in its original color scheme of natural metal with black edge trim and black radome.
Lockheed Martin via Jim Goodall collection

Hughes AN/ASG-18 radar. For the first time, ventral fins were introduced into the design, two being in the form of fixed surfaces attached to the rear underside of each engine nacelle, and a third being a large, hydraulically powered folding fin mounted on the fuselage centerline at the rear of the empennage.

The AN/ASG-18 was the first US coherent pulse Doppler radar designed for long-range, look-down, or look-up detection and single target attack. It was intended for use as an air defense interceptor system and was scheduled initially for the North American F-108 *Rapier*. Following termination of the F-108 program on September 23, 1959, Hughes continued research, development, and flight testing of the fire control system – including the Hughes GAR-9/AIM-47 air-to-air missile – on a specially modified Convair B-58A *Hustler*, 55-665.

The AN/ASG-18 employed a high average-power, liquid-cooled, traveling wave tube transmitter chain (consisting of two traveling wave tube amplifiers in tandem to provide the desired gain and analog circuitry for generation and processing of the coherent high pulse repetition frequency wave form. This system provided Hughes with much of the basic coherent high pulse repetition wave form experience that later enabled both the AN/AWG-9 and the AN/APG-63 programs to be accomplished successfully. The AN/ASG-18 radar consisted of 41 units and weighed 1,380 pounds. The entire package included a solid-state digital computer for navigation, attack, and BIT; integrated controls and displays; missile auxiliaries; an analog attack steering computer; and an infrared search and track set capable of cooperative usage with the radar.

Concurrent to the activity on the AF-12, a bomber version of the A-12, referred to as the RB-12, also was being studied. A forward fuselage full-scale mock-up had been completed by mid-1961 and on July 5, along with the AF-12 mock-up, was reviewed by Generals Curtis LeMay and Thomas Power. The two found the mock-ups of considerable interest and asked if either configuration could be modified to carry a terminal radar or an air-to-ground missile.

The AF-12 – as originally conceived by the *Skunk Works* engineering team – was a modified A-12 incorporating a fire control system integrated with a powerful new Hughes search and track radar. A second seat in the original sensor system bay was added to accommodate a fire control system operator. During December of 1960, a separate project group was organized in the *Skunk Works*, working independently of the A-12 team. On January 23 and 24, the first meeting with the Air Force's weapon system project office took place at Burbank and everyone was briefed on the *Skunk Works* aircraft design and development philosophy.

On May 31, the AF-12 mock-up review took place. Johnson noted, "I was very concerned when I learned that some 31 people were coming, but the mock-up group from the Air Force consisted of about 15 people. The different participants told me any number of times how pleased they were with the status of the mock-up, in general, and the ready answers they were getting from our engineering group."

By June, AF-12 wind tunnel tests had revealed directional stability problems that resulted from the revised nose and cockpit configuration mandated by the massive

Johnson responded favorably, stating, "We could do this within the aerodynamic configuration of the A-12 and, for the job that they outlined to do, which was to place a missile within 200 feet of a target, one could not argue about the use of a guided missile rather than our simpler approach in the RB-12 report." The latter referred to the use of conventional free-falling bombs.

The RB-12 study had in fact resulted from the then-recent development of small, high-yield nuclear warheads. Johnson, in an RB-12 proposal, had noted that the aircraft could result in a "very powerful striking force ... with little or no weight or space penalty..." to the aircraft. Four hypothetical 400 pound bombs based on the new warheads, or a single Polaris-type warhead, could be accommodated in the fuselage bomb bay while retaining the same fuel load as the reconnaissance A-12. No aerodynamic changes were required and the radar-attenuating features of the aircraft could be retained. The latter, coupled with the aircraft's extraordinary performance, almost certainly would make the chances of detection and interception close to none.

In addition to these queries, it was noted by Johnson that, "While Hughes was giving a presentation on a simplified air-to-ground weapon system, LeMay took me by the arm and we went to another office. He told me that he wasn't very sure that the RB-12 would become a model, but he felt sure 'we would get some fighters'. I asked him, 'What about reconnaissance airplanes like the A-12?' and he seemed surprised that the Air Force were not getting

any. He made a note on a yellow paper and asked me how soon we would have to know about A-12s to continue our production. I told him within two to three months."

In fact, the RB-12 program would never reach the hardware stage. This was not due to a capability shortfall, but rather because it was a threat to the ongoing North American XB-70A Valkyrie tri-sonic intercontinental range heavy bomber...a program with considerable political clout and one on which the Air Force had hung its hat for a Boeing B-52 replacement. Surprisingly, as noted on October 26, 1961, Johnson discovered the Department of Defense found the RB-12 more interesting than the AF-12. He noted, however, "The Air Force, from LeMay down, do want the AF-12."

Through mid-1962, Johnson continued to work on both the A-12 and AF-12 programs simultaneously. This was an intensive and difficult undertaking, primarily because the two programs were mutually exclusive and the security surrounding each required they be handled with great delicacy and little overlap.

The AF-12's fire control system and missile complement were major concerns for Johnson. No one had ever fired an air-to-air missile while flying at 3.0 Mach speeds, and there seemed to be little agreement as to how to eject the missile from the AF-12's weapon bays. Even the design of the missile pylon and trapeze assembly were ill-defined, and the company overseeing the fire control system, Hughes Aircraft, was as much in the dark as Lockheed. Paper studies verified it could be done, and wind tunnel tests confirmed these, but it would only be through testing of actual hardware that a realistic insight could be gained.

Air Force funding allocations for construction of three AF-12s by now had cleared the way for modification of three of the CIA's original order for ten A-12s, and by August 3, 1962, the major elements of the first AF-12 were in the jig at Burbank. During September,

Johnson, with Rus Daniell on engineering, began exploring what he called a "common market" A-12, "which would use one airframe to make either a reconnaissance and RS or an AF airplane. This would require folding the fins on the GAR-9 missile and use of a new radar antenna. It turned out very well. This version would simplify our production problems greatly and make a better fighter with more range and a better overall arrangement. It eliminates the necessity of the Air Force deciding which version they want to buy!"

From December of 1962 through early spring of 1963, construction of the three AF-12s, taking place in a segregated corner of the Burbank manufacturing facility, moved ahead with little difficulty. Discussions concerning the location of the flight-test program surfaced as a result of the security surrounding the ongoing A-12 program, and it appeared that Edwards AFB would be the best option. Regardless, at the last moment, initial flight-test activity was moved to Groom Lake/Area 51 and the final decision on undertaking flight testing at Edwards was delayed.

On August 7, 1963, several weeks after being moved by truck and trailer to Groom Lake/Area 51, the first AF-12 (aka YF-12A), with Lockheed's Jim Eastham at the controls, made its first flight. Johnson would note in his AF-12 log, "It is the first airplane I've ever worked on where the fire control system was checked out prior to the first flight." The latter was in reference to the successful Hughes-sponsored flight-test program wherein both the AN/ASG-18 radar and the AIM-47 missile were tested in flight aboard B-58, 55-665, in an operational high-Mach environment.

Flight testing proceeded without significant difficulty and during January, the aircraft was temporarily grounded while intake system upgrades and newer engines with increased thrust were installed.

On February 29, 1964 the wraps were pulled off the A-12 program, but only partially,

when President Lyndon Johnson announced the existence of the "A-11" program. His announcement, made in the form of a public speech broadcast on both radio and television, stated:

"The United States has successfully developed an advanced experimental jet aircraft, the A-11, which has been tested in sustained flight at more than 2,000 miles per hour and at altitudes in excess of 70,000 feet.

"The performance of the A-11 far exceeds that of any other aircraft in the world today. The development of this aircraft has been made possible by major advances in aircraft technology of great significance to both military and commercial application.

"Several A-11 aircraft are now being flight tested at Edwards AFB in California.

"The existence of this program is being disclosed today to permit the orderly exploitation of this advanced technology in our military and commercial planes. This advanced experimental aircraft, capable of high speed and high altitude, and long-range performance at thousands of miles, constitutes the technological accomplishment that will facilitate the achieve-

ment of a number of important military and commercial requirements. The A-11 aircraft now at Edwards AFB are undergoing extensive tests to determine their capabilities as long range interceptors. The development of supersonic commercial transport aircraft will also be greatly assisted by the lessons learned from this A-11 program. For example, one of the most important technological achievements in this project has been the mastery of the metallurgy and fabrication of titanium metal which is required for the high temperatures experienced by aircraft traveling at more than three times the speed of sound.

"Arrangements are being made to make this and other important technical developments available under appropriate safeguards to those directly engaged in the supersonic transport program.

"This project was first started in 1959. Appropriate members of the Senate and House have been kept fully informed on the program since the day of its inception.

"The Lockheed Aircraft Corp. at Burbank, California, is the manufacturer of the aircraft. The aircraft engine, the J58, was designed and built by the Pratt & Whitney Aircraft Division, United Aircraft Corp. The experimental fire control and air-to-air missile system for the A-11 was developed by the Hughes Aircraft Co.

"In view of the continuing importance of these developments to our national security, the detailed performance of the A-11 will remain strictly classified and all individuals associated with the program have been directed to refrain from making any further disclosure concerning this program.

"I do not expect to discuss this important matter further with you today but certain additional information will be made available to all of you after this meeting, If you care, Mr. Salinger will make the appropriate arrangements."

Johnson's reference to the A-11 was of course, the result of "Kelly" Johnson's input. There was no A-11, at least in hardware form, and the photographs released in conjunction with the President's announcement actually depicted the first AF-12. Compounding the confusion was the Air Force's decision to assign an "official" Air Force designation to the AF-12...and rename it YF-12A in concert with the most recent designation protocols which had gone into effect during 1962. Regardless, the first and second YF-12As, several hours before the actual announcement, were flown from Groom Lake/Area 51 to Edwards AFB in

Right: **Cockpit of YF-12A. All instrumentation was analog as this was a pre-digital era aircraft. Vertical display to left provided airspeed in Mach number and knots. Vertical display to right provided altitude reference data.** Lockheed Martin via Jim Goodall collection

Center: **YF-12A weapon system operator panel was perhaps the most advanced of its kind in the world at the time of its 1964 debut. No less than three CRTs had to be monitored during the course of an intercept.** Hughes Aircraft via Jim Goodall collection

Bottom: **YF-12A, 60-6935, in level flight with ventral fin extended. It was determined later that the vertical surface provided by the two vertical fins was sufficient to offset the loss of directional stability caused by the shortened nose-section chines. Once NASA acquired the aircraft, the folding ventral fin was removed.** Lockheed Martin via Jim Goodall collection

order to give credence to the President's claim they were operating from the California test center. According to "Kelly" Johnson, when the aircraft arrived and were hurriedly moved into a hangar, they were "so hot that the fire extinguishing nozzles came on and gave us a free wash job."

Now referred to as the YF-12A, test flights of the interceptor continued with increasing frequency as confidence in the aircraft grew. On April 16, 1964, the first AIM-47 air-to-air missile (an inert, ballasted shell) was ejected in flight. According to Johnson, "The launching was safe but the angle developed was poor. If it had been a powered missile, it would have come out through the cockpit. In spite of all our missile ejection tests without airflow, we muffed this one by a factor of three in nose-down pitching moment."

While the CIA's A-12 situation vacillated back and forth between an operational commitment and continued wait-and-see, flight testing of the Air Force's YF-12A moved ahead. On January 9, 1965, *Skunk Works* pilot Jim Eastham flew the first aircraft out to 3.23 Mach, sustaining 3.20 Mach for some five minutes. On the same day, Johnson would note in his log, "The airplane flies well and we actually set several speed records in the process of making a swing over Phoenix. I think we'll shortly get the go-ahead to go for the speed record, using Air Force pilots, of course."

Work with the YF-12A as an interceptor had remained a program priority. Difficulties with the Hughes fire control system had delayed actual missile firing tests, but finally, on March 18, Johnson wrote, "We finally fired a GAR-9 at a target. We hit it 36 miles away with a closing rate of well over 2,000 mph. We are scheduled to fire against many drones, including those at low altitude, this summer."

The various A-12s and the three YF-12As had routinely broken the then-existing world's absolute speed and altitude records during the nearly three years they had been flying. The Department of Defense, aware that the extant records were held by Russian aircraft, on August 12, 1964, informed Johnson of their desire to use the YF-12A to bring the records back to the US. The YF-12A was chosen over the A-12 primarily because it was the model with the greatest public exposure and the one with the least political and technological sensitivity.

The proposal languished as a result of ongoing technical difficulties, but the following April, the Air Force finally approved an official assault. In a September 30, 1967, CIA memo to Lt. Gen. James Stewart, the speed record was stated to be of the utmost importance by President Johnson and members of his staff. In light of the fact... "the President had publicly announced the DoD had been directed to break the speed record, every reasonable effort will be made in CY 1964 to do so. Further, it has been inferred that the speed would be in the vicinity of 2,000 mph.

"The best equipped and most capable aircraft in the overall fleet are Articles 129 and 121; these are the primary contractor test aircraft. Conversely, the least capable (and lowest priority aircraft) are the YF-12A's which are restricted to Mach 2.60 and are flying with fixed 'spikes'. The program currently is hampered by equipment shortages and deficiencies: hydraulic actuators, 'J-Model' afterburners and the latest model inlet controls.

"The probability of setting a new speed record on the first try is by no means a 90 percent certainty – even if the aircraft operates perfectly – since a high degree of flying precision is required at Mach 3 speeds and 80,000 ft. altitudes. The possibility of missing the 'gates' and 'corridors' is significant. The closed-course speed run (if a speed of 1,800 to 2,000 mph is desired) is a more difficult operation than a straight line run.

"The contractor believes he could prepare a YF-12A for the runs by the end of October without disrupting the flight-test program or slipping the A-12 interim operational capability. In this option, Article 121 or 129 (to be desig-

nated the XSR-71) could be used as a back-up and practice runs made in an unmodified YF-12A. If Article 121 or 129 had to used, there would be a certain amount of security risk to the A-12 program and some disruption to the flight-test program.

"The recommended course of action [is to] start preparing one YF-12A (actuators, afterburners, inlet controls, etc.) for the record attempt without disrupting the flight-test program and/or the interim A-12 capability. Conduct practice runs with the Mach-limited YF-12A's in mid-October. At that point in time, if the YF-12A up-dating is behind schedule, the possible use of 121 or 129 (designated as an XSR-71) can be re-evaluated."

As it turned out, all the various modifications required to bring the YF-12As up to an appropriate level of dependability for the record runs all came together in time for a May 1, 1965 attempt. Accordingly, the first (60-6934) and third (60-6936) YF-12As, flying from Edwards AFB, almost effortlessly set the following FAI-certified Class C Group III absolute records: sustained altitude (absolute) – 80,258 feet (crew, Col. Robert Stephens/Lt. Col. Daniel Andre); 15/25 kilometer closed circuit (absolute) – 2,070.102 mph (crew, Col. Robert Stephens/Lt. Col. Daniel Andre); 500 kilometer closed-circuit (Class C) – 1,643.042 mph (crew, Maj. Walter Daniel/Maj. Noel Warner); and 1,000 kilometer closed-circuit without payload and with 1,000 kilogram payload (absolute) and with 2,000 kilogram payload (Class C) – 1,688.891 mph (crew, Maj. Walter Daniel/ Capt. James Cooney).

Work on the YF-12A now took a slightly encouraging turn when, on May 14, 1965, the Skunk Works received a $500,000 contract for F-12B engineering. This aircraft, the proposed production version of the YF-12A, was configured for operational deployment and had improvements in aerodynamics and select systems. No production go-ahead was received with the engineering contract, but the expression of interest was sufficient to merit considerable optimism.

On September 28, a GAR-9 was fired from a YF-12A at 3.20 Mach at 75,000 feet, thus causing Johnson to note the program finally was "hitting the high speed corner of the design diagram". The missile missed its target at 40,000 feet and at a range of 36 miles by "6 feet 6 inches ... which is a very good shot".

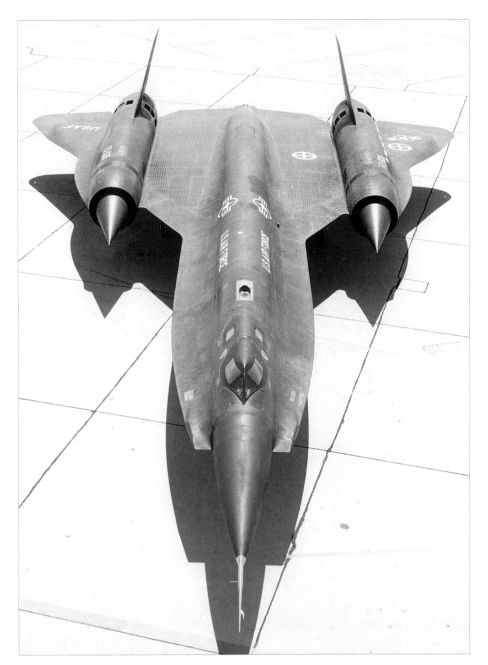

The Hughes fire control system was the heart of the YF-12A. The AN/ASG-18 fire-control system featured a long-range search capability and could detect low-flying targets down to ground level. With this system, the speed and combat radius of the YF-12A enabled it to cover a much greater area in its normal search pattern when compared to then-operational Air Defense interceptors, such as the Convair F-106A *Delta Dagger*.

The armament system performance related directly to aircraft maneuverability requirements. The air intercept missile AIM-47A carried by the YF-12A had a very long range and was highly maneuverable. It could engage high-altitude or low-altitude targets down to ground level while the YF-12A remained at its optimum cruise altitude. It could also be fired at targets on either side of the interceptor's flight path. Whereas then-current interceptors had to maneuver very precisely to get the target within their relatively small missile launch zone before it could fire, the YF-12A could take advantage of the range and maneuverability of the AIM-47A.

Because of the performance designed into the AIM-47A, the YF-12A was required to make only gross azimuth steering corrections during attack and did not require any changes in altitude. The combination of long-range search radar, state-of-the-art inertial navigation, on-board computers, and a long-range maneuvering missile allowed the YF-12A to operate, even in a degraded environment

While interceptor maneuverability was not as important during the attack phase with the YF-12A as it was with then-current interceptors, it became important for the re-attack. The speed of the YF-12A, coupled with its radar detection range and missile launch range, actually allowed it to re-attack sooner than the best-performing interceptors of its day despite its almost 100-mile turning radius. Against a subsonic bomber formation, the YF-12A would be in position to fire a second AIM-47A in one half the time required for the Convair F-106A. Against a supersonic dash bomber, it could re-attack in one fourth the time it would require in a Convair F-106A.

The success of the AN/ASG-18 was based as much on its extraordinary power as it was on its fire control system computer. As the time of its debut, the AN/ASG-18 was probably the most powerful system of its kind in the world. Its 40-inch diameter antenna was enormous by the standards of the day, and it generated enough radiation to be considered a hazard to ground crews and tanker crews alike.

Power for the AN/ASG-18 was provided by two 60 KVA alternators, one on each J58. The high temperatures generated by the radar "black boxes" caused Lockheed to install a Garrett-designed freon refrigeration system that required a 40 hp electric motor for power.

On November 10, another half-million dollar contract for basic F-12B design work was signed, thus kept the program alive a while longer. Hughes Aircraft also received a $4.5 million contract to continue development of the AN/ASG-18 radar and fire control system.

YF-12A work had moved ahead with some difficulty during this period. Its problems were compounded not only by propulsion system anomalies, but also by the complexities of the

Left: **On February 27, 1975, YF-12A, 60-6935, lost its ventral fin in flight. The accident occurred at 15,000 ft. and a speed of 0.90 Mach. Damage proved relatively minor and when it was determined the fin was redundant, it was not replaced. The aircraft flew the rest of its NASA career without it.** Lockheed Martin via Jim Goodall collection

Below: **A clean YF-12A, 60-6935, sans ventral fin and camera pods. This was the only YF-12A to survive the Air Force/NASA flight-test program. It is displayed at the US Air Force Museum in Ohio.** Lockheed Martin via Jim Goodall collection

AN/ASG-18 fire control system and the Hughes GAR-9 (AIM-47) air-to-air missile.

In between the various A-12 tests and political maneuverings, work on the YF-12A had continued in spurts. On March 29, 1966, Johnson noted in his log, "Had a long meeting with Col. Benjamin Bellis, Hughes Aircraft Company, test force members, etc., to talk about optimum use of the YF-12A for deriving information for the F-12B. The production airplane possibilities now look very good. At this meeting, Col. Bellis asked if we would take on the job of weapon systems integration going far beyond our normal responsibilities in that we would do major planning and programming not only of the aircraft but also of the missiles, radar, engines, and similar gear."

Johnson thought it over and replied that the *Skunk Works* would indeed be willing to handle the program from top to bottom. It was, in fact, quite reminiscent of what the *Skunk Works* already had done with the U-2...and what was, in most respects, being done with the A-12. It was to be a precedent the company would emulate for the following quarter century ...and which continues to this very day.

YF-12A flight testing had now continued to the point where actual fire control system tests against real targets could be undertaken. Over a six month period beginning with the first test over the Pacific Missile Test Range on March 18, 1965, seven launches were undertaken. Two of these, including one from Eglin AFB, Florida on April 25, were against Boeing B-47s.

During the March 25 intercept the attacking YF-12A (piloted by Jim Eastham), while flying at 75,000 feet and 3.20 Mach, fired a single AIM-47A at a B-47 flying at 1,100 feet on an opposite heading. The unarmed missile hit and destroyed some four feet of the B-47's horizontal stabilizer.

All but one of the missile test flights was deemed successful (the single miss was attributed to a missile gyro system failure). The launches are noted below.

Even in consideration of the successes realized by the YF-12A program, the Air Force found the aircraft hard to justify budgetarily and militarily. As the air-to-air missile program progressed, it became more and more apparent to Johnson that selling the aircraft to the Pentagon was going to be a difficult, if not impossible task.

During July of 1966, Johnson wrote in his log, "We were directed to give up further flying of the YF-12As, although we had proposed shooting down a drone at Holloman to get the effect of ground clutter for low altitude targets." The following August 5, he wrote, "We have laid off half of our test crew on the YF-12A and are maintaining only enough people to store the airplane or send it to Burbank. We are very near the end of this program". In fact, only one more missile launch would take place...just over a month after this entry.

Surprisingly, even in light of the declaration concerning continued flight testing of the YF-12As, Johnson remained somewhat hopeful the F-12B would be funded. During November of 1966, he wrote, "The F-12B is being opened up again as a result of a study made by the Air Force to get a modern air defense system." As late as January 27, 1967, he still was awaiting a decision. "In spite of favorable press releases, the President did not specifically spell out F-12B in his budget message, but did say that a start would be made on a new air defense system."

Lockheed had proposed production for the F-12B with a flyaway cost of $14 million in then 1967 dollars. This was for a production run of 100 F-12Bs, less government-supplied equipment, such as the Pratt & Whitney J58s,

Hughes AN/ASG-18 Fire Control System and the Hughes AIM-47A. If the contract had been let, the Air Force planned on three squadrons of sixteen F-12Bs each stationed on the East Coast at Otis AFB, Cape Cod, Maryland and three squadrons on the West Coast, at Paine AFB, Everett, Washington. Secretary of Defense, Robert S. McNamara elected not to support F-12B production and recommended that preliminary work on the F-12B be brought to a close.

Even in consideration of McNamara's declarations, the program stayed alive. On March 21, a call from Col. Bellis led Johnson to believe that the F-12B proposal had been accepted by the Air Force. And on March 4, Col. Dan Andre visited Johnson in Burbank and began discussing the security that would be required to cover the F-12B program. "I had a basic agreement with Gen. Bellis that externally, for drawings and manuals going to the Air Force, we would comply with DoD security requirements, but internally, we would not. Later on, we were given a thick document which would apply complete DoD security, internally and externally, to the *Skunk Works*. We couldn't begin to function; so I refused to sign our contract."

On November 13, Johnson noted, "We were asked to study the conversion of ten *Oxcart* airplanes to fighters and also ten SR-71s to fighters. We proposed the installation of Westinghouse radars and *Sparrow* missiles. Nothing came of this."

The writing now appeared to be on the wall. There would be no production A-12 interceptors. On December 29, Johnson wrote in his log, "I had a call from the SPO canceling all ADP air defense programs except a portion of the vulnerability study which was transferred to the SR-71. We were instructed to shut down, immediately, but I told them it would require at

Date	Place	YF-12#	L.Mach#	L.Alt.(ft.)	Target	Aspect	L.Range/RCS in M²	FlightTime	Miss Distance
03/18/65	PMR	'935	2.18	64,600	Ryan Q-2C (0.84 M/38K Ft.)	Nose 12°	36.2 Miles / 970	48.5 sec.	Hit
05/19/65	PMR	'935	2.16	65,000	Ryan Q-2C (0.84 M/20K Ft.)	Nose 5°	36.3 Miles / 670	55.0 sec.	Power Failed
09/28/65	PMR	'934	3.26	75,000	Ryan Q-2C (0.92 M/23K Ft.)	Nose 7.5°	32.2 Miles / 440	36.7 sec.	6.6 Ft.
03/22/66	PMR	'936	3.17	74,500	Ryan Q-2C (0.51 M/1.6K Ft.)	Nose	32.0 Miles / 40	41.6 sec.	9.0 Ft.
04/25/66	Eglin	'934	3.22	75,000	Boeing QB-47 (0.45 M/1.1K Ft.)	Nose on	30.6 Miles / 10-40	38.6 sec.	Hit
05/13/66	PMR	'936	3.17	74,000	Ryan Q-2C (0.77 M/18K Ft.)	Tail	34.1 Miles / 30	56.8 sec.	95 Ft.
09/21/66	White S.	'936	3.20	74,000	Boeing QB-47 (0.51 M/0.5K Ft.)	Nose	33.0 Miles / 10-40	39.0 sec.	44 Ft.

least a month. A termination notice, therefore, was not issued. We were asked to come in with a plan for an orderly shutdown." On January 5, 1968, an official wire "closing down the F-12B" was received from the Air Force. The YF-12A program would be formally terminated on February 1. As a parting gesture, Johnson left Air Force representatives with a proposal to convert two of the YF-12As to trainers for SAC use.

In a final disheartening move, the Air Force, on February 5, sent Johnson a letter instructing Lockheed to destroy the A-12/F-12 tooling (by the date of the letter, this also included the SR-71 tooling). "We have proceeded to store such items as are required for producing spare parts at Norton. The large jigs have now been cut up for scrap and we are finishing the clean-up of the complete area. Ten years from now the country will be very sorry for taking this decision of stopping production on the whole Mach 3 series of aircraft in the USA."

Prescient words from a truly prescient engineer.

NASA:
Though NASA facilities and select personnel had been used during the course of early A-12 and F-12 wind tunnel studies, the administration's access to information relating to the highly classified Lockheed program remained decidedly limited until 1967. That year, personnel at NASA Ames, California, initiated dialog with Air Force representatives concerning the possibility of allowing the NASA access to YF-12A wind tunnel data. In return, NASA would cooperate with and participate in the YF-12A flight-test program then under way at Edwards

AFB. Coincident to this it was noted also that the proposed activity would complement plans of the Office of Advanced Research and Technology which was tasked with high-speed research and its applicability to the proposed US supersonic transport.

Gene Matranga of the NASA now was assigned to the YF-12A test program. NASA personnel, believing this to be an indication of reduced propriety, requested the Air Force provide an instrumented SR-71A for NASA use. This was declined, along with a NASA request that, in lieu of the actual aircraft, a NASA research package be carried by the Air Force's Category II stability and control SR-71A test aircraft. The Air Force countered by offering the NASA use of the two remaining YF-12As then stored at Edwards AFB.

Using funding that had been coincidentally released following termination of the North American XB-70A and North American X-15 flight-test programs, NASA agreed to undertake support of the two YF-12As (with the help of an Air Defense Command maintenance and logistical support team) and immediately requested the aircraft be physically transferred to the NASA Dryden Flight Research Center facility at Edwards AFB.

A memorandum of understanding between the Air Force and NASA was signed on June 5, 1969, and a public announcement followed on July 18. Several months later, Matranga and his team undertook the first of what would be an extensive list of YF-12A modifications that included the installation of strain gauges and thermocouples in the wing and fuselage to

permit the measurement of dynamic loads, and the installation of thermocouples along the left side of the aircraft for temperature assessment and analysis.

Acquisition of the two YF-12As proved a windfall not only for the NASA research centers at Edwards AFB and Ames (Moffett Field, California), but also for those at NASA Langley (Langley AFB, Virginia...for high-speed aerodynamics and associated structures) and NASA Lewis (Cleveland, Ohio...for propulsion). Coincidentally, NASA had developed two computer programs, known as FLEXSTAB and NASTRAN, to predict loads and structural responses using finite-element analysis. It was predicted the YF-12As would make excellent subjects for exploring flight dynamics while setting up a baseline for future reference.

NASA and Air Force personnel completed three months of modification and test instrumentation installation in the second YF-12A during early December of 1969. On December 11, this aircraft, under the auspices of NASA (though manned by an Air Force crew) successfully completed its first post-modification flight. The first flight with a NASA flight-test engineer (Victor Horton) occupying the back seat took place the following March 26. The first flight with a NASA pilot (Donald Mallick) flying the aircraft took place on April 1.

Johnson, in contemplating the NASA's YF-12A operation, wrote on July 21, 1971, "Had a visit from the NASA test organizations who discussed their research to date. They haven't come up with anything that was new to us, but it seems to be a good program for them to keep

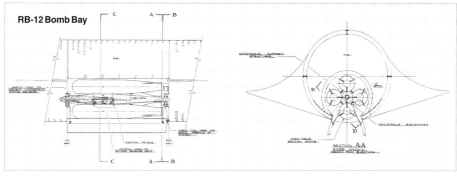

RB-12 Bomb Bay

RB-12

up their technical organizations. I am attaching a letter from Gene Matranga indicating our current relationship, which is excellent. I have two objections to the NASA program, the main one is that they will probably publish important data, which the Russians will be happy to receive as they always are with NASA reports. Secondly, they are repeating so many things we pioneered in and I gravely doubt our people will be given any, or sufficient, credit for solving the problems, first. We have continued to cooperate to the hilt with NASA in spite of the above."

NASA YF-12A research in fact had been modestly productive during this period, with the aircraft serving to permit exploration of a speed regime that had long been out of NASA's reach with its extant aircraft stable. The YF-12A's ability to cruise at speeds in excess of 2,000 mph made it an ideal platform for studying the unique aerodynamic and heating phenomenon which occurred at high Mach numbers. A large number of test specimens, systems, and equipment complements were heat-soaked and dynamically loaded at 3.0 Mach for sustained periods...a capability that had long been on NASA's wish list and remained unresolved until the arrival of Lockheed's now-retired high-speed interceptor.

In a further extension of the thermal studies, the NASA, during late February of 1972, took 60-6935 – by then the last YF-12A – and placed it in Dryden's High Temperature Loads Laboratory for airframe heating tests. This custom-built, oven-like structure, allowed NASA engineers to heat the airframe to temperatures approximating those that would be experienced in cruising flight at 3.0 Mach. The aircraft was used in this fashion for almost a year and did not fly again until July of 1973.

Prior to its transfer to the NASA, the third YF-12A, 60-6936, had been operated by Air Force crews. It was being flown in a series of tests where it was being used to simulate the Russian MiG-25 (a 2.80 Mach-capable interceptor) at various speeds and altitudes. On its sixty-third flight, taking place on June 24, 1971, an inflight fire in the right engine nacelle (caused by a fatigue failure of a high-pressure fuel line) led to its crew (Lt. Col. Ronald Layton and Maj. Billy Curtis) ejecting and the aircraft being written-off.

Propulsion system studies scheduled for the crashed aircraft now had to be rescheduled for the surviving YF-12A, 60-6935, thus causing schedule delays. A month after this loss, however, a redundant SR-71A, 64-17951, was placed on loan to the NASA from the Air Force inventory. This aircraft, at the Air Force's request, was redesignated YF-12C and given a bogus serial number, 60-6937 (see Chapter Five).

Among the many studies conducted using the surviving YF-12A during its NASA tenure were the *Coldwall* experiments using a ventrally suspended stainless steel tube equipped with thermocouples and a series of pressure sensors. Supported by NASA Langley, *Coldwall* was essentially a heat transfer experiment designed to acquire data applicable to future high-speed aircraft and transports. A special insulation coated the covered tube which, prior to flight, was chilled to extremely cold temperatures using liquid nitrogen. During an actual test flight, the insulation was expected to suddenly blow away at 3.0 Mach, thus exposing the tube to the ambient high temperature environment. The resulting data then was compared with similar data obtained from a similar *Coldwall* tube that had been tested in a wind tunnel. The final flight in this series took place on October 13, 1975.

By the beginning of 1977 the two YF-12s (one YF-12A and one YF-12C) had completed over 175 flights. Most had included time at speeds of 3.0 Mach or greater. Unfortunately, operating expenses for the two high-performance aircraft were becoming ever more difficult to justify as funding became tighter and research missions become more esoteric. As a result, during the spring of 1977, a decision was made by NASA directors to retire the YF-12A...though in fact, it would continue to fly sporadically until being turned over to the Air Force Museum at Wright-Patterson AFB, Ohio, on November 7, 1979. It flew its last official NASA flight, number 145, on October 31, 1979.

Earlier, residual funding had permitted additional test work with the YF-12C to be conducted through the fall of 1978. On October 27, 1978, however, it also was retired and returned to the Air Force inventory. The last official NASA YF-12C flight, the 88th, took place on September 28, 1978.

Chapter Four

Tagboard, Q-12, D-21, M-21

Of the various *Skunk Works* 3.0 Mach aircraft programs, the least-known to reach the operational hardware stage was undoubtedly the D-21 unmanned strategic reconnaissance drone. Developed for and operated by the Central Intelligence Agency and the Air Force under a veil of extreme secrecy not penetrated until long after the program had ceased to exist as a viable national reconnaissance asset, it entered the public domain only by accident.

During early 1977, the editor of *Aerophile* magazine, with the help of Benjamin Knowles of Tucson, Arizona, unexpectedly found seventeen D-21s in storage at Davis-Monthan AFB's Military Aircraft Storage and Disposition Center. This discovery resulted in the first public disclosure concerning the precedent-setting D-21 and the beginning of an ongoing curiosity about its history and operational service life.

Codenamed *Tagboard* by the Central Intelligence Agency, the D-21 was, in fact, an extension of the A-12 program. It was brought to life in response to an executive level US Government decision to discontinue overflights of unfriendly territories following the loss of Gary Powers in his U-2 on May 1, 1960.

Consequently, during October of 1962, "Kelly" Johnson made the first log entry in what was to become this enigmatic aircraft's long-hidden history: "Over the past several years, we have had a number of discussions on the feasibility of making a drone with the A-12 aircraft. I have steadily maintained that we should not do this, as it is a much too large and complicated machine. On several different occasions, we studied the use of a QF-104 air-launched from the A-12. It became obvious at an early date that the CIA was totally uninterested in this project, [but] others wanted to do it very much."

Regardless of the lack of interest, on October 10, 1962, authorization for a drone study was received by the *Skunk Works* from the CIA. Johnson noted the event as follows:

"We have now configured it to allow the use of plastic blankets overall for the basic structure. In order to avoid the F-104 problem of a high central vertical tail, I put two on the tips and one in the middle. Besides the aerodynamic benefits of this configuration, they will provide the basis for a landing gear during the flight-test operation."

Lockheed had extensive background with the ramjet-powered X-7A-1, X-7A-2 and X-7A-3 test vehicle series and a close working relationship with Marquardt, a neighboring company specializing in ramjet engines and located in the San Fernando Valley. On October 24, Johnson, Ben Rich and Rus Daniell met with representatives from Marquardt to discuss the use of a ramjet

Top: **Q-12 full-scale mock-up. Black leading edge was indicative of proposal to use composites in order to reduce the aircraft's radar return.** Lockheed Martin via Miller Collection

Right: **The first D-21 is fit-checked on M-21 dorsal pylon prior to completion.** Lockheed Martin via Jim Goodall collection

Top: **First mating of the Q-12 (D-21, 501) to the M-21, 60-6940. The D-21 was moved from production in Building 82 under cover of darkness to building 309/310 for this undertaking.** Lockheed Martin via Jim Goodall collection

Bottom: **During the conversion to the D-21B standards, all remaining D-21s were returned to the *Skunk Works* from Groom Lake/Area 51 in Burbank, California. Shown front to back, are D-21s, 507, 510 (in natural metal) 509, 511 and 508.** Lockheed Martin via Jim Goodall collection

propulsion system on the new Lockheed drone. Johnson wrote: "It is obvious that we cannot use the *Bomarc* engine without change. We will just do the best we can to use its major parts."

The Marquardt and Lockheed teams determined that the unmanned drone would most suitably be powered by a modified Marquardt RJ43-MA-11 ramjet engine similar to that used on Boeing IM-99 *Bomarc* surface-to-air-missile during cruising flight.

Using Marquardt's propulsion system experience, it was not difficult for the Lockheed team to execute a functional reconnaissance platform in a relatively short period of time. Concurrently, the technology base that had been generated by initial flight trials of the A-12 had given the engineering team (under Johnson) considerable confidence in the aerodynamic and low-observables precedent (i.e., reduced RCS) set by the chined delta. This configuration was a given by the time initial design options were studied for the D-21.

The new project was assigned to Art Bradley under the supervision of Dick Boehme. A small team was assembled to handle engineering and a section of the *Skunk Works* shop at Burbank was walled off specifically to accommodate the new drone activity,

The D-21 engine was properly identified as an XRJ43-MA20S-4 and was developed from the earlier RJ43 series of ramjets optimized for use on the Boeing IM-99 *Bomarc* series of surface-to-air anti-aircraft missiles. The RJ43 had the ability to function as an independent external power plant on any vehicle that could reach sufficient speed to allow efficient inlet operation. It was developed in supersonic wind tunnels at Marquardt's Van Nuys, California, test facility, flight tested on the Lockheed X-7A-3 at Holloman AFB, New Mexico, and, in its MA11 version, was deployed operationally on the *Bomarc B*.

The MA20S-4 engine employed in the D-21 used many MA-11 components but was modified to operate at lower pressures and higher temperatures. The S-4 was mounted internally in the D-21 and had no inlet structures of its own. Instead, it utilized the D-21's inlet system. The engine's center body and main structure were retained to house the fuel control, fuel pump, fuel injector nozzles and flame-holder assemblies. The latter was redesigned to allow for stable combustion at extreme high-altitude, high-temperature and low-pressure situations. Ignition was by a pyrophoric fluid known as tri-ethyl borane (TEB) to allow for re-ignition in the event of flameout. The combustion chamber/exit nozzle was redesigned to provide for the much greater expansion ratio required for high-altitude cruising. The design also incorporated an ejector system for engine structure cooling.

It is noteworthy that until the advent of the D-21, no ramjet had ever powered any craft for longer than fifteen minutes; the D-21's XRJ43-MA20S-4 routinely operated on missions lasting 1½ hours or longer.

During early November of 1962, while preliminary design work progressed with considerable rapidity (on what was then being referred to in the *Skunk Works* as the "Q-12"), miscellaneous subsystem problems, including those of the proposed optical sensor gear, surfaced to cause concerns about program progress. Johnson had favored the Hycon Company to win the contract to build the compact camera, but he was not the only one in the decision-making loop. About Hycon, Johnson would note, "I am very impressed by their recent design with a fast moving slit shutter arrangement I saw at their factory recently."

On November 5, Johnson noted: "The drone is developing without much discussion between Headquarters and us. I think I know what they want, but no one has spelled it out. We will try to get six-inch ground resolution photographically, a range of 3,000 nautical miles, and a payload of 425 pounds for the camera. We will attempt to save the expensive

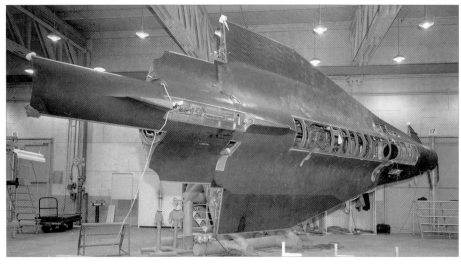

elements of the aircraft by parachute recovery of the nose."

The full-scale mock-up was completed on December 7. As it included the "anti-radar" characteristics of the actual drone, it was sent to Groom Lake/Area 51 on December 10 for eleven days of pole-model testing to measure its radar cross-section. When it was returned to Burbank, it was modified to correct some RCS shortcomings and concurrently used by Hycon to check-fit a mock-up of their new camera.

Propulsion system work began to accelerate at this time as well. A Marquardt RJ43-MA-3 engine was tunnel-tested at simulated "Q-12" operating conditions. Per Johnson: "We were all amazed, including Marquardt, that the engine could be shut off as long as 45 seconds and still restart, due to hot engine parts."

CIA and Air Force support, though restrained, continued to give Johnson and the rest of the Q-12 team encouragement. On January 3, Johnson noted in his log, "We are running wind tunnel tests and have revised the model to look exactly like the original proposal with the single tail, except that we have blended the leading edge of the chine into the basic wing. We also reduced the size of the vertical tail. We are going to plastics to reduce the anti-radar cross-section".

On March 20, 1963, a letter contract from the CIA arrived. "It makes us responsible for the navigation system and the ramjet engines, as well as the airframe," Johnson wrote. All was not copacetic with the new drone, however. On May 9, Johnson noted that engineering was having trouble with aerodynamic loads. "After investigating tunnel data, we find

we have a jury-rigged model that does not represent the configuration of either the A-12 or the R-12. Presence of the sting in the tail of the fuselage and a break in the fuselage to move the nose up 1.25 inch have resulted in the Q being placed in the wrong flow field and highly confusing loads."

Other difficulties included the size of the Hycon camera. The minor dimensional changes in the drone had led to dimensional changes in the ventral sensor system bay. As a result, Johnson noted that Hycon was going to be forced to change their camera's design if it were to fit the available space. On August 6, 1963, it was noted that Hycon was successful. The redesign effort had not impacted the quality of the imagery and the camera was dimensionally compatible with the Q-12's sensor bay.

By October, the Q-12's overall configuration had been finalized and the equally difficult task of defining the A-12 launch system and its configuration was nearing an end. By now, the somewhat unusual M-21 designation had been assigned to the two dedicated and purpose-built carrier A-12s. "M" stood simply for "Mother." At the same time, it was decided to rename the Q-12 "D-21", thus making it the "Daughter" aircraft. The numerals "1" and "2" of A-12 and Q-12, etc., were reversed so as not to confuse the "Mother/Daughter" combination with other "-12" variants.

Johnson, on October 1, wrote: "I proposed to Boehme that we simplify some of the load problems by letting the D-21 float at a zero moment incidence when attached to the M-21. While this concentrated the loads at one point, it reduces most of them and particularly the effect on the M-21. I also made sure that we can jettison the aircraft without power."

On December 31, 1963, Johnson noted that wind tunnel and paper studies were leading him to believe there would be launching difficulties with the M-21 "mother ship". According to Johnson: "Going through the fuselage shock wave is very hard. I am insisting on launching at full power, but there are problems regarding fuel-air ratio to the engine and engine blow-out in this condition."

A month later he would write: "Reviewed launch conditions again, and was very upset by recent tunnel tests which show we must make a pushover to launch. This is due to making the pylon too short. This was done for structural reasons, but got us into aerodynamic troubles which weren't recognized at once, although I suspected that we might encounter such troubles when it was done."

By late May of 1964, Johnson's impression of the D-21 had improved: "We have launch problems, transonic drag deficiencies in the basic airplane, and equipment problems as usual. But we can now haul the thing through

Mach 1.0, I believe, if we can get performance like A-12 #129. Launching must be done as an automatic pushover maneuver."

Concurrent to the D-21 work, the purpose-building of two M-21s to serve as launch platforms was also well under way at Burbank. A single, dorsally-mounted, low-drag pylon had been developed that was low drag…yet sufficiently strong enough to support the 11,000-pound D-21 at 3.0 Mach. The pylon contained a primary support post with locking hook, a secondary lock, provisions for emergency pneumatic jettisoning, and a refueling line that was used to cool D-21 sub systems and top off its fuel tanks prior to launch

A fit-check using M-21 #134 and D-21 #501 was completed successfully on June 19, 1964 in Building 309/310 at Burbank. Few problems surfaced during the mating and over the next several weeks, final assembly of the first carrier aircraft was completed. On August 12, it was delivered to Groom Lake/Area 51 to undergo initial flight testing. Concurrently, the initial D-21 static tests were successfully completed. Johnson wrote in his log: "Engine deliveries are in good shape but equipment, particularly cameras, is not so good. Trying to get out seven drones this year."

On December 22, 1964, the first flight of the M-21/D-21 combination (now referred to as the "M/D-21") was accomplished without difficulty from Groom Lake/Area 51. Per Johnson:

"Bill Park flew at the end of the day. It flew well and, in spite of having low-powered engines, went supersonic on the first flight." Interestingly, on this same day, the first SR-71A successfully completed its first flight from Lockheed's Palmdale, California facility.

Interest in the project, though supported by the CIA and the Air Force, remained difficult to ascertain. Johnson nevertheless doggedly pursued successful execution. He wrote, "We are aiming to launch one by my birthday – February 27, 1965." But Johnson's wish was not to be. His birthday came and went with little fanfare and no D-21 launch. "We have all kinds of troubles," he wrote, "Minneapolis-Honeywell came in with a terrible story on the Kollsman star tracker which they had purchased for the M-21 guidance system. It was a complete shambles from beginning to end."

Further flight testing of the mated M/D-21, in the meantime, continued…though without a launch During April of 1965, Johnson noted that one flight resulted in the loss of "… both elevons on the D-21 due to flutter. We are going to put on balance weights, and add control surface locks, etc."

By May, the M/D-21 combination had been flown out to 2.60 Mach. The flutter anomaly had been overcome but problems continued with the M-21s early YJ58s and their Hamilton Standard inlet control system. New "K" series engines with a thrust rating of 34,000 lb. were

requested, but they had not yet been made available. Johnson's frustration in not being able to consummate a D-21 launch was exacerbated by yet another problem when he noted, "We are ready to light the engine of the drone, but we must get a new course to run as we can not accelerate sufficiently in a turn. We are being restricted by lack of suitable test areas."

During July, the first of the only two Air Force officers to be assigned to *Tagboard*, Maj. Hal Rupard, was transferred from his B-58 assignment at Little Rock AFB to Groom. Rupard was followed 30 days later by Maj. Jack Reed. Both men had extensive experience as Bomber/Navigators in the Air Force's B-58 program.

Johnson now moved ahead with plans to convert from the Hamilton Standard inlet control system to a hydraulic system designed in-house by the *Skunk Works* engineering team. On October 21, he noted, "We have had great

Top: **D-21B, 501 during functional testing after undergoing extensive modifications to "B" standards.** Lockheed Martin via Jim Goodall collection

Bottom: **The first D-21 undergoing modifications for launch from the pylon of a *Senior Bowl* modified B-52H.** Lockheed Martin via Jim Goodall collection

difficulties in getting *Tagboard* to speed and range. We tried to run to Point Mugu for launch practice, but couldn't make the range. Transonic acceleration is very poor, particularly with high air temperatures. As of this day, we are putting in 34,000 pound thrust engines. Have had to convert from the Hamilton Standard inlet control to our own, and are having trouble blowing the nose cone and keeping parts out of the inlet. I believe I found a solution yesterday, involving the use of an aluminum ring. We are driving for a launch date of November 15. We seem to have the recovery system in hand, and have taken good pictures from the 'hot pod' (an externally mounted camera pod with special high-temperature glass ports optimized for photography) on #134. All D-21s have been built, but I cannot recommend construction of more until we prove the bird in flight".

By November, the transonic acceleration problem had yet to be overcome. Further complicating the situation was the inability of the instrumentation system strain gauges to measure separation forces accurately at the high temperatures associated with the 3.0 Mach-plus launch conditions. "We will not go until we know for certain that the separation maneuver will consist of," Johnson noted.

The solution to the frangible inlet cone problem was to eliminate it altogether. In addition to pieces of the cone entering the D-21's inlet and causing engine damage, they also caused unacceptable damage to the drone's wing leading edges, as well as to the fuselage of the M-21. By discarding the nose cone (and the aluminum exhaust nozzle fairing), the D-21's Marquardt ramjet now could be used to supplement the propulsive effort of the M-21's two J58s during the acceleration-to-launch conditions. The ramjet routinely was started at 1.24. Immediately prior to launch, fuel was transferred from the M-21 to the D-21 to replenish what had been used during acceleration.

By late January, most of the difficulties finally had been overcome. "We have now established that the separation forces, engine operation, and parachute recovery system work properly, and we have practiced the launch maneuver." With the exception of the Minneapolis-Honeywell inertial navigation system (critical to any operational D-21 mission, but not critical for the envisioned test launch), the time finally appeared ripe for an attempted launch. February 7 was declared the target date.

Delays inevitably set in and the February date came and went. Finally, on March 5, 1966, the first D-21 launch took place. "It was a great success," according to Johnson, "in terms of the launch. The airplane was lost 120 miles from the launch point. Mainly, we demonstrated the launch technique, which is the most dangerous maneuver we have ever been involved in any airplane I have worked on. Bill Park and Keith Beswick flew it. Everyone was greatly encouraged by the launch."

CIA and Air Force interest, even in light of the modestly successful first flight, remained lukewarm. Johnson had continued to emphasize the D-21 concept to the Air Force, and SAC officials had been kept apprised of progress. On April 22, 1966, Johnson wrote in his log, "Had a meeting with two SAC officers. We talked of using the D-21 and how to get it into service. If necessary, Lockheed will launch the early operational birds. We have been very strapped for money in the whole program, and training is difficult and time consuming."

Tagboard now was approaching a point where the program needed additional direction. Upon receiving orders from the Pentagon, Reed and Rupard flew to St. Petersburg, Florida. There, Honeywell was developing the D-21's inertial navigation system (Honeywell's INS was capable of updating coordinates from a one-of-a-kind, 60-star celestial catalog that was part of the M-21's navigation system; the other projects – A-12 and YF-12 – did not have this capability). The Honeywell team was making progress but additional test flights were required. Because of the scarcity of available test airframes, it was decided that the prototype Lockheed *JetStar* would be used as a Honeywell testbed. Approximately five flights were undertaken to verify the accuracy of their system.

The second flight now was successfully undertaken on April 27. "Boehme and I went to Pt. Mugu for the second launching…this was a dandy flight, going over 1,200 n. miles and holding course within a half mile for the whole flight. It reached 90,000 feet, Mach 3.3, and finally fell out of the sky when a hydraulic pump burned out. It turned out that the pump had been run unpressurized several times during checkout. At this time I have proposed the use of the D-21 with a rocket launch from the B-52. Our problem now will be to get wide usage of this new bird at low cost."

A second batch of fifteen D-21s was ordered on April 29, 1966, and the following month Johnson made a formal proposal to SAC to launch the new drone from Boeing B-52Hs. "This was based on great safety, lower cost, a nd great deployment range."

On June 16, 1966, the third D-21 was successfully launched. "It flew about 1,600 n. miles, making 8 programmed turns, to stay within sight of the picket ship. It did everything but eject the package, due to some electronic failure."

The fourth launch, attempted on July 30, 1966, was a disaster. The second M-21, piloted by Bill Park and with Ray Torick in the launch system operator's position, was lost over the Pacific Ocean off Point Mugu,

California, when D-21 #504 collided with the carrier aircraft moments after release. Observed by the first M-21 – which was flying chase – the D-21 and M-21 were seen to make contact moments after separation had begun. At 3.25 Mach, as the M-21 pitched up, its nose – just aft of the two cockpits – separated from the rest of the fuselage. Fuel sprayed outward in an enormous cloud as the two sections flew apart.

Both crew members ejected successfully and got good parachutes, but as a result of injuries sustained during bailout, Torick was unable to get into his one-man life raft. Having opened his helmet visor, his high-altitude flight suit rapidly filled with water as a result and he unfortunately drowned. Park survived and was rescued without serious incident.

Rupard, who was on hand at the time of the accident, noted, "It was on the 30th of July that Torick was launching, and this was the first time that we'd ever had the other Mother bird, #134, up and flying chase. They had been trying to do this ever since the first launch. Art ("Pete") Peterson and Beswick were in the

chase M-21 airplane. Park and Torick were in the launch airplane, and they were flying in formation at Mach 3.3. They had just launched the D-21 when it rolled sharply to the left and fell down on the wing. Beswick was getting all of this on film. When the drone hit the Mother bird, it pitched the nose up and caused the nose to break off at the 715 splice. Torick and Park were in that part of it. The launch airplane went out of view in a hurry because the speed went from ultrasonic to zip in nothing flat. This was on a Saturday and Reed and I were at the command post. The next thing we knew, Peterson came up on frequency. They had a code word for launching the rescue forces and he initiated that code word."

Torick's death served as the end of the *Tagboard* program involving launch of the D-21 from the M-21 carrier aircraft. Though additional studies of the M-21/D-21 combination were conducted, after the accident it was concluded that 3.0 Mach launches of a large vehicle like the D-21 were difficult to justify from the standpoint of safety. The interim studies calling for the use of rocket boosters to accelerate the

D-21 to ramjet ignition speed (as pioneered by the X-7) now were given renewed emphasis by Johnson. On August 15, after returning from a trip to Washington, DC wherein the accident was discussed primarily with the Air Force, Johnson noted "I proposed going to the B-52 and I believe we will get a go-ahead on this program." The D-21 now was grounded for a year while the new launch system was developed.

It is worth nothing that if *Tagboard* had gone operational, the launch location would have been staged from Groom Lake/Area 51. There had been some discussion to keep Peterson and Park as the pilots, and Reed and Rupard as the LCOs. It was assumed that in the event of the loss of an aircraft, they could claim it was manned by an Air Force crew.

With CIA and senior Air Force staffers working under Johnson's direction, plans were advanced for Lockheed to modify the D-21 to be launched from the more conventional Boeing B-52H *Stratofortress*. This program eventually evolved into project *Senior Bowl* (initially designated as "A"-Flight" and later as the 4200th Support Squadron based at Beale AFB, California). The 4200th, although officially a squadron, was actually a wing-level unit with direct and primary responsibility to Strategic Air Command (SAC) headquarters. Administrative functions were through the 14th Air Division at Beale, while operational functions were handled through SAC and other still-classified hierarchy.

As modified for B-52H carriage, the new D-21 configuration (now with dorsal mounting hooks rather than ventral) was redesignated D-21B (there was no D-21A, per se). The 4200th Support Squadron at Beale AFB, fol-

lowing a request from the CIA that D-21 operations be relocated to a place other than Groom Lake/Area 51, now assumed responsibility for the two modified B-52Hs, which had been commandeered by Gen. Leo Geary under orders from the Air Force Chief of Staff's office. These aircraft – the first of which, 61-0021, arrived at Lockheed's Palmdale facility on December 12, 1966, for modification – were the only readily available combat aircraft capable of transporting the heavy D-21Bs to within striking distance of a target. The second B-52H, 60-0036, arrived at Palmdale several months after the first.

During the changeover from *Tagboard* to *Senior Bowl*, the remaining D-21s were moved to Burbank for modification. It had been decided that all extant D-21s would be brought up to the D-21B standard. Lockheed C-5As were utilized to transport the remaining aircraft from Groom Lake/Area 51 to Burbank. All deliveries took place at night to minimize the chances of unauthorized personnel seeing the highly classified drone.

Following completion of the B-52 modifications at Palmdale and delivery of the first D-21Bs from Burbank, all hardware assets were initially moved back to Groom Lake/Area 51 for initiation of the flight-test program. As noted earlier, however, it was not long afterwards that the CIA requested that *Senior Bowl* be moved to Beale AFB, where it was deemed such operational activities would find a more appropriate home.

In an air-launch scenario, the D-21B was accelerated to ramjet ignition speed and altitude by a solid-propellant booster rocket developed by Lockheed Propulsion Company of Redlands, California. At 1.5 Mach, the booster was jettisoned with the D-21B then flying on the power of its own ramjet engine. The rest of the flight was thus a 3,000 nautical mile high-Mach cruise over a course which was preprogrammed in the inertial guidance system. At the end of the flight, a controlled descent was made to a lower altitude and a specific recovery point where the hatch containing the special Hycon camera and the inertial navigation unit was ejected. The hatch and its payload then were decelerated and lowered by parachute to an altitude where air retrieval was executed by a Lockheed JC-130B *Hercules*.

The operational D-21B consisted of three major elements: (1) the airframe and engine; (2) the recoverable hatch containing the camera and the high value electronic equipment: and (3) the solid-fuel booster including associated antenna, electrical and hydraulic power systems, and a folding ventral fin.

The recoverable hatch contained the reconnaissance camera, the inertial naviga-

tion system, the automatic flight control system, the command and telemetry electronics, the recovery beacons. and the recovery parachute system. Hatch ejection took place automatically at 60,000 feet and 1.67 Mach.

The solid fuel booster had a length of 531 inches, a case diameter of 30.16 inches, a weight of 13,286 pounds, an average thrust of 27,300 pounds, a burn time of 87 seconds, and an impulse of 2,371,600 pound seconds. Booster ignition took place shortly after release (always from the B-52H's left pylon; the right pylon was utilized, but only for transporting a spare drone) at an altitude of approximately 38,000 feet. The nose cone of the booster was fitted with a Marquardt B-4 supersonic ram-air turbine to provide the electrical and hydraulic power required during the drop and boost phase. Boost phase trajectory was preprogrammed in the inertial navigation system. Maximum forward acceleration during boost was 1.5 g.

Modifications to the two B-52Hs consisted principally of the following:

(1) Addition of a D-21B attach pylon to each wing. Each pylon bolted to the underside of the wing at existing attachment points and no structural modifications to the B-52H were required.

(2) Alteration of the flight deck area to accommodate two launch control officer (LCO) stations. The two stations were completely independent of each other and were located in the area normally occupied by the electronic warfare officer and the gunner.

(3) Addition of a stellar inertial navigation system and of telemetry and command sys-

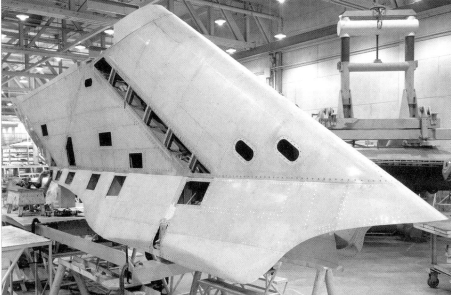

Top: **The first captive flight of the *Tagboard* M/D-21 took place on December 22, 1964. It is seen at Groom Lake/Area 51 immediately prior to first flight.** Lockheed Martin via Ron Girourd collection

Center: **During the changeover from the *Tagboard* M-21 launch system to the Boeing B-52H *Senior Bowl* launch aircraft, Lockheed manufactured four D-21 launch pylons. These were very similar to those used on the NASA NB-52A/B X-15 carrier aircraft.** Lockheed Martin via Jim Goodall collection

Bottom: **Lockheed Missile and Space developed the D-21B booster which was given the designation A-92. The *Skunk Works* developed the attachment hardware.** Lockheed Martin via Jim Goodall collection

D-21B INS position error accumulation was periodically updated to the B-52H's stellar INS.

The D-21B telemetry system provided space-positioning and speed data to the LCO aboard the B-52H launch vehicle during the boost phase for the first ten minutes of cruise. At that time, the telemetry system was turned off by an INS discrete and the mission was flown in radio silence. During the final phase of the mission, the telemetry system was turned on again by an INS discrete and the transmitted data was received by the recovery aircraft.

In addition to providing immediate data to the launch and recovery aircraft, the telemetry system transmitted other data, forty-one items in all, which were recorded for post-mission analysis. These items consisted of the following: automatic flight control measurements; propulsion system, fuel system, booster and hydraulic pressures; engine and equipment temperatures; electrical system voltages and frequencies; D-21B Mach number, direction, and location; and various systems event mark signals

The command system consisted of two command transmitters plus two antennas in the B-52H, and one command receiver plus two antennas in the D-21B. This system provided the launch and recovery aircraft with the means to command eight post-launch functions which were normally automatic (programmed in the INS) plus a destruct capability. The system provided a backup in the event of failure of any of the preprogrammed signals and it afforded the means to change the sequence or timing of the events should this become desirable. Provided functions included: fuel shutoff; engine ignition; destruct arm; beacons and TM on; booster jettison; hatch ejected; TM off; destruct disable; and destruct fire.

tems. Telemetry receiving and recording systems, including antennas, were duplicated for reliability.

(4) Addition of an air-conditioning system to supply air at the proper temperature and pressure to the D-21B for cooling and heating and for driving the auxiliary power unit.

(5) Two camera stations were installed in the left and right forward wheel wells. These held a set of 35mm high-speed cameras to record each D-21B launch. There was also a wide-angle, downward-looking, high-speed camera mounted inside each pylon. Once flight testing got under way, these cameras proved important tools for diagnosing some of the problems that eventually befell the program.

The inertial navigation system was accurate to 4.7 nautical miles over the course of an 18 hour 35 minute flight. During the flight, the

D-21 Events Sequence

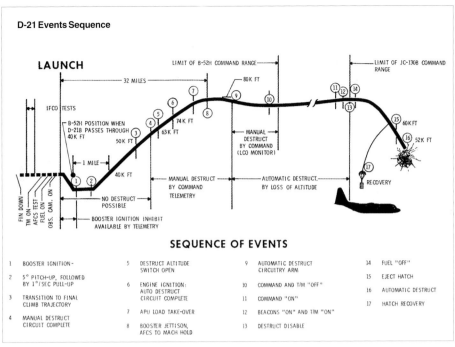

LAUNCH

LIMIT OF B-52H COMMAND RANGE
LIMIT OF JC-130B COMMAND RANGE

32 MILES
80 K FT

IFCO TESTS

B-52H POSITION WHEN
D-21B PASSES THROUGH
40 K FT

74 K FT
63 K FT
50 K FT

1 MILE
40 K FT

FIN DOWN
TM ON
AFCS TEST
FUEL ON
OBS. CAM. ON

NO DESTRUCT
POSSIBLE

BOOSTER IGNITION INHIBIT
AVAILABLE BY TELEMETRY

MANUAL DESTRUCT
BY COMMAND
TELEMETRY

MANUAL
DESTRUCT
BY COMMAND
(LCO MONITOR)

AUTOMATIC DESTRUCT
BY LOSS OF ALTITUDE

60 K FT
52 K FT

RECOVERY

SEQUENCE OF EVENTS

1	BOOSTER IGNITION	5	DESTRUCT ALTITUDE SWITCH OPEN	9	AUTOMATIC DESTRUCT CIRCUITRY ARM	14	FUEL "OFF"
2	5° PITCH-UP, FOLLOWED BY 1°/SEC PULL-UP	6	ENGINE IGNITION: AUTO DESTRUCT CIRCUIT COMPLETE	10	COMMAND AND T/M "OFF"	15	EJECT HATCH
3	TRANSITION TO FINAL CLIMB TRAJECTORY	7	APU LOAD TAKE-OVER	11	COMMAND "ON"	16	AUTOMATIC DESTRUCT
4	MANUAL DESTRUCT CIRCUIT COMPLETE	8	BOOSTER JETTISON, AFCS TO MACH HOLD	12	BEACONS "ON" AND T/M "ON"	17	HATCH RECOVERY
				13	DESTRUCT DISABLE		

Top left: **The Lockheed Missile and Space A-92 booster following removal from a cold soak canister and just prior to a static firing in the Santa Cruz mountains. Cold soaking was used to simulate the effects of a ten hour flight at temperatures of minus 50° F.** Lockheed Martin via Jim Goodall collection

Center right: **Hanging from the port pylon of the B-52H launch platform, the first D-21B, with its LMSC A-92 booster attached. Noteworthy is the folding ventral fin on the bottom of the booster.** Lockheed Martin via Jim Goodall collection

Above: *Senior Bowl* **B-52H with D-21B and boosters mounted on both pylons. Ventral fins folded to the right.** Lockheed Martin via Jim Goodall collection

On January 18, 1967, Johnson met with Deputy Secretary of Defense Cyrus Vance for one and a half hours in Washington, DC "He was very much for *Tagboard* and asked that we press forward vigorously on it. He also said we would never again fly a manned aircraft in peacetime over enemy territory, confirming the *Oxcart* decision."

During February, problems with longitudinal stability and control at 1.40 Mach surfaced. These were all booster related and not easily rectified. On September 28, a D-21 was accidentally dropped from a B-52H as a result of what Johnson referred to as "poor workman-

ship...a stripped nut in the forward right attachment to the pylon." Johnson noted that it was "very embarrassing". The booster in fact fired after the inadvertent launch (apparently caused by hydrogen embrittlement of explosive bolts), and was "quite a sight from the ground".

In the summer and early autumn of 1967, SAC began assembling the nucleus of the Air Force unit that would prepare, launch, fly, recover, and maintain the D-21Bs being carried by the modified B-52H aircraft. Assignments were levied throughout SAC for approximately 180 officers and airmen as follows:

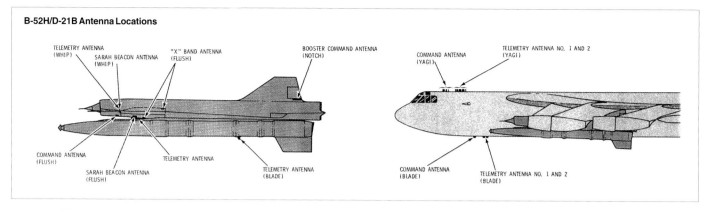

B-52H/D-21B Antenna Locations

1. Those personnel who would fly or work on the B-52H only.

2. Those personnel who would work on the D-21B only.

3. Those few personnel who would be involved in both the B-52H and D-21B programs.

4. A small, specially trained component of Security Police which would initially be responsible only to "A"-Flight (later they would support the 4200th Support Squadron).

5. Supply, administrative and other support personnel that would not be directly involved with either the B-52H or D-21B programs, but who would make important contributions to these projects.

In addition to Air Force personnel, many Lockheed, vendor-support and advisory personnel also were onboard, making up about 20% of staffing. During 1968, most of the cleared "A"-Flight personnel were sent out to Groom Lake/Area 51 each week where they were introduced to the D-21B and its systems, the modified B-52H, specifics about specialized equipment, and a view of how everyone fit into the program.

The team would meet at Beale AFB's Base Operations every Monday morning at about 0600 and board a civilian Fairchild F-27 for the flight out to Groom Lake/Area 51. While stationed there, the men were housed in mobile homes. They were not allowed to leave the test site but were free to wander within its boundaries. At 1730 hours each Friday, the team would again board the F-27 for the flight back to Beale. Their weekends were free, but come Monday morning the workweek away from home would begin all over again.

During late 1968, the unit gained operational status and the "A"-Flight designation was changed to the 4200th Support Squadron. With the change in designation, program members lost some of the priority treatment they had been enjoying, but they retained enough status (far more than SR-71 personnel) to know that they were in an elite outfit.

While the 4200th Support Squadron team had been stationed at the test site, civilian contractors had been busy remodeling the nose dock at Beale (located near the current site of the fuel cell and phase hangars) for the unit's new home. During December of 1969, the 4200th moved in and began setting up shop. The two *Senior Bowl* B-52Hs were also delivered and parked at the farthest point of the northern end of the ramp near the base alert facility.

The 4200th had its own cadre of security police staff who, like the rest of the 4200th, had been fully cleared for *Senior Bowl*. All team members (from E-2s to Colonels) were allowed exemption from the usual inspections, Maintenance Standardization and Evaluation Program (MSEP) inspections, base details and other irritants that everyone else at Beale AFB had to contend with. The 180 or so people who comprised the 4200th Support Squadron thus became a very close-knit group.

There were three land-based locations where the 4200th would most likely be sent to recover the mission payload: Anderson AFB, Guam; Kadena AB, Okinawa (as a backup to Anderson); or Hickam AFB, Hawaii. An assortment of Navy ships also served as destination points.

The first location (Anderson AFB, Guam) could receive and deploy the B-52H/D-21B as scheduled, allowing the aircraft to depart or recover from their mission. On all but one occasion, however, the missions commenced directly from and returned to Beale. If weather conditions prevented JC-130 mission recoveries at Anderson, then Kadena AB, Okinawa would be used as the alternate recovery site. The JC-130 would land at the closest of the three bases to off-load the recce system product into a waiting KC-135 for a flight back to Beale. The third location, a "floating TDY" (usually a Liberty Ship or Navy destroyer), could perform secondary recovery operations of the hatch in the event the JC-130B (codenamed *Cat's Whiskers*) was unable to snag the hatch in flight.

The first actual launch attempt from a B-52H took place on November 6, 1969. Johnson noted that it was not successful. "The rocket took it to altitude but it nosed over and dived-in within 150 miles." On November 28, a B-52H was flown for the first time with two D-21s (nos. 508 and 509) suspended from its wing pylons. This equated to a total payload weight of 24 tons...which was within the limits of the B-52H's capabilities, but an extremely heavy load nevertheless.

Following the move to Beale AFB, launches and launch attempts now followed with some regularity. Failures occurred on December 2 and January 19, and in between there were several aborts. On February 5, Johnson wrote, "I feel we must make this thing work on the next flight or the project will be canceled." In frustration, he convened a *Skunk Works* review. This took place from January 22 through February 14, 1968. "We made a careful study of all available data which ended up showing two things. The launches, whether from the *Oxcart* airplane or the B-52, got to identical altitudes but higher speeds with the rocket. The B-52 launch aircraft, however, flew 6,000 to 10,000 feet lower than they should have, compared to the *Oxcart* launches."

Another failure occurred on April 30, but on June 16, 1968, a successful flight was finally accomplished with D-21 #512. "It flew its design range, 3,000 nautical miles," Johnson

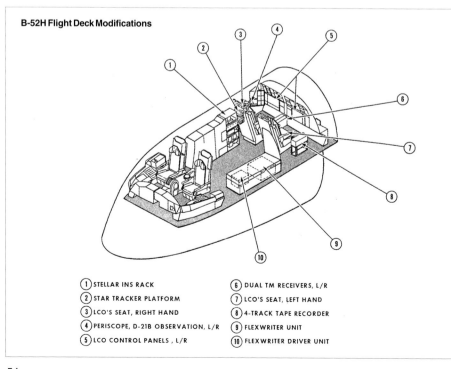

B-52H Flight Deck Modifications

1. STELLAR INS RACK
2. STAR TRACKER PLATFORM
3. LCO'S SEAT, RIGHT HAND
4. PERISCOPE, D-21B OBSERVATION, L/R
5. LCO CONTROL PANELS, L/R
6. DUAL TM RECEIVERS, L/R
7. LCO'S SEAT, LEFT HAND
8. 4-TRACK TAPE RECORDER
9. FLEXWRITER UNIT
10. FLEXWRITER DRIVER UNIT

wrote, and it reached an altitude of "over 90,000 feet and the package was recovered satisfactorily. The engine blew out in turns, but reignited in climb back."

More only partially successful flights followed, including several that Johnson flew to Hawaii to witness in person, and this continued to frustrate him. "We are overrunning costs obviously, working not only for zero budgets, but putting Lockheed money into the program. The *Tagboard* shows a great deal of promise, but it is a very tough technical job."

Still another failed flight took place on February 11...this being the first to attempt at a *Capt. Hook* mission wherein the inertial navigation system was programmed per an operational sortie. Johnson would later note, "Our best analysis for the reason was water in the autopilot, but we cannot definitely prove this."

A successful launch and flight took place on May 10 with modestly good photography resulting. Another good launch and flight took place on July 10. Johnson noted, "We have now met our design objectives to the point where the Air Force can consider the program successful and completed up to the operational phase. The remaining job will be to put the other birds in the same configuration as the last successful launch."

These successes now gave the *Skunk Works*, the CIA, and the Air Force renewed confidence in the program. On September 25, Johnson noted that the "decision to use *Tagboard* on a hot mission has now gone to President Nixon. I think there is a good probability that it will be used within the next six months. If we successfully do this, *Tagboard* should have a good future. We are studying how to recover the complete vehicle and it appears feasible." As an afterthought he would note, "I am very pleased with the technical success we have had with the bird since putting it on the B-52 for launching and I am very glad that we took our medicine at the time.*

On November 9, 1969, the first operational mission was launched but did not succeed. The D-21 simply disappeared. Johnson wrote, "It was lost. Subsequent to this failure, we went into the navigation system again and changed the programming to something I have wanted since the beginning of the program. This enables the airplane to miss a destination check point, but to continue to the following ones."

A non-operational mission was flown on February 20, 1970, this time with considerably more success, "We ran another *Captain Hook* mission with the new navigation programming flying over 3,000 nautical miles. The aircraft performed superbly, reaching altitudes over 95,000 feet, hitting all its check points within two to three miles. We were told to standby for another hot mission in March.

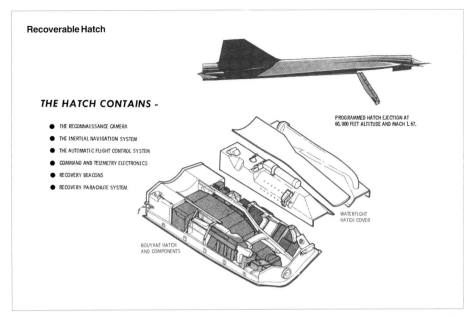

Recoverable Hatch

THE HATCH CONTAINS -

- THE RECONNAISSANCE CAMERA
- THE INERTIAL NAVIGATION SYSTEM
- THE AUTOMATIC FLIGHT CONTROL SYSTEM
- COMMAND AND TELEMETRY ELECTRONICS
- RECOVERY BEACONS
- RECOVERY PARACHUTE SYSTEM

PROGRAMMED HATCH EJECTION AT 60,000 FEET ALTITUDE AND MACH 1.67.

WATERTIGHT HATCH COVER

BOUYANT HATCH AND COMPONENTS

Political and other considerations now stepped in to curtail further D-21 activity. Between February 20 and mid-December, no further launches were attempted. The aircraft sat idle. Finally, after nearly a year of relative inactivity, a second "hot" mission was attempted on December 16. The D-21 apparently flew successfully, but the hatch was not recovered and no imagery resulted. Nearly three months later, on March 4, 1971, a third operational mission was flown resulting in a successful flight but a poorly managed hatch recovery effort. "The parachute was damaged during descent with

the hatch, it fell slowly into the water. The hatch floated – the Navy got there with a ship. During the recovery operation the hatch was damaged to the point where it sank. Another Navy ship found the *Tagboard* vehicle floating, but was unable to get cables around it before it sank."

Sixteen days later, the fourth operational mission was flown. The mission was a failure. The D-21 was lost "three-quarters of the way through...over a very heavily defended area". This was to be the last D-21 mission ever...though Johnson and the *Skunk Works* team did not know it at the time.

Right center: *Skunk Works* engineers and technicians perform the first pylon/D-21B mating at the Burbank production facility on June 1, 1967. The pylon was found to fit properly on the very first try. Lockheed Martin via Jim Goodall collection

Bottom: The B-52H launch platform drops one of its two D-21Bs on a *Captain Hook* mission west of the Hawaiian Islands. The A-92 booster ignited approximately two to four seconds after release. Lockheed Martin via Jay Miler collection

Operational Vehicle and Booster

- The D-21B Consists of Three Major Elements:
  - The Airframe and Engine
  - The Recoverable Hatch Containing
    - The Camera
    - High Value Electronic Equipment

- The Booster Including:
  - Antenna
  - Electrical and Hydraulic Power Systems
  - Retractable Fin

The D-21's problems had been many, and not easily resolved. Progress had been made throughout the course of the program, but four modestly successful missions out of a total of twenty flown did not a good track record make. This, when coupled with the ambivalence that had been shown by the CIA from the very beginning, spelled the end of the road by mid-1971. On July 15, Johnson received word of the program's cancellation, "Received wire canceling *Tagboard*. The birds will be placed in dead storage. We will work out the details of storing the aircraft later. We were already returning the birds and equipment from Beale AFB to ADP by means of a C-5A. We were ordered to destroy tooling, not only here, but at our vendors."

The real end came on July 23 when a very low key, but official termination get-together took place at Beale AFB near Sacramento, California. Johnson summarized the event with, "I flew up to Beale to make a speech to the 4200th Air Support Squadron who are being disbanded in SAC. It was a sad occasion for all.

I have four major feelings regarding the *Tagboard* program: (1) We will probably see the day when we will greatly rue the decision taken to scrap the program; (2) We did an excellent job on a program of the most difficult nature and at very low cost; (3) We had excellent cooperation from the Air Force, including SAC and our friends in the Pentagon; and (4) I am sad to see such a program, which actually had its inception back on the X-7 ramjet test vehicle, which developed the *Bomarc* engine and was based on some 20-odd years of technical development be canceled. The remarkable part of the program was not that we lost a few birds due to insufficient launches to develop reliability, but rather that we were able to obtain such a high degree of performance with such low cost compared to any other system."

The remaining D-21s were moved to Groom Lake/Area 51 and from there to Norton AFB in California. By 1977, they were all in storage at Davis-Monthan AFB, Arizona, eventually – some twenty years later – to be dispersed to various museums or scrapped.

Bottom left: **Two views of D-21Bs mounted under the inboard wings of one of two Boeing B-52Hs modified for the mission.** Lockheed Martin via Jim Goodall collection

Below: **A line up of seventeen D-21s in storage at the US Air Force AMARC facility, Davis Monthan AFB, Arizona. The fifth D-21 from the bottom is D-21, 503, damaged during the nose cone separation tests on the M-21.** Lockheed Martin via Jim Goodall collection

Chapter Five

Senior Crown, SR-71

Above: **Lined up at the *Skunk Works* in Bldg. 309/310, on November 20, 1964, are the first three SR-71As, (front to back), 61-7952, 61-7951 and the very first SR-71A, 61-7950.** Lockheed Martin via Jim Goodall collection

During the course of the A-12 program the US Air Force had been exceedingly helpful to the CIA. It provided financial support, conducted the refueling program, provided operational facilities at Kadena, and airlifted A-12 personnel and supplies to Okinawa in support of the Vietnam and North Korea overflight operations. Through it all, however, the Air Force remained frustrated that a strategic reconnaissance mission – historically its purview – had been given to another government agency. This umbrage had in fact been ongoing for nearly a decade by the advent of the R-12 – later formally designated SR-71 – and could be traced back directly to the Lockheed U-2 program and President Eisenhower's decision to turn control over to the CIA.

"Kelly" Johnson had first mentioned working on a "reconnaissance/strike" variant of the A-12 for the Air Force during April of 1962. However, preliminary discussions relating to a configuration of this type had been ongoing almost from the beginning of the program during 1958 and 1959. During March of 1962, the Air Force had been cleared to give Lockheed a study contract wherein the various Air Force mission options – including the ability to destroy ground targets – could be more precisely identified. The basis for the proposed aircraft was the CIA's A-12.

By April, two different mock-ups, an R-12 and an RS-12 (as Johnson referred to them), were under construction and mission definition work was well under way in the *Skunk Works*. On May 14, Johnson noted in the log, "Had mock-up review of RS-12 mock-up. Flew a simulated mission using 'quick check' radar photographs. The fifteen people we have had on this 90-day study under Daniell have done a most excellent job."

On June 4, the ninety-day study contract that had been granted the *Skunk Works* was reviewed by "Rus Daniell, Templeton, and a large number of aerial reconnaissance people." This was concluded satisfactorily, but no firm commitment to move ahead with hardware was immediately forthcoming...which frustrated the sometimes impatient Johnson.

On December 6, Johnson would note, "Working on R-12 Universal airplane, using company work order. Can get no decision on any military version of the aircraft, but there does seem to be considerable interest in it."

The idea of the Universal A-12 – which fundamentally could be field optimized to accommodate either reconnaissance or strike missions, had continued to appeal to Johnson. This utilitarian A-12 did, in fact, make sense, though political ramifications (i.e., one aircraft and one aircraft company doing all things for all requirements) eventually would prove too much for such pragmatism to prevail.

Seven days later, the *Skunk Works* was visited by SAC personnel. "They wanted to see what kind of a reconnaissance version would meet SAC's needs. There is a group of Air Force people who seem to be anxious that we do not exploit the A-12 to its maximum capability as a reconnaissance airplane. However,

became the project group on the R-12. By the advent of the R-12 the CIA had begun to diverge into other sensor platforms of a considerably more clandestine nature, including the first of the super-high-resolution optical systems then being merged for the first time with satellite technology. As the A-12s had been supported via Air Force (and Lockheed) expertise it was not surprising when the CIA capitulated to Air Force demands that the airborne strategic reconnaissance mission be returned to its jurisdiction.

In light of the Air Force's strong support for their mission-optimized R-12, it is interesting to note the CIA's A-12 remained, in many respects, the more capable aircraft. Its single-man crew left room for a much larger and higher-resolution camera as well as other collection devices which, when it was under development, could not be carried by the proposed R-12. Perhaps most importantly, it was operated in the civilian sector and thus could be employed covertly or at least without the number of personnel and amount of fanfare normally attending an Air Force operation. At the time, the A-12 was certainly the most effective reconnaissance aircraft in the world.

Once the Air Force had been approved to take over the A-12 mission, Johnson's *Skunk Works* team moved ahead with the slightly stretched and reconfigured A-12 which still was being referred to under the R-12 designator. The new aircraft would differ from its predecessor in one major respect...and several minor: it would be given a pressurized aft cockpit for a second crew member in the "Q-bay"

after they were here for a day or so, I believe we convinced them that we could carry all the reconnaissance gear that SAC felt was required. There is still a feeling that a reconnaissance/strike airplane larger than the R-12 is required, but I am going to be sure that our Universal airplane can do that job. We prepared our proposal for a 140,000 pound reconnaissance airplane capable of carrying 4,300 pounds of reconnaissance gear and gave it to Col. Templeton with a forwarding letter."

One week after SAC's visit, Johnson and several other *Skunk Works* engineers were off to Washington to continue their contract pursuit. "Presented our R-12 version, which Templeton and group presented to the Air Force in a closed session the next day. The outcome was that we were proposing too heavy an aircraft, with too much equipment, so we were requested to scale it down to 1,500 pounds of payload."

During this period, the *Skunk Works*, primarily under Rus Daniell, went through many

exercises in order to perfect the "R" model's design. Finally, on February 18, 1963, they were given pre-contractual authority to build six aircraft, with the understanding that an additional twenty-five would be ordered by July 1.

Interestingly, the first six aircraft were part of the A-12 order for the CIA, and the contract was through that agency and not the Air Force. Not coincidentally, the R-12 order eased the path of A-12 development by allowing the Air Force to share the program financial burden. Thus the cost per aircraft was somewhat reduced by the larger production quantity. In the long run, however, the R-12 funding spelled doom for the A-12. As noted in the A-12 chapter, government budgetary agencies determined two independent reconnaissance systems with basically similar capabilities could not be justified.

Col. Leo Geary was assigned as Weapon System Program Officer for the RS-12 in the Pentagon, and – after prolonged debate – Col. Templeton and the AF-12 project group

position normally occupied by sensor equipment; a slight fuselage stretch would result from adding another fuselage fuel tank along with other changes in the way sensors were carried; and the nose chine would be broadened to improve cruise characteristics and offset loss of directional stability resulting from the change in length.

On March 19, 1963, after receiving the Air Force go-ahead, Johnson would write in his log, "Having considerable problem with choosing the guidance system vendors. I have cautioned both Geary and Templeton not to proceed too fast in making hasty judgments. They are under pressure to use the Nortronics system from the GAM-87, which has been canceled. This leaves us with a problem on Motorola, Hughes, and Litton, who have proposed a system."

As the construction process gathered momentum and the first aircraft began to go together at Burbank, Bob Murphy had been sent to Site 2 at Palmdale in order to make arrangements with the Air Force and occupant Rockwell International to take over the facility. The *Skunk Works* needed the site for its own production program and it became Murphy's job to wrest it away.

In the meantime, a shortage of thin titanium sheet brought to light the sensitivity of the metalurgical side of the program. Titanium had, in fact, been a source of major concern for the *Skunk Works* from the very beginning. As it was far and away the single most important material utilized in the A-12 family, extraordinary means were used to control every facet of its manufacture and implementation. Johnson would summarize this in a paper written for "Lockheed Life" during December of 1981, "The *Skunk Works* traditionally avoids the snarls of excess report writing. However, with titanium, for an outfit that hated paperwork, we really deluged ourselves with it. Having made 13 million titanium parts to date, we can trace the history of all but the first few back to the mill

pour and, for about the last 10 million of them, even the direction of the grain in the sheet from which the part was cut has been recorded."

During the initial phases of the A-12 program, the *Skunk Works* engineering team discovered that titanium wing panels spot welded during the summer failed early in life, but those made in the winter lasted indefinitely. "We finally traced this problem to the Burbank water system, which heavily chlorinated water in the summer to prevent algae growth, but not in the winter. Changing to distilled water to wash the parts solved this problem."

Johnson also remained concerned about the crucial navigation system, noting, "I am not at all sold on the Nortronics guidance system. This device is not nearly as far along as Templeton and his people think. I look for nothing but trouble with this unit." And as a side note he added, "The mock-up is progressing well."

The first mock-up review took place on June 13 and 14, 1963. "Overall, it was a very successful meeting in all regards, including the

flight-test phase with Col. "Fox" Stephens," Johnson recalled. "I think the Air Force are well impressed with our operation to this point and I am very pleased at the high caliber of people Leo and Templeton are getting on the program."

Air Force interest in the strike capability of the new aircraft continued, even at this late date. On June 29, Johnson traveled to SAC Headquarters at Offutt AFB, Nebraska and met with Gen. Thomas Powers, then Commander of SAC. "We went over the problems of converting the R-12 aircraft to the RS version. I described the structural changes required and presented some Hughes Aircraft Company data on the new missile and went into discussions on side-looking radar. We also talked of several other items, such as the U-2 for satellite search, and the current status of the A-12 program."

Another mock-up conference took place on December 11, 1963, and was deemed a success by Johnson. By March 18, 1964, R-12 construction was moving along with consider-

able rapidity, but contract negotiations had yet to be concluded with the Air Force. Johnson noted in his log, "Spent several days...on...the first six R-12s. It is extremely difficult to get a reasonable profit for what we do and no credit is given for the fact we operate more cheaply than others."

All activity relating to the R-12 and RS-12 configurations had, of course, been kept completely under wraps in the *Skunk Works* and within the confines of the involved Air Force and CIA offices. On July 24, 1964, however, President Johnson publicly unveiled the existence of Lockheed's latest 3.0 Mach-capable aircraft. The full context of Johnson's speech was:

"I would like to announce the successful development of a major new strategic manned aircraft system, which will be employed by the Strategic Air Command. This system employs the new SR-71 aircraft, and provides a long range advanced strategic reconnaissance plane for military use, capable of worldwide reconnaissance for military operations. The Joint Chiefs of Staff, when reviewing the RS-70,

emphasized the importance of the strategic reconnaissance mission. The SR-71 aircraft reconnaissance system is the most advanced in the world. The aircraft will fly at more than three times the speed of sound. It will operate at altitudes in excess of 80,000 feet. It will use the most advanced observation equipment of all kinds in the world. The aircraft will provide the strategic forces of the United States with an outstanding long-range reconnaissance capability.

"The system will be used during periods of military hostilities and in other situations in which the United States military forces may be confronting foreign military forces.

"The SR-71 uses the same J58 engine as the experimental interceptor previously announced, but it is substantially heavier and it has a longer range. The considerably heavier gross weight permits it to accommodate multiple reconnaissance sensors needed by the Strategic Air Command to accomplish their strategic reconnaissance mission in a military environment. This billion dollar program was initiated in February of 1963. The first opera-

tional aircraft will begin flight testing in early 1965. Deployment of production units to the Strategic Air Command will begin shortly thereafter.

"Appropriate members of Congress have been kept fully informed on the nature of and the progress in this aircraft program. Further information on this major advanced aircraft system will be released from time to time at the appropriate military secret classification levels."

Though President Johnson's announcement had no impact on the status of the program, Air Force pressure was great to get the first aircraft completed and shipped from Burbank to Lockheed's Palmdale facility by October 21. Difficulties with vendors continued to plague the program, however, and as predicted by Johnson, the Nortronics guidance system was becoming a "big mess."

Finally, on October 29, 1964, the first R-12 was surreptitiously delivered by truck from Burbank to Palmdale for final assembly and pre-flight preparations. Much to everyone's surprise – in particular, Johnson's – the first aircraft, by now being referred to by its official Air Force SR-71 designation, initiated engine runs on December 18, 1964. Three days later, the first taxi tests were undertaken. Johnson would write in the log, "A large number of SAC people were here to see taxi tests of airplane #2001. They were very much impressed with the smooth operation. I delayed the flight on the aircraft one day, due to unfavorable weather and to get it in better shape to fly."

The next day, December 22, the first SR-71, 61-7950, with *Skunk Works* test pilot Bob Gilliland at the controls, took to the air for the first time. Departing from Lockheed's Air Force Plant 42 Site 2 facility at Palmdale, it remained airborne for just over an hour and reached a speed in excess of 1,000 mph..."which", Johnson noted, "is some kind of record for a first flight."

As a development of the now seemingly defunct RS-12, Johnson and the rest of the *Skunk Works* engineering team had continued to pursue an armed version of the A-12 configuration...in the form of a bomber SR-71. Referred to in-house at Lockheed as the B-71, on April 21, 1965, it was presented by Johnson to a small contingent of Air Force generals. Johnson had seen an opportunity in the form of the demise of the North American XB-70 and its proposed replacement with a bomber version of the experimental and highly controversial F-111. As Johnson so modestly described it, "I wanted them to know about our studies so they would not go too fast on the FB-111".

Though the SR-71 first flight had been completed with few difficulties, ongoing flight testing of the aircraft had not been comparably problem free. During April of 1965, fuel and

Top and upper right: **SR-71A, 61-7952, was lost on January 25, 1966 over Las Vegas, New Mexico, when it came apart at 3.17 Mach at an altitude of 80,000 feet.** Lockheed Martin via Jim Goodall collection

Lower right: **The fourth SR-71A, 61-7953 carries a white photo reference marking on the nacelle. Above the tail number is the Air Force Outstanding Unit citation.** Lockheed Martin via Jim Goodall collection

Bottom: **Covered with fire fighting foam, the fifth SR-71A, 61-7954, suffered a major wheel and tire failure at Edwards AFB, California on April 11, 1969. Repair costs exceeded value and the SR-71A was written off.** Lockheed Martin via Jim Goodall collection

hydraulic plumbing difficulties had lead to numerous test flight cancellations. "We are using a new fitting for better field installation", Johnson would note, "but poor workmanship due to our high labor turnover has rocked us back hard. We have made several landings with no hydraulic fluid in the left or right hydraulic system. Thank gosh we have an A and a B system to fly the airplane, or we would have been in real trouble. I put all the airplanes except one on the ground and we are doing a complete re-plumbing job. On one airplane we found 100 cases where tubes didn't fit, no seals were placed in the fittings, or two seals were in a fitting, bad scratches on the mating surfaces and every conceivable type of poor practice. This is a hard blow to take at this stage of the game, because we are delivering airplanes at almost one per month and we have really barely begun Category I testing. In April and again on May 11, I called numerous meetings with our shop and inspection personnel to set up ways and means for correcting and curing both the plumbing and the wiring problems due to workmanship."

Problems continued into October. "...We have gone through very expensive reworks of the electrical system and tank sealing on the SR-71s. Category I tests are way behind schedule, but so are Category II tests. The Air Force are very understanding. Our major problem now has to do with range, where we are about 25% short. We have made our speed, altitude, and are getting good results with the sensor packages."

On January 7, 1966, the first SR-71B trainer, 61-7956, with its elevated aft cockpit and associated flight controls and instrumentation changes, was delivered to Beale AFB from Palmdale. Daniell and Johnson flew to Beale to attend the acceptance ceremony.

This aircraft was the first to enter the operational Air Force inventory. It was the seventh aircraft completed and the first to go to the 4200th SRW at Beale AFB, California.

Following service introduction this unit was reorganized six months later as the 9th SRW at the same base. This occurred officially on June 22, 1966, and two squadrons, the 1st and the 99th SRS reformed to operate the SR-71A and SR-71B. Dedicated Boeing KC-135Q tankers continued to be operated by the 456th Bomb Wing's 907th Air Refueling Squadron in support of these special aircraft.

The SR-71 flight-test program – conducted at Palmdale – like that of its A-12 predecessor, was not without its accidents. The first, involving the third SR-71A, 61-7952, occurred on January 25, 1966, when *Skunk Works* pilot Bill Weaver miraculously escaped without using his ejection seat. His back seater, Jim Zwayer, was not so lucky and was killed.

At the time of the accident, the aircraft was in a right turn and the right inlet forward bypass doors were being controlled manually by Weaver. Approximately 15° into a turn, at between 77,000 ft. and 78,000 ft. and 3.17 Mach, a right inlet un-start was experienced and the bank angle immediately increased from 35° to 60°. The aircraft started to pitch up. Weaver attempted to regain control, but the effort proved futile. The aircraft continued to pitch until – as Weaver later noted – "the horizon disappeared and there wasn't anything left but blue sky to look at..." Moments later, the forward nose section, including the cockpits, departed the rest of the fuselage.

The first operational SR-71A, 61-7958, the ninth aircraft completed, was delivered to Beale AFB on April 4, 1966. Problems continued to plague the program, however, and these delayed actual operational integration of the aircraft into the day-to-day activities of the military intelligence community. Johnson, in recounting this period, would write in his log, "We have a backlog of airplanes at Palmdale for many reasons, particularly fuel leaks, plumbing problems, etc. The Air Force is very understanding and sympathetic to our problems."

The following month, the program took a turn for the better. "We have broken the log jam and are getting airplanes to Beale, with tank

61

Yet another aircraft, SR-71A, 61-7965, number 16, crashed in Nevada on October 25. "The pilot (Maj. Roy L. St. Martin and RSO Capt. John F. Carnochan) became completely disoriented. The crew bailed out safety, but a large part of the problem came about due to confusion between the crew members and their inability to read the standard Air Force standby attitude indicator, which is really not suited for night flying."

The Air Force had maintained a position of patience with Lockheed from the SR-71's inception. There was no question it was a major rework of the original A-12 and in many respects, because of the operational criteria around which it had been conceived, it was a significantly different aircraft. These factors had adversely impacted the flight-test program and problems had resulted.

During the beginning of the Category I testing of the SR-71, a bulk of the test objectives were spelled out in Air Force Regulation 80-14 and labeled Cat. I/II/III. Cat. I Tests utilized SR-71As, 61-7950, 61-7951, and 61-7952 and Cat. II Tests utilized 61-7953, 61-7954, and 61-7955. Cat. III tests involved the majority of the SR-71 fleet.

During the Cat. I tests, Lockheed was responsible for verifying the aircraft was safe to fly, that all systems and subsystems worked per specification, that the engines were suitable and reliable, and that all sensors, electronics, communications and navigation equipment worked in concert with one another and per specification.

Maj. William Lusby, an SR-71 flight-test engineer who participated in the Cat. I tests, noted, "I have a vivid memory of the dynamic lateral directional test in the SR-71. The airplane is naturally instable in the directional axis with the (Honeywell) Stability Augmentation System (SAS) off. With the SAS on there was no problem. However, it was necessary to turn the SAS off and put in a slight rudder pulse to obtain the unaugmented damping derivatives. I watched the flight instruments and saw the yaw angle slowly increase with each cycle. The inlet spikes began to cycle in and out as the airflow changed direction going into the inlet (this was due to the SR-71 yawing from side to side at Mach 3+). We needed several cycles of motion to get enough data...needless to say, the pilot had his finger on the SAS re-engage trigger waiting for a signal to end the test."

The allocation of flight-test assets with regard to Lockheed were: SR-71A, 61-7950, instrumented for performance, stability, and control studies; SR-71As, 61-7951 and 61-7952, assigned to systems trials and other items related to system flight tests and follow-on programs.

The Air Force assigned three SR-71As to category-series testing in addition to the three assigned to Lockheed. SR-71As, 61-7953,

leaks being our biggest problem. They are released to go to Mach 3.0. This includes the second trainer, aircraft number 8. We have not completed our Category I or II tests, but have made good progress." On June 15, a small but notable change also was made to the aircraft's aerodynamics, "Laid out a program for changing the nose tilt on the SR-71 2° up to improve the trim characteristics."

Though SR-71s finally were beginning to enter operational service, the miscellaneous subsystem problems remained difficult to overcome. Tank sealing and range deficiencies continued to plague the aircraft, including those considered operational at Beale AFB, and corrective action was painfully slow in coming.

On January 10, 1967, the first SR-71, 61-7950, was accidentally written-off during a brake testing exercise. The drag chute failed on an artificially wetted surface. According to Johnson, "The airplane ground off the right-hand wheels until they had a one foot long flat spot. Going out on the overrun at 100 knots, the right gear broke off, then all the others. The airplane burned completely. Art Peterson escaped with a cracked disc in his back." Braking on wet surfaces would continue to be a problem with the initial production aircraft.

On April 13, another SR-71A, 61-7966, Article 2017, crashed in New Mexico. Johnson noted it in the log with, "After a night refueling, the pilot had some engine stalls and the airspeed drifted down to about 170 knots at 37,000 feet. Both crew members, (Capt. Earle M. Boone and Capt. Richard E. Sheffield), escaped. It was a bad time to have another accident."

Top: **With its forty foot drag chute fully deployed, SR-71A, 61-7955, touches down on the runway of Air Force Plant 42, Palmdale, California.** Lockheed Martin via Jim Goodall collection

Center: **NASA SR-71B, 61-7956/NASA 844, undergoes testing in the fuel barn at the Lockheed's Palmdale, California facility.** NASA via Mike Relja

Bottom: **The first SR-71B, 61-7956. This aircraft was turned over to the NASA at the end of SR-71 operations.** Lockheed Martin via Jim Goodall collection

61-7954, and 61-7955, plus the three YF-12As that were still in a combined Air Force/Lockheed test program at Edwards AFB, were the total number dedicated to Category II tests and were then stationed at Edwards AFB, California...this making a total of nine aircraft in the series at Edwards. (As a note of interest, only three of the original nine aircraft survived: YF-12A, 60-6935, now displayed at the Air Force Museum, Wright-Patterson AFB, Ohio; SR-71A, 61-7951, now displayed at the Pima Air Museum, Tucson, Arizona; and SR-71A, 61-7955, now displayed at the Flight Test Museum, Edwards AFB, California.) SR-71 Cat. I flight testing ran from December 22, 1964 through 1967; SR-71 Cat. II flight testing ran from July 1, 1965 through 1967.

Though select aircraft were finally operational at Beale AFB, the Air Force had long envisioned deploying the SR-71 to detachment facilities near critical hot spots around the world. First among these was Kadena Air Base, Okinawa, which would permit quick response overflights of sensitive areas. Flights into denied airspace required not only the SR-71's superior performance, but also a host of advanced electronic countermeasures systems. Installation of the latter proved a difficult, if not demanding task and it was not until late 1967 that the first effective systems were installed and declared operational.

While work on solving operational problems with the standard production SR-71 was ongoing at Lockheed, "Kelly" Johnson and his team had not failed to explore other variant options. On December 4, 1967, Rus Daniell, Dan Haughton, and Johnson went to SAC Headquarters in Omaha, Nebraska, and made a presentation on yet another A-12 model, the FB-12. A common airframe for an air defense fighter or bomber, it was noted by Johnson as being, "...a strong case for high altitude bombing." Though the trio were well received, the FB-12, like its other Universal predecessors, proved short-lived. There were simply too many other bomber projects with stronger lobbying teams in Congress.

By late 1967, all thirty-one SR-71s on order from Lockheed had been completed and delivered. On February 14, 1968, Johnson wrote in the log that Col. Benjamin Bellis was "trying to have us store SR-71 tools". *Skunk Works* activity related to the SR-71 was then

limited to getting the aircraft ready for their initial deployment to Kadena AB and keeping them serviced in the field. On March 4 and 5, the final SR-71 construction contract termination negotiations were concluded and the company concomitantly was given an ongoing service contract in its place.

On July 31, 1967, the eleventh SR-71A, 61-7960, piloted by Maj. Ben Bowles, was severely damaged after flying 300 miles with an engine fire. It was eventually repaired and returned to service, but not without great expense.

On April 11, 1969, the number five SR-71A, 61-7954, also was severely damaged. Like number eleven, it was repairable, but the cost was estimated to be $5 million. In both cases, the crews escaped without injury.

By late September of 1969, the SR-71 was well on its way to a long and illustrious operational career. SAC already had flown well over one hundred "hot missions" out of Kadena, and many more were in the pipeline. Most importantly, the reconnaissance cameras and other electronic sensor systems were functioning with considerable dependability, and the intelligence product they were producing was extraordinary. All levels of the US intelligence community benefited from the new aircraft's extraordinary capabilities and the fact that it, unlike satellites, could be directed to a specific hot spot and deliver imagery in near real-time, was a significant plus in its favor.

NASA, for the first time, formally inquired into having an SR-71 for test purposes on December 29, 1970, when a query was received by the *Skunk Works* concerning possible use of the aircraft to launch scale models of the forthcoming Rockwell International *Space Shuttle*. This query was the result of general acknowledgment that SR-71 assets were greater than the intelligence community's needs – or the Air Force's operating budget – and that redundant aircraft might be made available to the NASA, at least temporarily, if funding could be found.

Top: **SR-71B, 61-7957, was lost on January 11, 1968, after suffering a total electrical failure during a training flight.** Lockheed Martin via Tony Landis collection

Center: **SR-71A, 61-7958, with photo reference markings on bottom.** Lockheed Martin via Jim Goodall collection

Bottom: **SR-71A, 61-7958, bearing low-visibility markings.** Lockheed Martin via Jay Miller collection

Top: **SR-71A, 61-7959, at Edwards AFB and prior to conversion to** *Big Tail* **modification.** Lockheed via Jim Goodall collection

Right and below: **Two views of SR-71A, 61-7959, following conversion to** *Big Tail* **configuration. This was the only aircraft to be equipped with this experimental package which provided space for additional sensors and electronic countermeasures upgrades.** Both Lockheed via Tony Landis collection

Funding was indeed found and during July of 1971 a single SR-71A, 61-7951, was transferred from the Air Force inventory to the NASA...where it was promptly and ironically redesignated YF-12C. Underscoring the airframe redundancy problem, however, was a decision to store six select aircraft at Palmdale. Johnson attributed the decision to a "lack of missions and money".

On July 28, 1971, Johnson noted in his log, "Nothing new on the SR-71 operation. SAC made a ten hour flight a short time ago on which about half the time was over Mach 3 and 80,000 feet. They flew 10,000 miles."

The Vietnam War had successfully justified the SR-71's existence from the time of its operational debut during 1968 through 1973. But as the war wound down, additional aircraft were placed in storage, even after their return to Beale AFB. Some 600 missions had been logged during the course of Vietnam operations, and the aircraft had logged an enviable record of dependability and mission successes.

SR-71 deployments to Kadena and to RAF Mildenhall in the United Kingdom were made at regular intervals during the 1970s and 1980s, and a permanent facility maintaining at least two SR-71As on a round-the-clock availability basis eventually was activated at the latter. Temporary deployment to Forward Operating Locations (FOLs...or OLs) worldwide were undertaken with considerable alacrity and during the course of its service career, the aircraft overflew almost every major

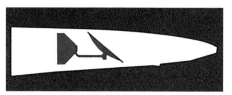

political and militarily significant hot spot in the world while gathering intelligence data of inestimable political and military value. At least one mission in excess of 14,000 miles was flown, and though unrefueled range continued to be a limiting tactical factor, the availability of the Air Force's large KC-135Q fleet allowed the aircraft to overfly targets anywhere on the globe.

Johnson and the *Skunk Works* team, in the meantime, had continued to pursue alternative missions for the SR-71 in an attempt to keep the program alive and justifiable. One study, dated November 9, 1970, called for "experimental development of an airborne system to destroy heavily defended point targets". This required a modification to the SR-71 which had "proven to be invulnerable to the types of surface-to-air missiles and interceptors used by Soviet satellite countries and Communist China". The *Skunk Works* engineering team estimated that with laser-guided bombs, the circular error probable (CEP) was about fifteen feet against fixed targets and mobile radiating targets such as surface-to-air missile radars.

On October 23, 1973, Johnson spoke with representatives from the Defense Advanced Research Projects Agency (DARPA) about the possibility of using the SR-71 as a 3.0 Mach bomber "for dropping a streamlined iron bomb with a guidance system on hard targets". As Johnson envisioned it, the aircraft would have become a "national crises control force". Eventually, a small study contract resulted, but no hardware was ever built.

The last SR-71 log entry was dated June 26, 1974. Johnson wrote, "Generally in 1974 the SR-71s played a vital role in the *Yom Kippur War* flying missions out of the east

coast in the US over the eastern Mediterranean battle lines. In fact, based on SR-71 photographic and other takes, the Israelis were advised where to strike. Made many missions using several refuelings. Aircraft and crews operated very well."

It was at approximately this time that the Air Force, during 1974, released a requirement calling for ways to augment the then-current SR-71 fleet capabilities. In turn, this need was a result of the premature decision to end production in 1967.

The *Big Tail* configuration, as it was nicknamed, grew out of a need for aft ECM coverage and real-time data transmission. Numerous studies were evaluated that allowed for an expanded complement of sensors and additional systems without remanufacturing the entire SR-71 fleet. Several options, including conformal housings, ventral and dorsal pods, and an extended tail, were considered. It eventually was concluded by the Lockheed team that the extended tail option was the most suitable in terms of aerodynamics and the desire to retain the aircraft's performance characteristics at their existing levels. During early 1975, with a decision by Air Force to proceed, Lockheed selected SR-71A, 61-7959/Article 2010, as the technology demonstrator.

The final design as implemented was capable of containing a variety of sensors, cameras, satellite up- and down-links, ECM gear and/or and SIGNET equipment. The new tail consisted of an 8 ft. 10 in. extension that was hinged just aft of the trailing edge of the inboard ailerons. It could move vertically, +/- 8.5° to ensure clearance during take-off and landing.

Weighing 1,273 lb., the *Big Tail* structure was constructed of titanium rings, stiffened with honeycomb sheer panels and advanced composites manufactured with high-temperature polymers. It had modular payload provisions, a self-contained air-conditioning system, fuel dump provisions and electrical connections built-in. A new, articulated, faring was required to match the fuselage contours to the new assembly.

Big Tail's payload comprised 49 cubic ft. of environmentally controlled space with a maximum payload weight of 864 lb. The modifications, which initially consisted primarily of test requirement, served to validate the 24 in. optical bar camera (OBC) and the aft-facing ECM system.

On December 3, 1975, Lockheed test pilot, Darrell Greenamyer flew the *Big Tail* aircraft for the first time, flying two legs and accumulating two hours and fifteen minutes at or above 3.0 Mach. Greenamyer reported in a post flight debriefing that, "*Big Tail* flew fine and there was no compromise in performance when compared with operational SR-71As."

The first Air Force flight test, piloted by LTC Tom Pugh, served to validate high-resolution photography through the aircraft's boundary layer with the 24 in. OBC while concurrently testing the aft-facing ECM pallet. Additional flights served to certify additional *Big Tail* sensors such as an updated ELINT package, the DEF A2 package, electro-optical cameras, photographic cameras, and a satellite data link antenna. The latter was for real-time data transmission to field commanders, intelligence centers, the Pentagon and other entities in need of quick access to data gathered by an SR-71 during an operational overflight mission.

When interviewed about the *Big Tail* program, Tom Pugh noted, "*Big Tail* was also configured with oversized chine bays that were large enough to carry the 24 inch OBC, and that on one of the last flights, we carried four OBC cameras, one in the nose, two in the chines, and a fourth one in the tail." Pugh also noted, "The advantage to the *Big Tail* configuration, you could trim SR by simply adjusting the position of the tail."

Above: **SR-71A, 61-7961, as it flies over the Sierra foothills to the east of Beale AFB.** Lockheed Martin via Jim Goodall collection

Right: **At a location referred to as "Last Chance", SR-71A, 61-7961, prepares for take-off at Beale AFB, California. Position of the all-moving rudders is noteworthy.** Lockheed Martin via Jim Goodall collection

Bottom: **Carrying the distinctive white photo reference markings on the underside, SR-71A, 61-7962, departs from Beale AFB.** Lockheed Martin via Jim Goodall collection

Lockheed had delivered the *Big Tail* increased capability SR-71 to the Air Force on time and on budget. However, with hostilities in Southeast Asia coming to an end and the associated downsizing of the military by the Carter administration, the Air Force no longer was interested in the increased capabilities the aircraft offered or in a production program. Stricken from the inventory, with only 866.1 hours of flight time, *Big Tail* flew for the last time on October 29, 1976, and was temporarily stored, minus engines, sensors and extended empennage, at Lockheed's Palmdale, California facility. During the winter of 1991/92, the aircraft was disassembled and moved, via a truck operated by World Wide Aircraft Recovery, to the Air Force Armament Museum, Eglin AFB, Fort Walton Beach, Florida.

The previously mentioned YF-12A speed and altitude records were eclipsed by the SR-71A during a series of *Fédération Aéronautique Internationale* (FAI) monitored flights during 1976. As of this writing, all of these records still stand, including the world's absolute speed and sustained altitude records.

The flights had been approved by the Air Force during early 1976, and on July 27, the following records were set: height in sustained horizontal flight – 85,069 feet (crew, Capt. Robert Helt/Maj. Larry Elliot); speed in a straight line – 2,193.17 mph (crew, Capt. Eldon Joersz/Maj. George Morgan, Jr.); and speed over a 1,000 kilometer closed circuit – 2,092.294 mph (crew, Maj. Adolphus Bledsoe, Jr./Maj. John Fuller).

Other records set by the SR-71A include:
April 26,1971 – a non-stop 15,000 mile mission flown in 10.5 hours (crew, Maj. Thomas Estes/Maj. Dewain Vick – awarded the 1971 Harmon and McKay Trophies)

September 1, 1974 – a nonstop flight in SR-71A, 61-7972, from Beale AFB to RAE Farnborough in which the New York to London (3,490 miles) segment was flown in 1 hour 54 minutes 56.4 seconds (crew, Maj. James Sullivan/Maj. Noel Widdifield)

September 13, 1974 – a non-stop flight from London to Los Angeles (5,645 miles) in 3 hours 47 minutes 35.8 seconds at an average speed of 1,487 mph including in-flight refuelings (crew, Capt. Harold Adams/Maj. William Machorek)

During the late 1980s, as major international political and economic changes began to manifest themselves throughout the world, the US intelligence community began to

reassess priorities and in particular, the way it was going to spend its enormous but nevertheless limited financial resources. Virtually every program, including the SR-71, was reviewed with the intent of determining its long-term viability and in particular, its simple cost-effectiveness.

As a result of this review, and in light of advances in other sensor systems, on October 1, 1989, all SR-71 activities, with the exception of crew proficiency training and associated training flights, were suspended while the Air Force awaited release of the 1990 Fiscal Year budget. When this was unveiled several weeks later, it stated that funding for the SR-71 program had been eliminated. Accordingly, all Air Force SR-71 operations were formally terminated on November 22. The SR-71 was officially retired during an emotional ceremony at Beale AFB the following January 26. Many of the Lockheed, Air Force, and CIA personnel

who had been involved in the program during the preceding twenty-four years were on hand to say farewell to what many viewed as the single most significant military aircraft of the post-World War Two period.

In a September 1991 interview with Ben R. Rich, he was quoted as saying…"In August 1989, General Larry Welch (Air Force Chief of Staff) had ordered us to give him a cost to destroy all existing SR-71s and A-12s in storage both here at Palmdale and at Beale. He doesn't want the SR-71s dispersed, but destroyed! It took us about ten days to address

his request. Lockheed's response to General Welch for a figure on the destruction of the SR-71 fleet, was approximately $67 million dollars per aircraft. When Welch heard that, he changed his mind and said, 'Maybe we should just send them all to museums'."

Rich went on to note, "In September 1990, DoD asked us how long it would take to re-activate one SR-71A, with crew and a full complement of sensors (this would have been in support of *Desert Storm*). I called DoD back about a week later and said that we could have a fully mission-capable SR-71 with crew and

sensors in fifteen days. But to do this, we need top priority on all of our requests, we will need to spend whatever it takes to get the job done, no questions asked. DoD said that they would get back to us in a few days. About two weeks later, DoD asked how long it would take to re-activate a second SR-71. I said an additional fifteen days.

"After waiting until mid-November, the DoD finally got back to us and said, "Since the SR-71 program was ultimately canceled at the Secretary of Defenses office, to reinstate it now would make the Secretary look bad."

Lockheed, Pratt & Whitney, and in particular, the *Skunk Works* could take great pride in their many accomplishments relative to the SR-71. Besides the more noteworthy aerodynamic, subsystems, materials, and airframe advances, the *Skunk Works* team demonstrated highly successful systems engineering/integration on the aircraft. Included were optical film cameras (both visual and infrared); imaging radar systems; electronic intelligence equipment; air-to-ground data linking; analog and digital recording devices; design of a real-time satellite data link; design of a global positioning system (GPS); captive test of radar for reentry vehicles; and laser communications systems.

Other successful tests and demonstrations included: overland sonic boom characterization; *Space Shuttle* reentry flight path emulation; extended high-heat profile development; digital automatic flight/inlet control development; advanced sensor/electronic warfare interoperability; high-altitude turbulence characterization; and high-temperature structure and thermal-protection materials.

The SR-71's record in service had been inspiring, to say the least. SAC operations had resulted in 53,490 flight hours, 17,300 missions, 3,551 operational missions, 11,008 operational hours, 25,862 in-flight refuelings, and a staggering 11,675 hours of operation at 3.0 Mach or greater. No other conventional fixed-wing aircraft in the world had ever sustained speeds of 3.0 Mach-plus and 80,000 feet – much less operated routinely for long periods at such velocities and altitudes.

High-time crew member of the SR-71 program was Lt. Col. Joseph Vida, a reconnaissance systems operator who had first flown in

Top: **Trailing its forty foot orange Nomex parachute, SR-71A, 61-7962 lands at Beale AFB after a training flight.** Lockheed Martin via Jim Goodall collection

Left: **Prior to hook up with a dedicated KC-135Q tanker, SR-71A, 61-7963, maneuvers into position to take on JP-7.** Ben Bowles via Jim Goodall collection

the aircraft on June 18, 1975. By the time of program termination, he had logged no less than 1,392.7 flight hours in the SR-71. High-time pilot was Col. Robert Powell, who had first flown the aircraft on July 5, 1967. He logged no less than 1,020.3 flight hours and received two Distinguished Flying Crosses by the time of program termination.

Of the thirty-one original aircraft, twenty had survived to the program's finish. With the formal termination during January of 1990, fourteen of the remaining SR-71s were released to the jurisdiction of the US Air Force Museum at Wright-Patterson AFB, Ohio, where plans were placed in motion to allocate them to various aviation museums around the US and in Europe.

On March 6, 1990, the 1974 record-setting SR-71A, 61-7972, was given to the Smithsonian Institution's National Air & Space Museum in Washington, DC. During its delivery flight from Beale AFB to Dulles International Airport, Maryland, this aircraft set four world class records, including: US coast-to-coast in 1 hour 7 minutes 53.69 seconds with an average speed of 2,124.5 mph; Los Angeles, California to Washington, DC in 1 hour 4 minutes 19.89 seconds with an average speed of 2,144.8 mph; Kansas City, Kansas to Washington, DC in 25 minutes 58.53 seconds with an average speed of 2,176.08 mph; and St. Louis, Missouri

to Cincinnati, Ohio in 8 minutes 31.97 seconds with an average speed of 2,189.94 mph. All four records were set on the same flight. The Air Force crew consisted of Lt. Col. Edward Yielding and Lt. Col. Joseph Vida.

Of the six aircraft not assigned to various museums, three, 61-7962, 61-7967 and 61-7968, were placed in storage at Lockheed's Site II facility at Palmdale, California, and three, 61-7956, 61-7971, and 61-7980, were assigned to the NASA, at their Dryden Flight Research Center, Edwards AFB, California. All of the six remaining SR-71s were later placed with museums.

Prior to the final termination of the program, discussions were held concerning a proposal that select SR-71s be retained by the Air Force and assigned to the NASA to be used for contingency situations and research projects. Among the latter, SR-71A, 61-7980 and SR-71B, 61-7956, were turned over to NASA Dryden (and maintained by Lockheed) to accommodate a variety of proposed research programs.

Proponents of the SR-71's use by NASA argued that the aircraft could become a cost-

effective high-altitude platform for scientific experiments and engineering development of space instruments. They felt it was much cheaper to conduct tests at 85,000 ft. than to launch them via the *Space Shuttle* and have them fail in space.

The first official NASA project utilizing the SR-71's unique capabilities was undertaken on March 9, 1993, when the aircraft flew the first of a series of high-altitude ultraviolet spectrometry missions from NASA Dryden, Edwards AFB. Other research flights planned at the time included: evaluations of two ultraviolet spectrometers; a University of California physics department study of *Aurora Borealis*; the testing of sensors specifically optimized for volcano plume and lava-flow studies; chasing a planned 1994 launch of the Strategic Defense Initiative Organization's (SDIO) *Clementine* lunar fly-by module while carrying special ultraviolet spectrometers; studies of atmospheric pollutants; and combining the most recent advances in laser resonant fluorescence techniques with ultraviolet spectrometry to sense substances such as chlorine monoxide.

Top: **SR-71A, 61-7963, bearing distinctive photo reference markings, departs on training mission.** Lockheed Martin via Jim Goodall collection

Center: **SR-71A, 61-7964, in subsonic cruising flight. Photo accurately depicts extraordinary aesthetics of this magnificent aircraft.** Lockheed Martin via Jay Miller collection

Right: **Crew exits SR-71A, 61-7964, on the Offutt AFB ramp after a high-speed flight from Beale AFB. Brake cooling fans on the main landing gear and open parachute doors are noteworthy.** Charles Mayer

Additionally, one of the last NASA SR-71 projects involved using SR-71A, 61-7980, to serve as the testbed for the proposed linear aerospike engine scheduled for the Lockheed X-33 single-stage-to-orbit (SSTO) research vehicle. As a precursor to the proposed, larger, *VentureStar* SSTO, the X-33 was considered a critical stepping stone to what Lockheed viewed as a potential *Space Shuttle* replacement.

The test unit contained eight thrust cells (four upper and four lower) of an aerospike engine and was mounted dorsally on the SR-71A on a platform referred to as a "canoe". The latter contained tanks for gaseous hydrogen, helium, and instrumentation. Altogether, the unit was referred to as a "pod". The entire assembly was 41 ft. long and weighed 14,300 lb. The first mating of the LASRE (Linear Aerospike SR-71 Experiment) pod took place on August 26, 1997.

The first LASRE flight, lasting 1 hr. 50 min and reaching a maximum speed of 1.19 Mach at an altitude of between 27,000 ft. and 33,000 ft.,

took place on October 31, 1997, with Ed Schneider and Robert Meyer as crew. Altogether, seven flights of the one tenth-scale, half-span, 7,000 lb. thrust Boeing-Rocketdyne J2-S engine were completed, but the engine was never operated. Only three of the flights involved cold-flow operations which cycled the gaseous helium and liquid nitrogen systems. Leaks of the cryogenic propellants dictated that actual ignition not be attempted. These technical difficulties, coupled with concerns over the eventual success of the X-33, led to the project (and program) being canceled during November of 1998.

As noted in the YF-12 chapter – and as a result of a cooperative arrangement between NASA Ames, California, and the US Air Force that could be traced back to 1967 – a single SR-71A was loaned to the NASA Dryden team at Edwards AFB, following the loss of YF-12A, 60-6936.

On June 16, 1970, YF-12A, 60-6935, still in use by the NASA, was grounded for nine

months to accommodate instrumentation upgrades. In part, this led to the NASA placing increased emphasis on the need for a second 3.0 Mach-capable platform to accommodate the test load that continued unabated at NASA Dryden. On July 16, 1971, the Air Force placed on loan SR-71A, 61-7951, and requested that, for public disclosure purposes, the aircraft be referred to as an YF-12C and be assigned a fictitious serial number, 60-6937. Its first NASA flight took place on May 24, 1972.

Among the more significant flight-test programs requiring the NASA YF-12C's services was the Central Airborne Performance Analyser (CAPA) which served to isolate faults and record (on .5 in. magnetic tape) the status of up to 170 subsystems (mostly associated with the propulsion system and inlet). Pre- and post-flight analysis of CAPA data permitted a detailed assessment of required maintenance issues. As a result of maintenance time and cost savings realized via the CAPA system, the operational SR-71 fleet was retrofitted with the device.

Following completion of its 88th NASA test flight on September 28, 1978, the YF-12C was retired and placed in storage at Lockheed's Palmdale, California, facility. It eventually became a static display item at the Pima Air Museum outside Tucson, Arizona.

Besides the three aircraft acquired in 1993, the NASA also received the Air Force's cockpit simulator. This unit initially had facilitated crew transitions but long-term plans included utilizing it to explore specific mission objectives without exposing crews to hazardous flight conditions. NASA's SR-71 program manager was David Lux. Project pilots were Stephen Ishmael and Rogers Smith. Flight-test engineers included NASA's first husband and wife flight-test engineering team, Robert Meyer and Marta Bohn-Meyer.

During 1994, the US Congress, noting a shortfall in intelligence-gathering capability and considerable angst among many Air Force intelligence community officials who thought retiring the aircraft from the active inventory to be premature, elected to return the SR-71 to operational status. As a result, three SR-71As were picked for refurbishment and upgrading. Aircraft 61-7967 and 61-7968, came from Lockheed long-term storage at Palmdale, and a single aircraft, 61-7971, was recalled from the NASA.

Congress tentatively approved a total budget of $100 million for the refurbishment effort. Successful reconditioning of the first aircraft, 61-7971, was completed during mid-1995. It was handed over to the Air Force at Palmdale on June 28. The second aircraft, 61-7967, was delivered during August of 1995. Funds for the

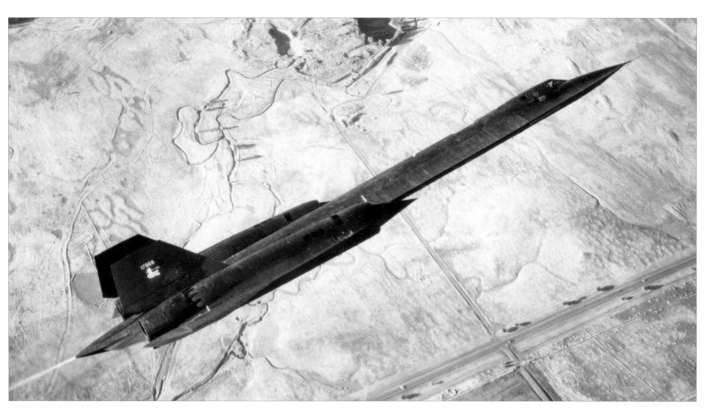

third aircraft, 61-7968, were tentatively committed for inclusion in the fiscal year 1996 budget with the aircraft being delivered during that year. As it would turn out, this last aircraft would never make it to the refurbishment stage. Corrosion problems resulting from poor storage practices had adversely impacted cockpit equipment and instrumentation, and upon review, it had been determined that making the aircraft flightworthy was not practical within the time and money constraints dictated by Congress.

Funding for the first and second SR-71As planned for reintegration into the Air Force under the auspices of the 9th Reconnaissance Wing were approved for release by Congress on September 21, 1996.

The second SR-71A, 61-7967, was the first of the three to be equipped with a Unisys air-to-ground data link which allowed the aircraft's intelligence-gathering systems to work in concert with those found in *Senior Span*-configured U-2Ss. At a later date, the first SR-71A also was upgraded to the Unisys system.

The Unisys system was designed to accept digital input from a Loral advanced synthetic aperture radar system (ASARS) and associated digital and analog electronic intelligence system inputs from the other parts of the reconnaissance system. This permitted the near-real-time down-linking of collected data to appropriate analysis entities.

Top: **SR-71A, 61-7968, bearing "Dolby" tail art.**
Lockheed Martin via Fred Carmody collection

Center: **SR-71A, 61-7969, was lost on October 18, 1966 over Thailand shortly after a successful aerial refueling. The loss was due to a subsonic stall or pitch-up.** Lockheed Martin via Jim Goodall collection

Bottom: **SR-71A, 61-7970, shown here with a Beale-assigned KC-135Q and a B-52G, was lost on June 17, 1970, near Biggs Army Air Field, El Paso, Texas.** US Air Force via Jim Goodall collection

The first refurbished SR-71A, the former NASA SR-71A, 61-7971, reached a speed of 0.94 Mach on its initial flight following modification on April 26. On May 23, it reached a speed of 3.30 Mach (just 13.5 knots short of the world speed record for class set during July of 1976) at 81,000 feet.

In the interim, the two refurbished aircraft at Palmdale had been delivered to their new home at Edwards AFB, California. It was from there that they were scheduled to fly their operational missions, rather than the 9th RW's home base at Beale AFB.

On January 1, 1997, the SR-71As were declared operational under the auspices of Det 2. On April 18, 1997, Col. Charles Simpson assumed command of the 9th RW, taking over from Brig. Gen. Robert Behler. On August 19,

the first new Air Force SR-71 crew in nine years, Maj. Bert Garrison (pilot) and Capt. Domingo Ochotorena (RSO) soloed while undertaking a practice sortie. A second new crew, Capt. Craig Barker (pilot) and Capt. Dale Zimmeman (RSO) followed in September.

Frustratingly, the SR-71's return to service proved extremely short-lived. Following a small number of operational training missions and a marked lack of support from the Air Force and national intelligence communities, the aircraft lost funding when President Clinton killed it with a line item veto on October 15, 1997. In limbo while Congress debated whether to reinstate the funding, a final verdict came on June 30, 1999, when a lack of Congressional support officially removed the SR-71 from the Air Force inventory and Det 2

Top: **World speed record holder, SR-71A, 61-7972, on the ramp at RAF Mildenhall, England.** Lockheed Martin via Jim Goodall collection

Center: **SR-71, 61-7972, taxis down the ramp at RAF Mildenhall, in preparation for a training flight.** Lockheed Martin via Jim Goodall collection

Bottom: **In a hangar at Andrews AFB, Maryland, SR-71A, 61-7973, sports its low-visibility markings.** Tony Landis

was shut down as a result. This forever ended the US Air Force's SR-71 program.

As noted earlier, SR-71A, 61-7967 was sent to Barksdale AFB, Louisiana, and SR-71A, 61-7971, was turned over to the Evergreen Museum in McMinnville, Oregon. The Imperial War Museum at Duxford, England acquired 61-7962. The 19th SR-71A, 61-7968, was moved to the Virginia Aviation Museum, near Richmond, Virginia.

The two NASA SR-71s, including SR-71A, 61-7980/NASA 844 and SR-71B, 61-7956/ NASA 831 also were allocated for display. The SR-71A was given to NASA Dryden to serve as a gate guard and the SR-71B was shipped to Kennedy AFS, Cape Canaveral, Florida.

The following is a listing of all units to which the SR-71s were assigned during the course of their operational careers:

4786th Test Squadron, Edwards AFB, North Base, California – designated January 16, 1970 (ex SR-71/YF-12 Test Force, established June 1965) with YF-12 and SR-71.

Det 1, 9th SRW, Kadena Air Base, Okinawa, Japan – known as OL-8; SR-71s began arriving at Kadena (nicknamed "The Rock") during March of 1968. The operation to transfer the SR-71s from Beale to Kadena was codenamed *Glowing Heat*. The first Detachment Commander was Col. Charles Minter with Col. Carl Estes as the Director of Maintenance. On March 15, 1968, OL-8 was declared Operationally Ready for SR-71 sor-

ties. The first aircraft to deployed to OL-8 – on March 8, 1968 – was SR-71A, 61-7978, piloted by Buddy Brown and RSO Dave Jensenon. Five days later, SR-71A, 61-7974, arrived at OL-8 piloted by Bob Spencer and RSO Keith Branham.

The final SR-71A delivered to OL-8, was SR-71A, 61-7976, piloted by Jerry O'Malley and RSO Ed Paine. On standby as the back-up SR-71, at Beale AFB, California, were Jim Watkins and Dave Dempster in SR-71A, 61-7980 (three times, 61-7980, taxied to the end of the runway as a backup aircraft for the deployment).

Det 1 had four Detachment designations from March 1968 to the end of operations during January of 1990 as follows: OL-8 was established during early March of 1968; this followed SAC's designation change for Reconnaissance Overseas Locations, with OL-8 becoming OL-RK (OL-RK stands for "Operating Location – Ryukyus"; the latter are a chain of islands in which Okinawa is situated) on October 30, 1970. Less than a year later, OL-RK became OL-KA (OL-KA stands for "Operating Location – Kadena") on October 26, 1971. Det 1 OL-KA then became simply Det 1 during August of 1974. For the following 16 years it remained Det 1 until the SR-71 fleet was retired during January of 1990.

The first SR-71 combat mission was scheduled for March 16, 1968, but canceled due to weather. On March 18, SR-71A, 61-

7978 departed to fly the first scheduled operational mission but diverted into Ching Chuan Kang (CCK), Taiwan due to adverse weather. SR-71A, 61-7978, returned to Det 1 on March 23, 1968.

On March 19, 61-7976 became the next scheduled aircraft to fly an operational mission but did not fly. Finally on March 21, 1968, SR-71A, 61-7974, flew the first operational sortie over Vietnam, piloted by Jerry O'Malley and RSO Ed Paine. Upon returning to Kadena, O'Malley found the base fogged in and was forced to divert to CCK. Regardless, the mission was successful in achieving usable imagery. Included in the latter was the first indication the North Vietnamese had established emplacements around the Khe Sanh area. These previously had been undetected.

The second operational mission was flown by the same crew in 61-7976 on April 10, 1968. Upon descent from 80,000 ft., both engines flamed out. Col. O'Malley succeeded in restarting them somewhere around 20,000 ft. Altitude and speed were quickly regained and after refueling, the flight continued on to a normal landing at Kadena.

One week later, pilot Buddy Brown and RSO Dave Jensen flew the third operational North Vietnamese sortie. Upon descent from altitude, the left generator failed and both engines flamed out. A restart was accomplished and the aircraft landed at Takhli RTAFB, Thailand. Maintenance crews from Kadena

Top: SR-71A, 61-7973, on October 10, 1991, waiting for disposition at Lockheed's Palmdale, California, facility. Aircraft was written off after being over-stressed during an airshow in the UK. Jim Goodall

Center: SR-71A, 61-7974, lands at RAF Mildenhall, UK during March of 1983. Tom Long

Bottom: The last SR-71A to be lost, 61-7974, carried the name *Ichi Ban* while assigned to Det 1, Kadena AB, Okinawa. Lockheed Martin via Jay Miller collection

flew in and performed the repairs. The aircraft later returned uneventfully to Kadena AB.

The fourth flight also was flown by Brown and Jensen. Again as they descended from altitude, they experienced a double engine flameout as well as a generator failure. Engine restart was successfully accomplished and the aircraft again landed at Takhli.

On April 19, 1968, SR-71A, 61-7974, piloted by Jim Watkins and RSO Dave Dempster took off for the fifth operational mission. Descending from altitude they experienced a double engine un-start and flameout. Jim Watkins finally solved the flameout problems by holding engine rpm a couple of hundred higher than the checklist had recommended as the engines were brought out of afterburner. The problem was related to fuel control scheduling and to non-standard ambient air temperatures that were not the norm for the Far East. The fuel system was modified to accommodate the differences and the problem effectively disappeared.

During the course of Det 1's operational mission history, surface-to-air missiles (SAMs) were constantly fired at the SR-71s in an attempt to bring one down. "Kelly" Johnson stated in a *Time Magazine* interview that, "over 1,000 missiles have been fired at the 'Blackbird' without a loss of plane or crew". Superior DEF electronics and crew skills certainly contributed to the success and accomplishment of the operational sorties.

During the SR-71's twenty-two years flying operationally out of Kadena, combat missions were flown over all of Vietnam, Laos, Cambodia, Thailand, and North Korea. Additionally, the airspace of the former Soviet Union and China was penetrated on numerous occasions. Four eleven-hour operational missions to the Persian Gulf took place during the Iran-Iraq War in 1987 and 1988. A total of 2,410 SR-71 missions were flown from first deployment in 1968 to Detachment 1 closure in 1990.

Det 2, 9th SRW, Edwards AFB, California – September 1, 1995, saw the reactivation of two SR-71As, 61-7971 and 61-7967, and the SR-71B, 61-7956, at Beale's Detachment 2 at Edwards Air Force Base, CA. The planes were operated by Air Combat Command.

Det 4, 9th SRW, RAF Mildenhall, UK – 99th SRS, 9th SRW, established March 31, 1979 and equipped both with the U-2R and the SR-71A. From 1980 through 1991 only SR-71s flew out of Mildenhall.

SR-71 operations at RAF Mildenhall ran from 1976 to 1990. Prior to Det 4 being established, UK permission was required for each sortie flown. The SR-71's stay was to be no longer than 20 days for each visit. On April 5, 1982, Prime Minister Thatcher announced that Det 4 would be a permanent SR-71 Detachment with two aircraft assigned. The United Kingdom retained control of the more sensitive missions.

The two-aircraft Detachment ceased operations on November 22, 1989. The last aircraft, SR-71A, 61-7964, departed the UK on January 18, 1990.

During *Operation El Dorado Canyon*, U-2Rs of Det OL-OH, RAF Akrotiri, Cyprus, were

during August of 1977 and was redesignated Detachment 6.

Det 6, Norton AFB, California – Supply Depot at Palmdale, California, Air Force Plant 42, Lockheed Plant 10, (ex Site II). Home of the 2762nd Logistics Squadron, AFLC, (ex Det 51) for the U-2 and SR-71.

Det 8, 9th SRW, Diego Garcia, British Indian Ocean Territory (BIOT) Chagos Archipelago – SR-71 operations were conducted for a short time in 1978/79 from Diego Garcia. An Air Force *Prime Beef* team dismantled one of the SR-71 shelters at Beale AFB, shipped it to Diego Garcia, and then reassembled it there for use by the 9th Strategic Reconnaissance Wing. Diego Garcia is the largest island of the Chagos Archipelago, SW of Sri Lanka. Diego Garcia is part of the British Indian Ocean Territory (BIOT). The archipelago consists of 2,300 islands. Diego Garcia, the largest and southernmost island, occupies a strategic location in the central Indian Ocean.

supplemented by several TR-1As from the 95th RS, 17th RW, RAF Alconbury, and together with SR-71A, 61-7980, Detachment 4, Mildenhall engaged in the reconnaissance of possible target areas in Libya.

Det 5, 9th SRW, Eielson AFB, Alaska – Sporadic operational missions were per-

formed during 1979/80. Additionally, cold weather performance tests were undertaken.

Det 51, Palmdale, California – Air Force Plant 42, Lockheed Plant 10, (ex Site II), 2762nd Logistics Squadron, AFLC (U-2 and SR-71; before December 31, 1970, operations were part of AFSC). This was reorganized

Top: **SR-71A, 61-7975, departs Beale AFB on February 11, 1981.** Jim Goodall

Center: **SR-71A, 61-7975, at a March AFB, California, open house during the late 1970s.** Mick Roth

Bottom: **SR-71A, 61-7976, makes a low-speed pass at Kelly AFB, Texas.** Jay Miller

Top: **SR-71A, 61-7976, prepares for take-off from Kadena AB, Okinawa.** Steve Myatt

Center: **SR-71A, 61-7978, nicknamed** *Rapid Rabbit*, **was lost on landing at Kadena AB, Okinawa, on July 20, 1972.** Air Force via Jim Goodall collection

Bottom: **SR-71A, 61-7979, departs on a training flight from Kadena AB, Okinawa, during January of 1981.** Tom Long

The island is site of a joint US-UK military facility. The 11-sq-mi (28 sq. km) island was leased to the US in 1970. It later was developed as a major US naval base to guard the Persian Gulf oil routes and to counter increased Soviet military activities in South Asia and Africa.

On July 1, 1980, SR-71A, 61-7962, departed Kadena AB, Okinawa with Pilot Bob Crowder and RSO Don Emmons at the controls. The 4.5 hour flight to Diego Garcia was to test and validate the readiness of the facility.

OL-KB, 9th SRW, Griffiss AFB, Rome, New York – Operations were set up for flights during the *Yom Kippur War* but moved to OL-SB due to adverse weather conditions.

The Air Force Systems Command deployed SR-71A, 61-7955, to Griffiss AFB, New York, under the code name *Black Knight*. Using the cover story of evaluation of a new Electronic Counter Measures (ECM) suite of sensors, the operation provided a series of 11.4 hour round-robin sorties to the Middle East. Plans were originally made to fly these flights from Beale AFB and recover at Mildenhall, UK. At Mildenhall to set up recovery operations, Col. Patrick Halloran, 9th

Strategic Reconnaissance Wing Commander, was informed that the British Government had second thoughts about the operation and had denied authority to operate from the United Kingdom. The reasoning was a possible Arab oil embargo against Great Britain. The two SR-71's assigned to perform the 11.4 hour round-robin flights, were 61-7964 and 61-7979. The code name for the missions was *Giant Reach*.

On October 13, 1973, Pilot Jim Shelton and RSO Gary Coleman in SR-71A, 61-7979, departed Griffiss AFB, New York, on the first of a series of flights to the Middle East. After 11.13 hours (including 5 hours above 3.0 Mach) and six refuelings the aircraft landed back at Griffiss AFB. The mission was highly successful and provided considerable insight into the critical military situation in Syria.

Again on October 25, 1973, pilot Al Joersz and RSO John Fuller flew 61-7979 on another 11.13 hour non-stop round-robin sortie to assess the situation around the Sinai and Galilee. On November 2, 1973, Pilot Bob Helt and RSO Larry Elliott, once again in 61-7979, flew a similar sortie into the *Yom Kippur War* zone in a mission lasting 11.22 hours.

Top: **SR-71A, 61-7979, heads back to hangar after a training flight on February 11, 1981.** Jim Goodall

Center: **Waiting its turn for take-off, SR-71A, 61-7979, does an engine run-up at "Last Chance" on the north end of the Beale AFB runway.** Jim Goodall

Bottom: **The very last SR-71A built, 61-7980, flies over the central England countryside after being reactivated during the mid-1980s.** Air Force via Jim Goodall collection

Top: **On a rainy day at Beale AFB, SR-71A, 61-7980, taxis for take-off.** Lockheed Martin via Jay Miller collection

Above: **The only SR-71C, 61-7981, was created by mating the forward fuselage of a functional engineering mock-up with the back half of the first YF-12A, 60-6934.** Lockheed Martin via Tony Landis collection

Right: **The SR-71C, 61-7981, just prior to launch at Beale AFB, during early 1974.** Brian C. Rogers

Below: **The second SR-71A, 61-7951, as flown by the NASA.** NASA via Marty Isham collection

The last of these Middle Eastern flights from Griffiss AFB was November 11, 1973, in SR-71A, 61-7964, flown by pilot Jim Wilson and RSO Bruce Douglass. Because of inclement weather, Wilson chose to revert to Seymour Johnson AFB, North Carolina. This sortie lasted 10.49 hours. As snow fell in Rome, New York, Col. Pat Halloran opted for a warmer climate and moved operations to Seymour Johnson AFB, North Carolina.

These SR-71 flights were instrumental in defusing the war situation in the Middle East and provided positive intelligence photos to the deeply distrusting Israelis and Arabs. With the shooting war over, OL-SB, Seymour Johnson became the base of operation for continued surveillance of the war zone to ensure compliance with the peace accord.

OL-SB, 9th SRW, Seymour Johnson AFB, North Carolina – From here the SR-71 was used for operational non-stop reconnaissance flights over Egypt, Israel, and Syria during the *Yom Kippur War* (1973/74), under the code name *Operation Giant Reach* beginning on October 11, 1973. The first mission was flown on October 13, 1973. On December 2, pilot Jim

Sullivan and RSO Noel Widdifield flew the first SR-71 to the Middle East from the Seymour Johnson AFB location in SR-71A, 61-7964. The mission lasted 9.56 hours.

On December 10, pilot Pat Bledsoe and RSO Reggie Blackwell flew SR-71A, 61-7979, to the Middle East and back in 10.0 hours. On January 25, 1974, pilot Buck Adams and RSO Bill Machorek flew SR-71A, 61-7971, in a round-robin sortie to the Middle East in 10.04 hours. On March 7, Pilot Ty Judkins and RSO John Morgan flew 61-7979 on a mission lasting 9.45 hours.

The final *Giant Reach* flight occurred on April 6, 1974, in SR-71A, 61-7979, piloted by Lee Ransom and RSO Mark Gersten. The mission lasted 9.46 hours.

In all, four *Giant Reach* sorties were flown from Griffiss AFB, New York, averaging 11.4 hours; five *Giant Reach* sorties were flown from Seymour Johnson AFB, North Carolina, averaging 10 hours each.

OL-Bodo, 9th SRW, Bodo AB, Norway – The SR-71 operated from a variety of overseas locations. Although Bodo was not a Detachment, it was an emergency recovery base for European flights.

Top: **SR-71A (aka YF-12C) 61-7951, flies over the Edwards AFB range.** NASA via Marty Isham collection

Center: **The last SR-71A built, 61-7980/NASA 844, carried the old-style NASA "worm" logo that then NASA Administrator ordered removed.** NASA via Tony Landis collection

Bottom: **Trailing its forty foot drag chute, NASA SR-71A, 61-7980/844, lands at Edwards AFB after a training flight.** NASA via Tony Landis collection

Top: **The NASA YF-12C (aka SR-71A, 61-7951) is pre-pared for launch by Lockheed/NASA technicians at the Dryden Flight Research Center, Edwards AFB, California.** NASA via Tony Landis collection

Center: **In a move to displace the controversial NASA "worm" logo, SR-71A, 61-7980/NASA 844, was given an interim logo that eventually proved short-lived.** NASA via Tony Landis collection

Bottom: **NASA's SR-71B, 61-7956/NASA 831, just after being refueled over the lower Sierra Nevada range in California.** NASA via Tony Landis collection

On August 12, 1981, pilot, B.C. Thomas and RSO Jay Reid made an emergency landing at Bodo AB after their SR-71A, 61-7960 was determined to have an engine oil problem. A recovery team left Beale AFB at 5:00 PM on August 13 in a KC-135Q and flew to Pease AFB, New Hampshire.

After refueling, the aircraft flew a polar route to Bodo and landed at 7:00 AM the following morning. Four days later, following a series of problems and one minor accident, the SR-71 was refueled statically from a KC-135Q and departed for a relatively uneventful return flight home.

OL-Warner-Robins, Warner-Robins AFB, Georgia – *Senior Year* Program Office

4200th SRW, Beale AFB, California – Established January 1, 1965, with SR-71s and T-38s, redesignated 9th SRW June 25, 1966.

9th SRW, Beale AFB, California – Established on June 25, 1966, combined all operational SR-71 and U-2 assets during March/April 1976. All SR-71 activity ended at Beale on March 6, 1990, after flying 3,551 missions over a span of 22 years with no losses. Redesignated the 9th Wing during 1990 when SAC became a part of ACC operating U-2R/S models and T-38s. The 9th Wing was redesignated the 9th Reconnaissance Wing during October of 1992, with the U-2R/S and T-38.

2762nd Logistics Squadron, Palmdale, California – Air Force Plant 42, Site II, (belonged to AFLC) servicing U-2 and SR-71 assets.

"A" Flight / 4200th Support Squadron, Beale AFB, California – Formed January 1, 1965, with its first operating location, Det 1, Area 51, also referred to as "A" Flight, flying two B-52H launch aircraft and the D-21B.

Top: **NASA's SR-71B, 61-7956/NASA 831, during checkout at Lockheed's Air Force Plant 42, Site II, Palmdale, California, facility.** Tony Landis

Center: **The end of all SR-71 activities at Beale AFB resulted in eleven surviving Beale AFB aircraft being pulled out for a special photo event on January 10, 1990. This was the first and last time this was ever done.** Lockheed via Jay Miller collection

Bottom: **The first A-12, 60-6924, and the twenty-fourth SR-71A, 61-7973, on display at Blackbird Air Park, Palmdale, California.** Tony Landis

The SR-71 in Detail:

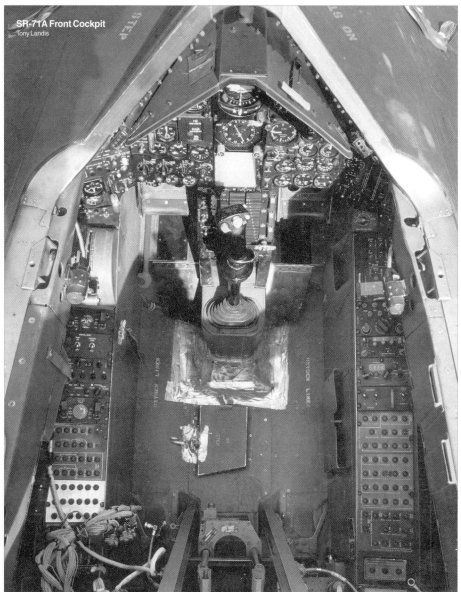

SR-71A Front Cockpit
Tony Landis

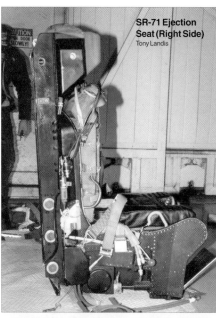

SR-71 Ejection Seat (Right Side)
Tony Landis

SR-71 Ejection Seat (Left Side)
Tony Landis

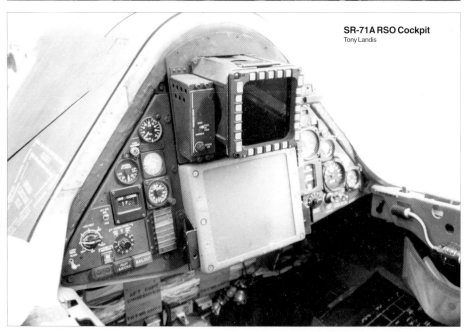

SR-71A RSO Cockpit
Tony Landis

David Clark S-901J Suits (Early SR-71 Suit)
Jim Goodall collection

SR-71A Front Cockpit
Jim Goodall collection

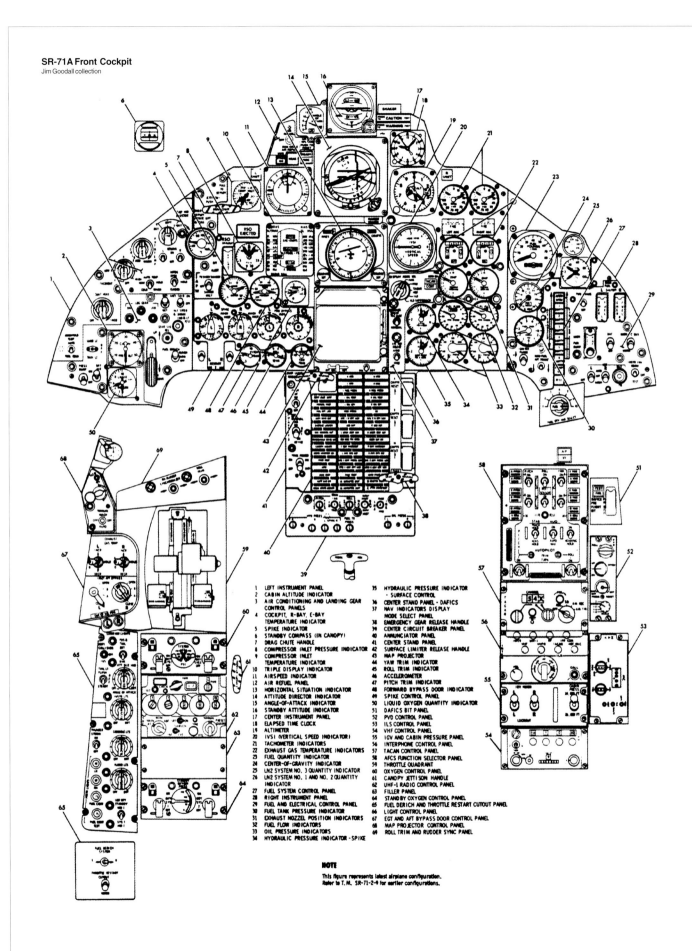

1 LEFT INSTRUMENT PANEL
2 CABIN ALTITUDE INDICATOR
3 AIR CONDITIONING AND LANDING GEAR CONTROL PANELS
4 COCKPIT, R-BAY, E-BAY TEMPERATURE INDICATOR
5 SPIKE INDICATOR
6 STANDBY COMPASS (IN CANOPY)
7 DRAG CHUTE HANDLE
8 COMPRESSOR INLET PRESSURE INDICATOR
9 COMPRESSOR INLET TEMPERATURE INDICATOR
10 TRIPLE DISPLAY INDICATOR
11 AIRSPEED INDICATOR
12 AIR REFUEL PANEL
13 HORIZONTAL SITUATION INDICATOR
14 ATTITUDE DIRECTOR INDICATOR
15 ANGLE-OF-ATTACK INDICATOR
16 STANDBY ATTITUDE INDICATOR
17 CENTER INSTRUMENT PANEL
18 ELAPSED TIME CLOCK
19 ALTIMETER
20 IVSI (VERTICAL SPEED INDICATOR)
21 TACHOMETER INDICATORS
22 EXHAUST GAS TEMPERATURE INDICATORS
23 FUEL QUANTITY INDICATOR
24 CENTER-OF-GRAVITY INDICATOR
25 LN2 SYSTEM NO. 3 QUANTITY INDICATOR
26 LN2 SYSTEM NO. 1 AND NO. 2 QUANTITY INDICATOR
27 FUEL SYSTEM CONTROL PANEL
28 RIGHT INSTRUMENT PANEL
29 FUEL AND ELECTRICAL CONTROL PANEL
30 FUEL TANK PRESSURE INDICATOR
31 EXHAUST NOZZLE POSITION INDICATORS
32 FUEL FLOW INDICATORS
33 OIL PRESSURE INDICATORS
34 HYDRAULIC PRESSURE INDICATOR - SPIKE

35 HYDRAULIC PRESSURE INDICATOR - SURFACE CONTROL
36 CENTER STAND PANEL - DAFICS
37 NAV INDICATORS DISPLAY MODE SELECT PANEL
38 EMERGENCY GEAR RELEASE HANDLE
39 CENTER CIRCUIT BREAKER PANEL
40 ANNUNCIATOR PANEL
41 CENTER STAND PANEL
42 SURFACE LIMITER RELEASE HANDLE
43 MAP PROJECTOR
44 YAW TRIM INDICATOR
45 ROLL TRIM INDICATOR
46 ACCELEROMETER
47 PITCH TRIM INDICATOR
48 FORWARD BYPASS DOOR INDICATOR
49 SPIKE CONTROL PANEL
50 LIQUID OXYGEN QUANTITY INDICATOR
51 DAFICS BIT PANEL
52 PVD CONTROL PANEL
53 ILS CONTROL PANEL
54 VHF CONTROL PANEL
55 IGV AND CABIN PRESSURE PANEL
56 INTERPHONE CONTROL PANEL
57 TACAN CONTROL PANEL
58 AFCS FUNCTION SELECTOR PANEL
59 THROTTLE QUADRANT
60 OXYGEN CONTROL PANEL
61 CANOPY JETTISON HANDLE
62 UHF-1 RADIO CONTROL PANEL
63 FILLER PANEL
64 STAND BY OXYGEN CONTROL PANEL
65 FUEL DERICH AND THROTTLE RESTART CUTOUT PANEL
66 LIGHT CONTROL PANEL
67 EGT AND AFT BYPASS DOOR CONTROL PANEL
68 MAP PROJECTOR CONTROL PANEL
69 ROLL TRIM AND RUDDER SYNC PANEL

NOTE
This figure represents latest airplane configuration.
Refer to T.M. SR-71-2-9 for earlier configurations.

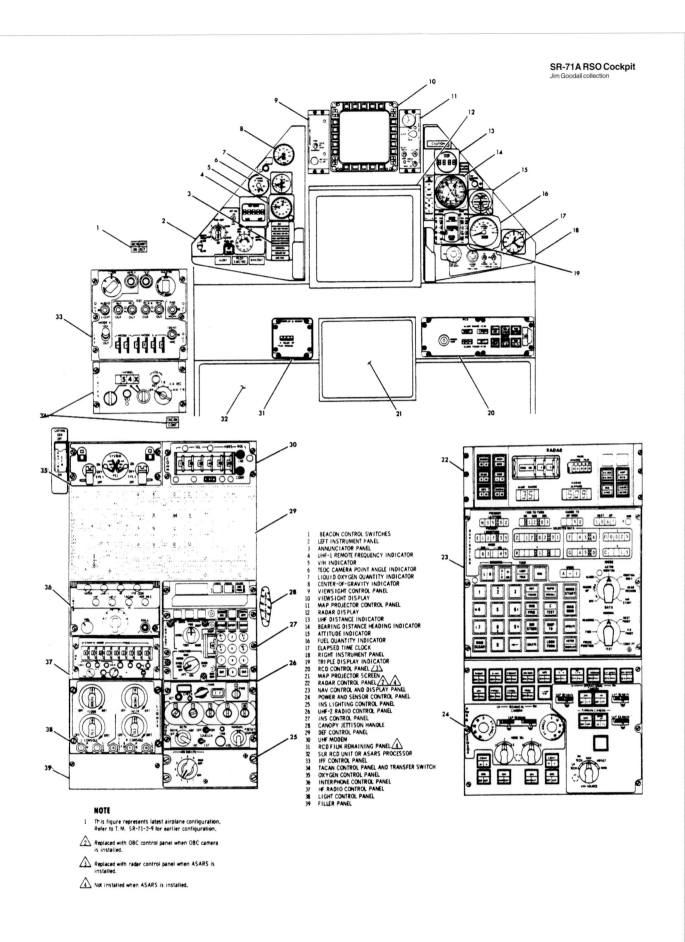

1   BEACON CONTROL SWITCHES
2   LEFT INSTRUMENT PANEL
3   ANNUNCIATOR PANEL
4   UHF-1 REMOTE FREQUENCY INDICATOR
5   V/H INDICATOR
6   TEOC CAMERA POINT ANGLE INDICATOR
7   LIQUID OXYGEN QUANTITY INDICATOR
8   CENTER-OF-GRAVITY INDICATOR
9   VIEWSIGHT CONTROL PANEL
10 VIEWSIGHT DISPLAY
11 MAP PROJECTOR CONTROL PANEL
12 RADAR DISPLAY
13 UHF DISTANCE INDICATOR
14 BEARING DISTANCE HEADING INDICATOR
15 ATTITUDE INDICATOR
16 FUEL QUANTITY INDICATOR
17 ELAPSED TIME CLOCK
18 RIGHT INSTRUMENT PANEL
19 TRIPLE DISPLAY INDICATOR
20 RCD CONTROL PANEL /3\
21 MAP PROJECTOR SCREEN
22 RADAR CONTROL PANEL /2\ /4\
23 NAV CONTROL AND DISPLAY PANEL
24 POWER AND SENSOR CONTROL PANEL
25 INS LIGHTING CONTROL PANEL
26 UHF-2 RADIO CONTROL PANEL
27 INS CONTROL PANEL
28 CANOPY JETTISON HANDLE
29 DEF CONTROL PANEL
30 UHF MODEM
31 RCD FILM REMAINING PANEL /4\
32 SLR RCD UNIT OR ASARS PROCESSOR
33 IFF CONTROL PANEL
34 TACAN CONTROL PANEL AND TRANSFER SWITCH
35 OXYGEN CONTROL PANEL
36 INTERPHONE CONTROL PANEL
37 HF RADIO CONTROL PANEL
38 LIGHT CONTROL PANEL
39 FILLER PANEL

NOTE

1   This figure represents latest airplane configuration.
    Refer to T.M. SR-71-2-9 for earlier configuration.

/2\ Replaced with OBC control panel when OBC camera
     is installed.

/3\ Replaced with radar control panel when ASARS is
     installed.

/4\ Not installed when ASARS is installed.

SR-71A Dimensions
Jim Goodall collection

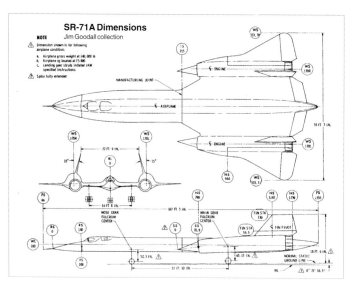

SR-71A High-Temperature Composites
Jim Goodall collection

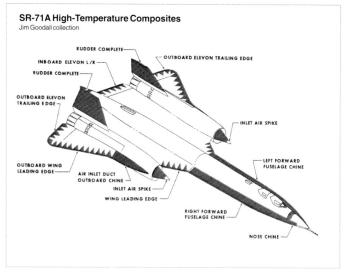

SR-71A Interior Details
Miller Collection

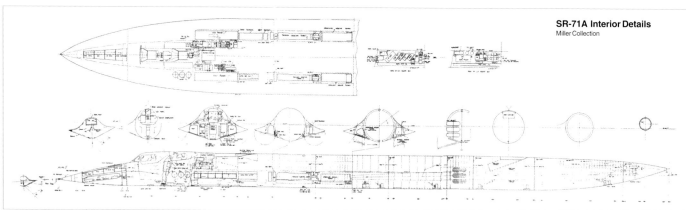

SR-71B/C Component Details
Jim Goodall collection

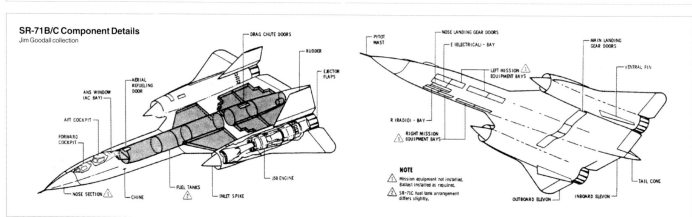

SR-71B/C Static Pitot Sensor
Jim Goodall collection

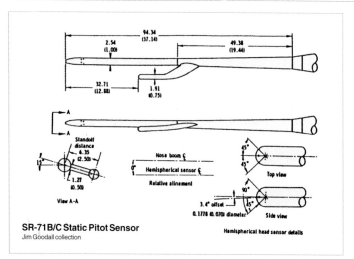

SR-71 Payload Capability
Lockheed Martin

Payload Capability

Internal Payloads: Internal payloads are carried in detachable nose and equipment bays in forebody of airplane.

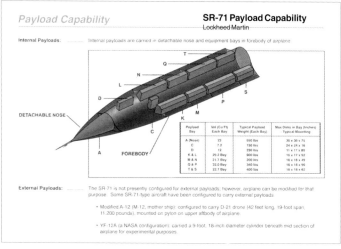

Payload Bay	Vol (Cu Ft) Each Bay	Typical Payload Weight (Each Bay)	Max Dims in Bay (Inches) Typical Mounting
A (Nose)	23	550 lbs	30 x 36 x 76
C	7.2	150 lbs	24 x 24 x 16
D	12	230 lbs	11 x 17 x 80
K & L	29.2 Bay	900 lbs	16 x 17 x 92
M & N	21.7 Bay	200 lbs	18 x 18 x 49
Q & P	32.0 Bay	340 lbs	18 x 18 x 90
T & S	22.7 Bay	400 lbs	18 x 18 x 62

External Payloads: The SR-71 is not presently configured for external payloads; however, airplane can be modified for that purpose. Some SR-71-type aircraft have been configured to carry external payloads.

• Modified A-12 (M-12, mother ship): configured to carry D-21 drone (42 feet long, 19-foot span, 11,200 pounds), mounted on pylon on upper aftbody of airplane.

• YF-12A (a NASA configuration): carried a 9-foot, 18-inch diameter cylinder beneath mid section of airplane for experimental purposes.

SR-71 Sensor Bays
Jim Goodall collection

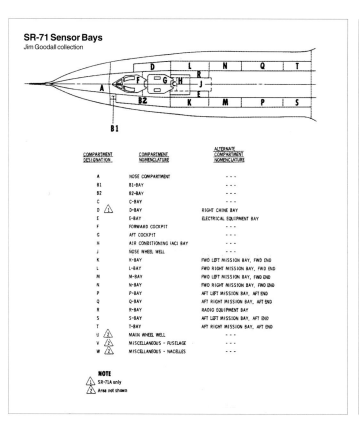

COMPARTMENT DESIGNATION	COMPARTMENT NOMENCLATURE	ALTERNATE COMPARTMENT NOMENCLATURE
A	NOSE COMPARTMENT	- - -
B1	B1-BAY	- - -
B2	B2-BAY	- - -
C	C-BAY	- - -
D ⚠	D-BAY	RIGHT CHINE BAY
E	E-BAY	ELECTRICAL EQUIPMENT BAY
F	FORWARD COCKPIT	- - -
G	AFT COCKPIT	- - -
H	AIR CONDITIONING (AC) BAY	- - -
J	NOSE WHEEL WELL	- - -
K	K-BAY	FWD LEFT MISSION BAY, FWD END
L	L-BAY	FWD RIGHT MISSION BAY, FWD END
M	M-BAY	FWD LEFT MISSION BAY, FWD END
N	N-BAY	FWD RIGHT MISSION BAY, FWD END
P	P-BAY	AFT LEFT MISSION BAY, AFT END
Q	Q-BAY	AFT RIGHT MISSION BAY, AFT END
R	R-BAY	RADIO EQUIPMENT BAY
S	S-BAY	AFT LEFT MISSION BAY, AFT END
T	T-BAY	AFT RIGHT MISSION BAY, AFT END
U ⚠2	MAIN WHEEL WELL	- - -
V ⚠2	MISCELLANEOUS - FUSELAGE	- - -
W ⚠2	MISCELLANEOUS - NACELLES	- - -

NOTE
⚠ SR-71A only
⚠2 Area not shown

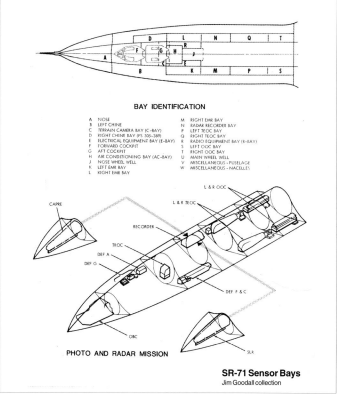

BAY IDENTIFICATION

A	NOSE	M	RIGHT EMR BAY
B	LEFT CHINE	N	RADAR RECORDER BAY
C	TERRAIN CAMERA BAY (C-BAY)	P	LEFT TEOC BAY
D	RIGHT CHINE BAY (FS 305-389)	Q	RIGHT TEOC BAY
E	ELECTRICAL EQUIPMENT BAY (E-BAY)	R	RADIO EQUIPMENT BAY (R-BAY)
F	FORWARD COCKPIT	S	LEFT OOC BAY
G	AFT COCKPIT	T	RIGHT OOC BAY
H	AIR CONDITIONING BAY (AC-BAY)	U	MAIN WHEEL WELL
J	NOSE WHEEL WELL	V	MISCELLANEOUS - FUSELAGE
K	LEFT EMR BAY	W	MISCELLANEOUS - NACELLES
L	RIGHT EMR BAY		

PHOTO AND RADAR MISSION

SR-71 Sensor Bays
Jim Goodall collection

SR-71A Dissemination of Sensor Data
Lockheed Martin

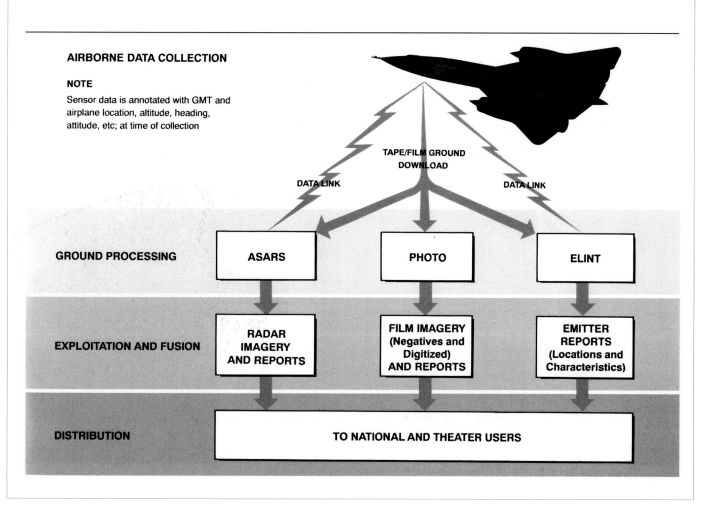

AIRBORNE DATA COLLECTION

NOTE
Sensor data is annotated with GMT and airplane location, altitude, heading, attitude, etc; at time of collection

TAPE/FILM GROUND DOWNLOAD

DATA LINK   DATA LINK

GROUND PROCESSING — ASARS · PHOTO · ELINT

EXPLOITATION AND FUSION — RADAR IMAGERY AND REPORTS · FILM IMAGERY (Negatives and Digitized) AND REPORTS · EMITTER REPORTS (Locations and Characteristics)

DISTRIBUTION — TO NATIONAL AND THEATER USERS

SR-71A Sensor Data Collection (Terrain Coverage at 80,000 Feet)
Lockheed Martin

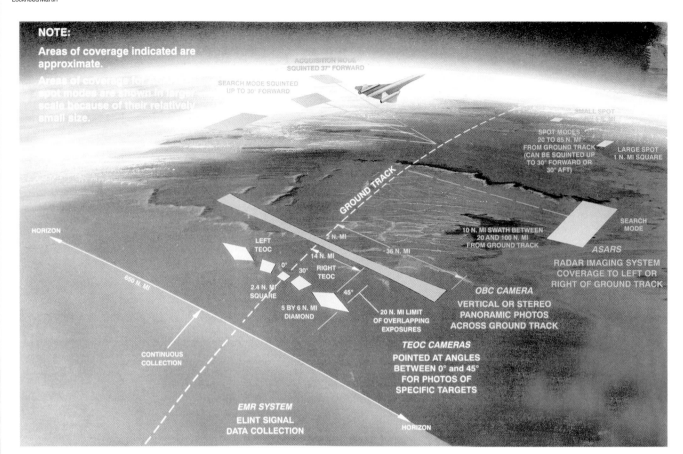

SR-71A Optical Bar Camera Nose
Jim Goodall collection

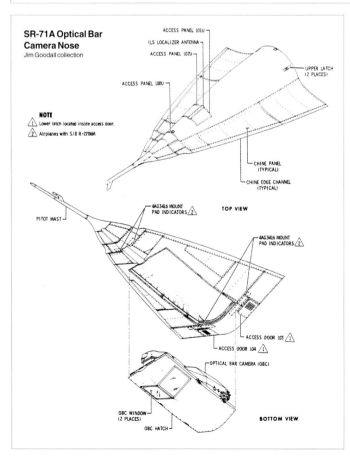

SR-71A Advanced Synthetic Aperture Radar Nose
Jim Goodall collection

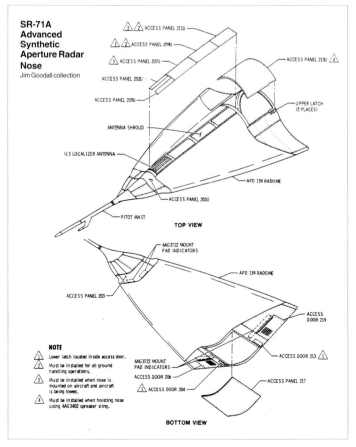

SR-71A CAPRE Nose (Capability, Reconnaissance [Radar System])
Jim Goodall collection

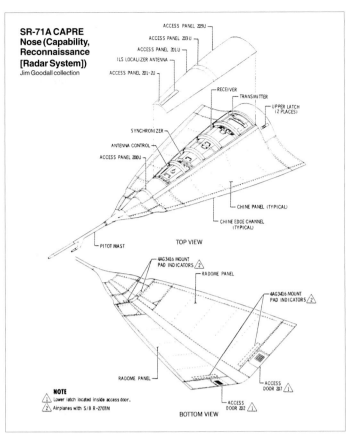

ACCESS PANEL 205U
ACCESS PANEL 203U
ACCESS PANEL 201U
ILS LOCALIZER ANTENNA
ACCESS PANEL 201-2U
RECEIVER
TRANSMITTER
UPPER LATCH (2 PLACES)
SYNCHRONIZER
ANTENNA CONTROL
ACCESS PANEL 200U
CHINE PANEL (TYPICAL)
CHINE EDGE CHANNEL (TYPICAL)
PITOT MAST

TOP VIEW

4AG3416 MOUNT PAD INDICATORS ⟨2⟩
RADOME PANEL
4AG3416 MOUNT PAD INDICATORS ⟨2⟩
RADOME PANEL
ACCESS DOOR 207 ⟨1⟩
ACCESS DOOR 202 ⟨1⟩

NOTE
⟨1⟩ Lower latch located inside access door.
⟨2⟩ Airplanes with S/B R-2707M

BOTTOM VIEW

SR-71A Optical Bar Camera Nose
Jim Goodall collection

The OBC is a high-resolution panoramic camera. In operation the camera takes photographs while scanning from left to right across the airplane ground track. Camera operation is automatic. Camera turn-on/turn-off and operating mode are controlled manually by the Reconnaissance Systems Officer.

Camera Location	....	Camera is installed in a specially-configured detachable nose.
Operating Modes	....	Three selectable modes provide vertical exposures, with two different along-track exposure-overlap coverages, and stereo photography. Camera can be operated in turns.

Terrain Coverage in Straight and Level Flight at 80,000 Feet:

Each Photograph	....	2 nautical miles along ground track by 36 nautical miles to each side of ground track. (Distance to one side increases in banks or turns.)
Along-Track Terrain Coverage	....	Determined by film supply and operating mode. Approximately 2,952 nautical miles with 10,500-foot supply of film, at 10% exposure overlap; 1,476 nautical miles at 55% overlap and in stereo.

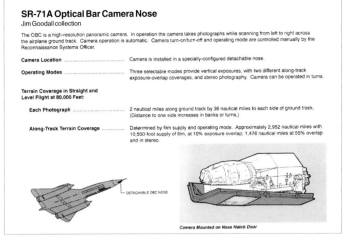

DETACHABLE OBC NOSE

Camera Mounted on Nose Hatch Door

***Big Tail* on 61-7959**
US Air Force

Optical Bar Camera
Jim Goodall collection

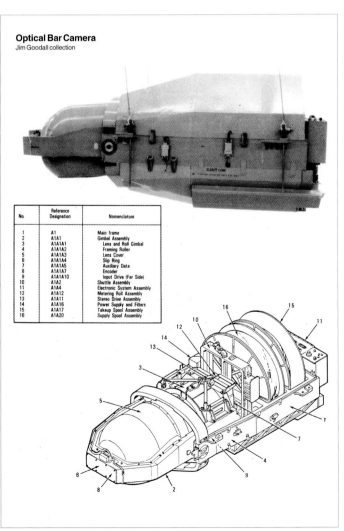

No.	Reference Designation	Nomenclature
1	A1	Main frame
2	A1A1	Gimbal Assembly
3	A1A1A1	Lens and Roll Gimbal
4	A1A1A2	Framing Roller
5	A1A1A3	Lens Cover
6	A1A1A4	Slip Ring
7	A1A1A5	Auxiliary Data
8	A1A1A7	Encoder
9	A1A1A10	Input Drive (Far Side)
10	A1A2	Shuttle Assembly
11	A1A4	Electronic System Assembly
12	A1A12	Metering Roll Assembly
13	A1A11	Stereo Drive Assembly
14	A1A16	Power Supply and Filters
15	A1A17	Takeup Spool Assembly
16	A1A20	Supply Spool Assembly

Optical Bar Camera
Jim Goodall collection

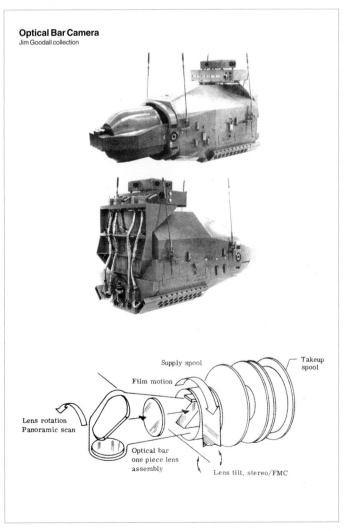

Supply spool
Takeup spool
Film motion
Lens rotation Panoramic scan
Optical bar one piece lens assembly
Lens tilt, stereo/FMC

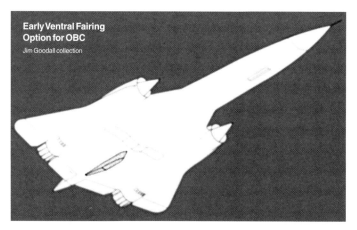

Early Ventral Fairing Option for OBC
Jim Goodall collection

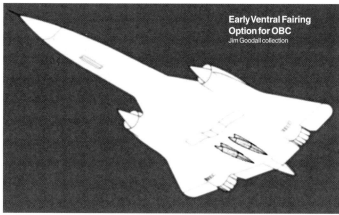

Early Ventral Fairing Option for OBC
Jim Goodall collection

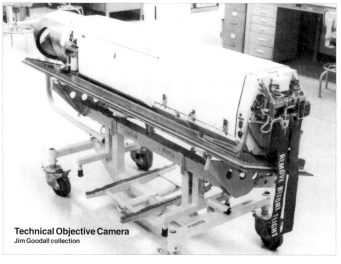

Technical Objective Camera
Jim Goodall collection

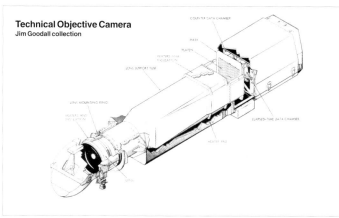

Technical Objective Camera
Jim Goodall collection

Technical Objective Camera System Schematic
Jim Goodall collection

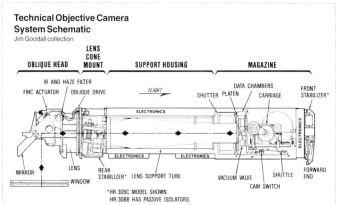

*HR-308C MODEL SHOWN
HR-308B HAS PASSIVE ISOLATORS

Technical Objective Camera
Jim Goodall collection

The TEOC is a very high-resolution, pointable camera. In operation the camera takes photographs of specific target areas at angles that vary from 0° (along airplane vertical) to 45° to the side. Camera operation is automatic. Camera turn-on/turn-off, operating mode and pointing angle are controlled automatically by the ANS navigation system or manually by the Reconnaissance Systems Officer. Left and right equipment-bay-configured cameras provide coverage to the left and to the right of the airplane ground track.

Camera Location	Left, right or both cameras can be installed in equipment bays as required for a specific mission.
Operating Modes	Three selectable aiming modes provide different exposure-overlap coverages in along-track and cross-track directions. Camera can be operated in turns.
Terrain Coverage in Straight and Level Flight at 80,000 Feet:	
Each Photograph	At 0° pointing angle, a 2.4 nautical-mile square area, centered on ground track. At 45° pointing angle, a 5 by 6 nautical-mile diamond-shaped area, centered 14 nautical miles to side of ground track. Distance and area of coverage to the side can be increased in banks or turns.
Along-Track Terrain Coverage	Determined by film supply and pointing angle. Approximately 1,428 nautical miles with 1,500-foot supply of film and 0° pointing angle.

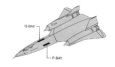

Camera Mounted on Bay Door Left Camera Shown, Right Similar

Electromagnetic Reconnaissance System
Jim Goodall collection

The EMR is a computerized broad-band electronic intelligence (ELINT) signal collection system. During system operation it continuously scans a broad portion of radar spectrum to the left and right of the airplane flight path. Characteristics of all received radar signals are digitized. Also, characteristics of special preprogrammed signals, when received, are reproduced in analog form as well as digitized. EMR digital and analog ELINT data are supplied to the data link system. That system has the capability to downlink ELINT data when flight path permits, as well as record that data in the DCRsi recorder, a functional part of the data link system (see Data Link System). The EMR system is manually placed in operation by the Reconnaissance System Officer. The computer-controlled system operates automatically in straight and level flight and in turns.

Component Location	The system includes left and right multi-antenna, signal-collection and analysis units, installed in the equipment bays.
Emitter Coverage	Signal acquisition extends to the horizon, depending on received signal strength. Signal collection and processing permit the accurate determination of emitter locations. The airplane's presence may bring up emitters that could otherwise remain silent.
Along-Track Terrain Coverage	Limited by capacity of DCRsi recorder. (See Data Link System.)

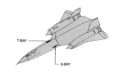

Left EMR (S-Bay) Shown, Right EMR (T-Bay) Similar

Data Link System
Jim Goodall collection

The data link system accepts digital inputs from ASARS-1 and digital and analog ELINT inputs from the EMR. ASARS and/or ELINT data is recorded and, when flight path permits, downlinked in near-real-time, recorded for later playback and downlink or recorded for later playback and ground download.

Components	The system includes a down-looking antenna and various electronic components for ground station uplink connection and data transmission. A digital cassette recorder system (DCRsi), consisting of an electronics unit and a tape transport unit, provides for recording and playback of ASARS and ELINT data. The antenna is located below the C-bay, data link system electronic components are located in the C-bay and DCRsi components are located in the L-bay.
Operating Modes	Three modes: record and near-real-time downlink data to ground station, record data then downlink at later time, record data only.
Recording-Time Capacity	DCRsi records only when data is being received. Capacity for recording ASARS and/or ELINT data is approximately 1 hour total; about 2,000 nautical miles along-track coverage.

NOTE

* Data-link system electronic components are not shown.

DCRsi Electronics and Tape Transport Units (On L-Bay Door)   *Antenna (In Radome Below C-Bay)*

Advanced Synthetic Aperture Radar System
Lockheed Martin

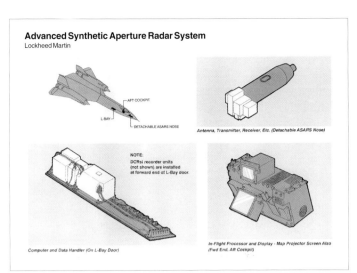

AFT COCKPIT

L-BAY

DETACHABLE ASARS NOSE

Antenna, Transmitter, Receiver, Etc. (Detachable ASARS Nose)

NOTE:
DCRsi recorder units
(not shown) are installed
at forward end of L-Bay door.

Computer and Data Handler (On L-Bay Door)

In-Flight Processor and Display - Map Projector Screen Also
(Fwd End, Aft Cockpit)

Cart Starter (Mechanical)
Jim Goodall collection

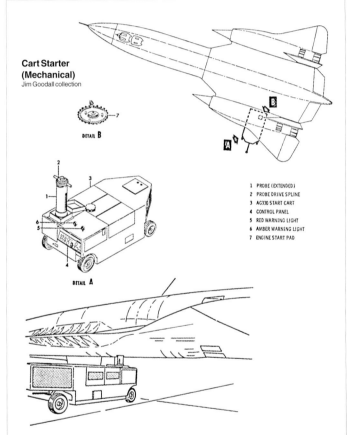

DETAIL B

DETAIL A

1 PROBE (EXTENDED)
2 PROBE DRIVE SPLINE
3 AG330 START CART
4 CONTROL PANEL
5 RED WARNING LIGHT
6 AMBER WARNING LIGHT
7 ENGINE START PAD

Chemical Gas Starter
Miller Collection

Astro-Navigation System.
Tony Landis

DO NOT SET ON BOTTOM SURFACE

Cart Starter (Pressurized Air)
Tony Landis

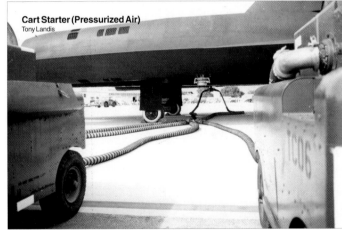

Mach Three Plus Club Card
Jim Goodall collection

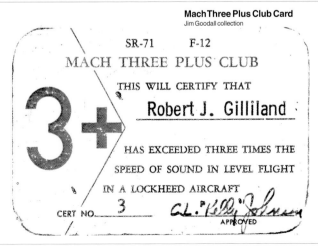

SR-71   F-12

MACH THREE PLUS CLUB

THIS WILL CERTIFY THAT

Robert J. Gilliland

HAS EXCEEDED THREE TIMES THE

SPEED OF SOUND IN LEVEL FLIGHT

IN A LOCKHEED AIRCRAFT

CERT NO. 3   C.L. "Kelly" Johnson
                     APPROVED

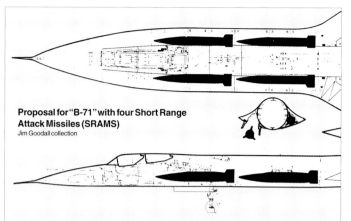

Proposal for "B-71" with four Short Range Attack Missiles (SRAMS)
Jim Goodall collection

Proposal Calling for Carriage of a Hypersonic Testbed to Launch Speed/Altitude
Miller Collection

Installation of LASRE on NASA SR-71A, 844
Tony Landis collection

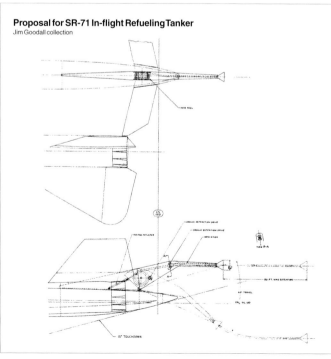

Proposal for SR-71 In-flight Refueling Tanker
Jim Goodall collection

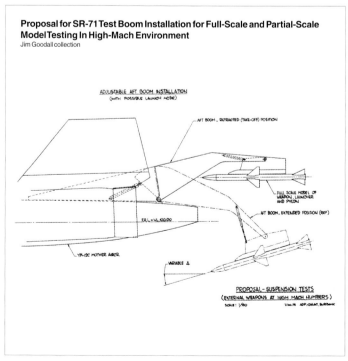

Proposal for SR-71 Test Boom Installation for Full-Scale and Partial-Scale Model Testing In High-Mach Environment
Jim Goodall collection

Chapter Six

Pratt & Whitney JT11D/J58
Bleed Bypass Turbojet Engine

Above: **The Pratt & Whitney FX-114 was the prototype engine that led to the development of the JT11D/J58 series engines.** Pratt & Whitney via Jim Goodall collection

Pratt & Whitney's historically and technologically significant JT11D/J58 series engines can trace their origins back to the company's highly successful J57 and J75 and the little-known JT9 (FX-114) and later J58-P2/P4 prototype engines designed for the North American B-70 and several Navy aircraft programs, respectively. Additionally, the company's work on boron-fueled powerplants and the earlier Project *Suntan* Model 304 hydrogen-fueled engine also had influential developmental roles.

P&W's first attempt to build a 3.0 Mach engine was the JT9 (which, in prototype form, was referred to as the FX-114). A single-spool 8-to-1 pressure ratio turbojet with a total mass flow of approximately 400 lb. per second, it was designed to accommodate the requirements specified for the North American XB-70.

When General Electric won the XB-70 competition with their J93, P&W took their basic JT9 design, reduced it in size by 20%, and offered it as a powerplant under the J58 designator for the Vought F8U-3 which, during the 1957/1958 time period, was entering a major Navy competition with McDonnell's F4H-1. Rated at 26,000 lb. thrust, this first-generation J58 was a relatively conventional turbojet with a large afterburner. By the advent of the A-12 program during 1959, P&W had completed approximately 700 hours of static bench testing on this engine.

Concurrent to development of the first-generation J58 had been work on a separate high-energy engine using boron-based fuels.

This design took advantage of the higher density heating value of boron and thus the associated improvements in range performance.

Boron's adverse impact on the environment and an ongoing and seemingly unsolvable problem with the formation of solids in the engine fuel system led to the program's early termination.

Project *Suntan* and its hydrogen-fueled engine noted earlier in this book also contributed to J58 development. Though terminated in 1958, the Model 304 and its predecessor studies provided rationale for a hydrocarbon-fueled 3.0 Mach cruise aircraft. It also left the legacy of a relevant materials and engineering data base that held the engineering staff in good stead during the J58's early development period.

The P&W propulsion team working on the J58 had a staff of approximately twenty-five engineers during the initial stages of the project. Working with P&W's chief engineer, William H. Brown, the key personnel consisted of Don Pascal, Norm Cotter, Dick Coar, Ed Esmeier, and William Gordon. Gordon, who at the time was in-charge of P&W's West Palm Beach test facility, enjoyed an excellent professional relationship with the *Skunk Works*.

P&W's engineering team worked like their counterparts at Lockheed, using minimal documentation and shunning written contracts. By interfacing directly with the *Skunk Works* they were able to reduce both paper output and security requirements to a minimum. The relationship thus fostered between Lockheed and Pratt & Whitney eventually would last for almost fifty years.

During initial design of what would become the JT11D/J58 series engines, it was ascertained that a straight turbojet operating at what then were considered to be normal turbine temperatures (as exemplified by the J57 and

J75) would not provide enough thrust to meet the A-12's mission requirements. Additionally, problems with the predicted cruise speed thermal environment became evident when the original J58-P2 was tested.

Because of the shortcomings of the first-generation J58s, the engine was completely redesigned. Only the basic airflow rates and the compressor and turbine aerodynamics were retained. At a later date, even those would go through a major redesign.

Among the innovations developed by P&W in response to the high Mach environment in which the JT11D/J58 was expected to function routinely were:

(1) The external/internal compression inlet used for high inlet recovery at high speed required engine airflow control and inlet/engine airflow matching. This led to the development of a method to discharge inlet bleed air and surplus inlet air while minimizing drag.

(2) High inlet temperatures led to high turbine temperature requirements and an air-cooled turbine.

(3) High temperatures required a fuel capable of no-coking operation at over 600° F.

(4) Engine lubricants were developed that would not break down at temperatures approaching 1,000° F.

(5) Weldable sheet metal made from turbine blade materials was used.

(6) An engine ignition system that would operate without electrical power was created.

(7) A variable camber inlet vane was developed.

(8) Fuel was used as hydraulic fluid.

(9) Variable-geometry spray bars were developed.

(10) Blow-in-doors to increase transonic thrust were developed.

(11) An exhaust nozzle offering variable area capability was developed.

(12) Fuel was used as a heat sink.

(13) Dual temperature sensors were developed.

(14) Bypass bleed ducts to vary the engine cycle were developed.

(15) A variable throat area was created to control airflow.

(16) An ejector that was part of the airframe structure was developed; it provided thrust augmentation and low drag exhaust of surplus inlet air.

Engine design requirements included a continuous cruise speed of 3.0 Mach-plus; a corrected airflow turndown ratio (cruise/maximum; turndown ratio describes the reduction in mass flow speed) of 60%; an altitude capability of 80,000 ft.-plus; a compressor inlet temperature of -40° F. to 800° F.; a combustor exit temperature of 2,000° F. (continuous); a maximum fuel inlet temperature of 350° F.; a maximum lubricant inlet temperature of 550° F.; a thrust-to-weight ratio of 5.2; and the ability to operate continuously in either military or afterburner throttle settings.

Material selection was of course critical. Eventually, after considerable trial and error, utilization of the data resulting from the J57 and J75 experience permitted the following material choices to be made:

Titanium – It was desired to use a titanium alloy for the front stages of the compressor. Titanium is considerably lighter than steel and stronger than aluminum, but possesses limited temperature capabilities. An existing tita-

nium alloy was modified to give good creep properties at temperatures up to 850° F. Ti-8-1-1 was used for the first stage blades. The welded inlet case was made from Ti-5-2.5.

Materials possessing the necessary fatigue and tensile properties were sometimes found to be brittle and susceptible to other failure modes. Galling of titanium first compressor blade roots resulted in the installation of a thin shoe or shim covering the contact area of the blade with the disk. The shim was plated with nickel which tended to distribute the load on the blade root and reduce stress concentrations.

Waspaloy was the material chosen for most components. Waspaloy was a nickel-base alloy that retained strength and oxidation resistance characteristics to temperatures up to 1,400° F. It was, however, very tedious to weld and heat treat.

At the time that materials were chosen for the JT11D-20 engine, Waspaloy was available only as a forging. The Hamilton Watch Company manufactured the first experimental Waspaloy sheets for P&W. They were approximately 12 in. by 48 in. but were too small to make most parts on a JT11D-20 engine.

Because of their high strength at high temperatures, very thin Waspaloy sheets could be used in some applications. The thinness aggravated the inherent fabrication problems, however. Forming of the .012 in. thick corrugated skin for the inner burner case required development of special explosive forming techniques.

Inconel 718 was a nickel-base alloy widely accepted for weldments and castings in static applications up to 1,250° F. Among the

nickel-base alloys, Inconel 718 was one of the easier materials to weld and was therefore selected as the material for the diffuser case when fabrication of this intricate weldment from Waspaloy proved too difficult.

Hastelloy X was a non-hardenable nickel-base alloy that was suitable for low stress applications requiring high oxidation resistance up to 2,000° F. It readily lent itself to most standard manufacturing processes and to plasma-sprayed thermal barrier coatings. It was, therefore, a logical choice for burner components.

Astroloy was a nickel-base, precipitation hardenable alloy possessing creep and tensile properties superior to Waspaloy at temperatures up to 1,500° F. It was available as a forging and was particularly suitable for turbine disk applications. This was a very expensive material specified for only the most rigorous applications.

Powder Metallurgy AF2-1DA was used to produce high-temperature compressor tie bolts from near-net-shape isothermal forgings. This material provided improved creep strength over Astroloy.

Top: **The first true J58s were the prototype P2 and P4 series engines. The latter, shown here, was optimized for use in the aborted Vought F8U-3 Super Crusader.** Pratt & Whitney via Jim Goodall collection

Below: **J58/JT11D-20 cutaway.** Pratt & Whitney via Jim Goodall collection

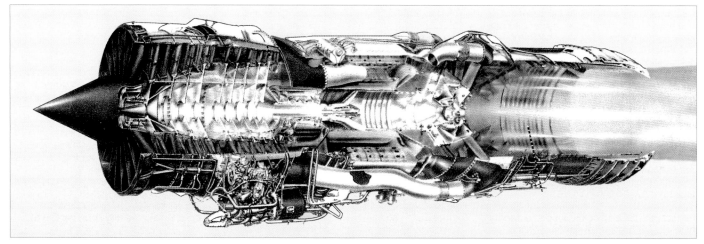

Mar-M-20ODS was a new material that was developed for first-stage turbine vanes. It was a nickel-base super alloy with columnar material grains. A new casting process caused the material crystals to be directionally solidified so that the grains grew span-wise. The complete absence of chord-wise grain boundaries minimized the possibility of leading and trailing-edge thermal shock cracks characteristic of other nickel alloy castings.

IN-100 was a cast nickel-base alloy used for first and second-stage turbine blades, second-stage turbine vanes and JT11D-20 afterburner nozzle flaps. Process control was established to consistently produce fine grain castings for engine-ready turbine blades.

L-605 (*Haynes 25*) was a cobalt-base alloy which was available in sheets and possessed good weldability and formability. It was specified for applications similar to *Hastelloy X* but was reserved for parts requiring greater resistance to buckling and sliding wear. L-605 was replaced in most applications by later-generation alloys such as *Haynes 188* and *Haynes 230*, which had improved oxidation resistance without sacrificing other properties.

Silver-impregnated carbon bushings were used in lubrication pumps when all conventional bushing materials and lubricating schemes failed to produce durable pumps.

These high-temperature materials were expensive. In engines designed for subsonic or supersonic *dash* operations, titanium was considered to be a relatively expensive material. Titanium eventually was replaced both in the rotor and static structure by even more expensive high-temperature alloys. An example of the increased material costs could be found in the first-stage *Astroloy* turbine disk forgings, which originally cost $8,300 (in 1962 dollars) compared to $250 for AMS 5616 disk forgings used in other engines. These high-temperature alloys were not only more expensive as raw material, but also required more time to machine and fabricate.

A number of ways to increase the JT11D/J58 engine's thrust at cruise speed were explored during the course of the engine's development. Included were studies using pre-compressor section cooling, building a larger compressor-engine combination, and rotation of the stator vanes mechanically to improve air angles in both the front and rear stages. However, after these studies were completed it was concluded a bypass system permitting the afterburner to be used as a ramjet was the best option. This configuration, later referred to as a turbo-ramjet by some, was large and heavy as a result of the requirement that it have the capacity to pass about equal corrected volume either through the turbojet or around it. Furthermore, the combustion efficiency was low when compared to that of a turbojet. The solution was to duct part of the inlet air around the gas generator with most of the air going through the engine core. This conserved frontal area and heated the air for more efficient combustion.

At the beginning of the development cycle, it was determined that a variable-geometry exhaust ejector would be utilized as an integral part of the airframe. It was decided jointly that Lockheed would be responsible for the design and integration as part of the airframe in an

Top: **A J58/SR-71B nacelle installation. The engine was easily accessed by lifting the integral outer wing panel/engine nacelle cowling.** Pratt & Whitney via Jim Goodall collection

Right: **J58/JT11D-20 inlet bleed and bypass system detail.** Pratt & Whitney via Jim Goodall collection

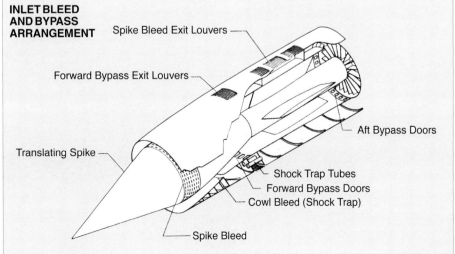

INLET BLEED AND BYPASS ARRANGEMENT

Spike Bleed Exit Louvers

Forward Bypass Exit Louvers

Translating Spike

Aft Bypass Doors

Shock Trap Tubes

Forward Bypass Doors

Cowl Bleed (Shock Trap)

Spike Bleed

effort to keep the dimensions within acceptable limits. Pratt & Whitney would be accountable for the design of the nozzle, post-combustion chamber section, gears, bearings and welding.

The J58 went through numerous design modifications through the end of 1960. These included major changes to the design of the bypass ducts, increasing the number of compressor stages from eight to nine, augmentation of the rather low compression rate, and adoption of an afterburner intended for continuous operation throughout a typical mission.

The original J58-P4 design for the A-12 had few common parts with the initial J58-P2 studied for the Navy. Only the overall dimensions, the aerodynamics of the compressor blades and the turbine unit were retained. At a later date even these items were changed.

The bleed bypass cycle that became unique to the J58 permitted the engine to be a conventional afterburning turbojet during take-off and transonic flight, a low-bypass-ratio augmented turbofan during supersonic acceleration, and a ramjet during high-speed supersonic cruise. During subsonic loiter, it also became a low-bypass-ratio turbofan.

The bleed bypass cycle ducted air from the compressor middle stages into the afterburner, thus bypassing the flow restriction that existed in the rear compressor stages during supersonic flight or during subsonic flight at low power. This improved turbine blade airfoil incidence and thus engine efficiency. Bleed air entered the afterburner at the same static pressure as the main flow and was heated in the afterburner during supersonic flight. The bleed air thus produced almost as much thrust per lb. of air as the main flow which passed through the rear compressor, burner, and turbine. When compared to a standard turbojet engine operating at the installed thrust level required for cruise flight, the bypass bleed engine had a 20% advantage in fuel consumption over the turbojet.

High energy was required to ignite a fuel-air mixture at the low pressures experienced at high altitude. Because of the extreme difficulty in implementing a high-temperature, high-energy electrical system, the engine ignition system used the pyrophoric (ignition took place on contact with ambient air) fluid triethyl borane (TEB) that had been explored during the days of P&W's borane-fueled engine studies. This required the development of a chemical ignition system (CIS) that would meter TEB into the burner for both ground and air starting of both the main engine and the afterburner. As a result, a multiple delivery system, inert in itself, but capable of operating throughout the flight envelope, was developed. A catalytic ignition system was provided in the afterburner as a TEB system back-up.

Plumbing was another critical engine design issue. The high-temperature environment precluded the use of rubber hoses. The plumbing thus was all made from high-temperature nickel base alloys and was routed and clipped to allow for thermal expansions and contractions.

Design of the JT11D/J58 turbine and its blade and vane cooling were accommodated in an extensive engine development test program. More than 14,000 hours of test operation at turbine inlet temperatures at or above 1,900° F. were accumulated. Of these, more than 7,300 hours were at temperatures at or above 2,000° F. Over 200 compressor blade, compressor diffuser, burner can and transition duct configurations were tested before a required stable temperature inlet pattern was established.

Design of the afterburner was equally critical. For subsonic operation all the air entering the afterburner came from the turbine section discharge. When the bleed bypass was opened above 2.10 Mach, this bleed air entered in an annulus surrounding the turbine discharge. Part of this bleed air mixed with the turbine discharge air and was burned in the

Top: **The J58, being an even-numbered engine, originally was intended for Navy use. Odd-numbers usually were reserved for US Air Force aircraft.** Jim Goodall

Left: **J58/JT11D-20 afterburner assembly and exhaust nozzle.** Jim Goodall

afterburner. Part of the cool bleed air then passed behind the cooling liner and provided improved cooling at the high supersonic flight speed where the ambient temperature surrounding the afterburner was highest. There were four annular spray rings, manifolded together to a common fuel supply and four annular flame holders in the afterburner.

Virtually everything about the J58 was beyond what Pratt & Whitney had experienced in past engine designs. Maximum fuel temps rose from 110/130° F. to 350° F. Engine lubricant temps increased from 250° F. on the J75 to over 550° F. on the J58, and engine inlet temperatures exceeded 800° F. under certain conditions. The fuel inlet temperature was normally below 300° F., but increased to 350° during temperature transients. The fuel temperature at the main and afterburning fuel nozzles ranged from 600° to 700° F. The lubricant temperatures rose from 700° F. to a high of over 1,000° F. in some localized parts.

The magnitude of the problem can best be understood when such things as continuous afterburning operation, normally measured in minutes was, with the advent of the J58, suddenly being measured in hours. This capability resulted in inlet temperatures that were greater than the melt temperatures of the materials in similar inlets in other engines..

Performance increments of the bleed bypass cycle compared to the same engine without the bleed bypass operating at the same rotor speed at a supersonic cruise of 3.0 Mach-plus gave the J58 22% more airflow and a 19% increase in net thrust.

Another key set of assumptions was that the inlet and nacelle be sized for the bleed bypass cycle and that surplus air be discharged through the forward bypass duct which in turn discharged it through the exhaust ejector.

The bleed bypass opened at approximately 1.90 to 2.00 Mach and was a function of the compressor inlet temperature (CIT). The bleed bypass would open anytime the CIT exceeded 275° F. At the aircraft's design speed of 3.24 Mach, the bleed bypass system passed a maximum of 12% of the airflow around the engine and into the exhaust ejector.

The operation of the bleed bypass doors was through the engine hydraulics. The working fluid for the engine hydraulic system was JP-7 fuel.

Afterburner cooling was accomplished by taking the relatively cool bleed bypass air routed from the fourth compressor stage and ducting it ahead of the afterburner liner when the bleed bypass duct was opened. This airflow was 20% of the total moving through the engine.

Engine rpm was maintained by modulating the exhaust nozzle. This arrangement provided nearly constant airflow at a given Mach number...from below military power to maximum afterburner. This was very desirable when operating behind a supersonic mixed compression inlet.

Fuel consumption at cruising Mach number was approximately 8,000 gallons per hour. During the continuous operation of the afterburner, the fuel flow was 2.4 times that of subsonic fuel flow. This penalty was offset by the increased thrust and velocity, so in fact, at 3.0 Mach-plus the range was greater than the subsonic range. In addition to providing the best fuel consumption for this engine cycle, afterburning also provided the additional thrust to climb and operate at altitudes above 80,000 ft.

The fuel type was JP-7. Also designated PWA 523B, it had an extremely low vapor pressure and a very high flash point. JP-7 was a triple-distilled kerosene with a liquid Teflon additive needed to lubricate the engine hydraulics, pumps and engine accessories. Weight was 6.6 lb. per gallon. Freezing point was -50° F.

Ignition required the use of TEB (see page 94). TEB delivery to the J58 comprised a gaseous nitrogen unit that powered a piston and delivered a specific amount of TEB to the main engine burner or afterburner, regardless of engine operating conditions.

One of the problems that plagued Pratt & Whitney throughout early CIS development was the plugging of the probe where the TEB was injected into the burners. The solution ultimately selected was to continuously "drip" fuel into the TEB plumbing line near the CIS, which assured purging of the plumbing and probe. This, however, was not without certain risks. If the fuel drip were too little, the fuel would evaporate and cake up; if it were too much, it would cause a "hot" streak in the burner. An acceptable level to prevent all problems eventually was found through extended testing.

The J58 in continuous afterburner, either on the test stand or during flight, expanded some six inches in length and just over two and a half inches in diameter as a result of heat. This growth led to the requirement that a very specific schedule be maintained during descent to permit the engine's internal parts to cool at the same rate as the external casing.

The problem of ground starting the J58 initially was solved by using two Buick *Wildcat* high-performance engines in a specially designed ground cart. Each engine pair combined for a total of some 700 hp and was manually connected to the J58 via a hydraulically-actuated shaft prior to engine start.

The shaft was inserted vertically through the bottom of each engine nacelle and connected to the J58's accessory drive unit. The automobile engines were then started and their power was transmitted through the shaft to spool the J58 to the proper rpm. Once the latter was reached, TEB was injected and the ignition process got under way.

Two different versions of the piston-engined starter cart eventually were developed: one was equipped with Buick 401 cubic inch *Wildcat* engines of 350 hp each, and one had Chevy 454 cubic inch LS-6 engines of 450 hp each. During the early years of the pro-

Below: **A standard JT11D-20/J58 on its transport trailer. Noteworthy are distinctive bypass tubes.**
Pratt & Whitney via Jim Goodall collection

gram, the Buick-based carts were used. These later were replaced by the Chevrolet carts.

The engines were accessible through hinged hoods on both sides of the cart. The exhaust for the engines was routed through individual, unmuffled exhaust pipes. The two side-by side engines were connected via a 12 in.-wide Gilmer belt.

There were other methods considered for starting as well. Two were devised for the ill-fated F-12B program. The Air Force had required the F-12B to be suitable for alert status and thus to be launched in the shortest possible time. A one-shot chemical starter was developed by Lockheed to meet this requirement (see page 89). Consisting of a removable twin turbo unit mechanically attached under each nacelle it was basically a chemically powered steam turbine that transferred power through a shaft, which was much like the carted gasoline engine system.

A third starter system was considered but never built. This would have been a unit similar to the gas-engined power carts but powered by a small APU-type turbine.

Eventually, the V-8-powered start carts were phased out at Beale AFB, California, and Kadena AB, Okinawa, when a permanent high-pressure starting system was installed in each hangar. This consisted of a compressed air unit of considerable size that powered a detachable starter under each nacelle. Interestingly, portable compressed air carts were still servicing SR-71s at remote operating locations late in the aircraft's operational life. When NASA took over SR-71 flight operations at Edwards AFB, these second-generation starter carts were once again brought back into service.

The early YJ-58's thrust ratings were limited to 20,000 pounds of thrust in military power to 31,500 pounds of thrust in after-burner at sea level. The later, upgraded, Model "K" engines were rated at 32,500 pounds of thrust.

The SR-71's inlet consisted of a translating 26° cone which acted as the initial deceleration or compression surface producing a series of shock waves up to the inlet throat. The purpose of the inlet was to supply the air required by the engine at the highest recovery and the lowest drag, with a minimum of distoraton.

The inlet spike regulated the amount of air entering the inlet by moving progressively rearwards as the aircraft's speed increased. Up through 1.40 Mach, the spike remained at the fully-forward position. Above 1.40 Mach, the spike began its transition back to the fully-aft position. This was also the configuration of the inlet at 3.0 Mach and above.

Inlet control was accomplished by an automatic spike-and-bypass-door system, which influenced the individual engine spike inlet shock position. The spike was locked at full forward up to an altitude of 30,000 feet. Boundary layer air was trapped within each nacelle and was bled off into the ejectors, which were part of the airframe structure. Each engine exhausted through an afterburner and variable-area nozzle supplied with the engine. Ejector flaps were designed specifically to operate in conjunction with the nozzle position and were mounted on the aft end of each nacelle.

The inlet spike function was in effect an air throttle that provided adequate area ratio to match the flow requirements of the J58. The bypass doors positioned the shock while also controlling the position of the oblique shock and the contraction ratio.

There were a number of items that controlled the spike position including: principally the local Mach number, and as a bias, the aircraft's altitude. Within the inlet was a sensor that would sense when the shock was inadvertently expelled. This "shock expulsion" sensor detected a decreased pressure ratio and would automatically move the intake spike to its full forward position. At the same time, the inlet bypass doors also would go into the full open position. As soon as the shock had been swallowed by the duct, the spike and inlet bypass doors would begin to schedule normally.

Expulsion of the shock was known as an "un-start". Early in the flight-test program, un-starts were deemed very serious and considered potentially life threatening. As experience with un-starts was gained, it was realized that the event – though significant – was not catastrophic and that it was in fact, reversible in flight.

The purpose of the inlet duct bypass doors was to position the shock wave by increasing or decreasing the pressure aft. In addition, the bleed bypass doors helped maintain correct flow through the inlet. Excess bleed bypass air was dumped overboard through the forward nacelle louvers.

Inside the inlet, positioned about eight feet into the inlet, were a series of canoe-shaped devices informally referred to as "mice". Their purpose was to decrease the initial subsonic diffusion rate to minimize the flow separation at high subsonic duct Mach numbers. This eliminated duct rumble and/or turbulence.

To the rear of the inlet was a device commonly referred to as the "onion slicer". Its purpose was to provide additional inlet bypass area for low engine and wind-milling rotor speeds. The secondary use was to provide additional secondary ejector flow if this proved to be advantageous. It also provided initial bypass area to dump air internally rather than externally which resulted in less drag at low supersonic speeds.

The SR-71 engine air inlet was a mixed external and internal compression axisymmetric inlet with gradual isentropic compression approaching the throat.

At 2.20 Mach, the inlet produced some 13% of the overall engine thrust. The engine and ejector accounted for 73% and 14% respectively. At 3.0 Mach, the corresponding figures were: inlet – 64%; engine 17%; and ejector 29%. Thus, at cruising speed, most of the thrust actually came form the inlet.

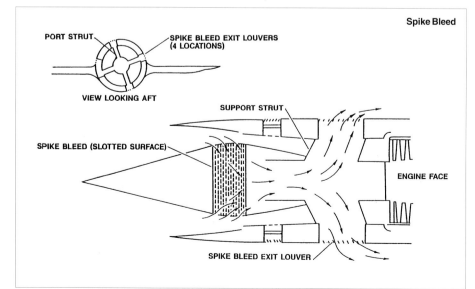

Top: **Heated inlet test facility at Pratt & Whitney's West Palm Beach, Florida location was equipped with a J75 to provide a realistic temperature environment.** Pratt & Whitney via Jim Good all collection

Left: **J58 intake bypass illustration.** Pratt & Whitney via Jim Goodall collection

The inlet utilized the DAFICS computers for control of spike and bypass doors. Spike movement was controlled by Mach number, angle of attack, angle of yaw, and load factor.

Terminal shock position was controlled and regulated for forward and aft bypass doors which matched the inlet air-swallowing capability of the engine requirement.

The compression ratio at cruise speed was 40 to 1. The inlets were canted inboard some 3° out of respect for the impact of the chines on overall aircraft aerodynamics.

From the lip of the inlet, translating back twenty feet to the face of the J58's first-stage compressor, the air temperature rise, due to compression and friction, was an amazing 900° F. (from an ambient air temperature of -70° F. to just over 800° F.).

The exhaust ejector was an integral part of the airframe and was designed by Lockheed. The engine nozzle moved to hold the scheduled rpm with the latter being biased by the CIT. Each exhaust nozzle was actuated via engine hydraulics and received its position setting from the main fuel control.

The ejector flaps formed an optimum divergent section aft of the engine and were at fully closed at approximately 1.70 Mach, opening completely at approximately 2.40 Mach. The position also was influenced by the power setting and equivalent airspeed.

The ejector flaps were free floating and their position was a function of the delta between the local and ejector area pressure.

The ejector performed the reverse function of the inlet. It accelerated the air coming out of the turbine at 0.40 Mach up to 3.0 Mach. Because exit velocity must match flight speed, the variable exit flaps stayed fully closed until about 1.20 Mach. By 2.40 Mach, they were fully open.

Located just forward of the ejector flaps were a series of free-floating tertiary doors that opened or closed with the varying internal nozzle pressure. The latter was a function of Mach and engine power settings. At approximately 1.10 Mach, the tertiary doors were in the fully closed position.

The main ejector was supported downstream on streamlined struts and a ring of *Rene 41* steel alloy on which were hinged free-floating trailing-edge flaps of *Hastelloy X*.

Hydraulics:

The SR-71 had four independent, closed-center hydraulic power systems which operated at a nominal 3,000 psi and were powered by take-offs from the J58 engines. A and B systems for flight control, and L and R system for the utility subsystems and air inlet control. Primary flight controls were operated by conventional stick and rudder inputs from the cockpit by an electronic stability augmentation system. The flight controls were powered through electro-hydraulic servo valves. Independent hydraulic systems A and B each supplied pressure fluid to six flight control dual

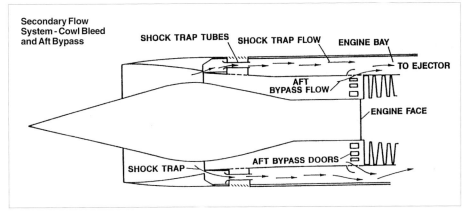

servo valves; the left and right rudder, and the inboard and outboard elevon systems. The L hydraulic system powered the left engine air-inlet and air-bypass controls and these additional circuits – normal brakes, landing gear, nose wheel steering, and an aerial refueling door. The R system powered the right engine air inlet and air-bypass controls and furnished emergency power to operate an alternate brake system. It also provided emergency

retraction of the landing gear if the L system became inoperative.

The flight control system, operated by the hydraulic system, was extremely simple. There were two thin, movable slab vertical stabilizers which were movable and thus served as the aircraft's rudders. There were also four elevons with two being positioned inboard and two being positioned outboard on the wing trailing edges. These acted as both elevators and

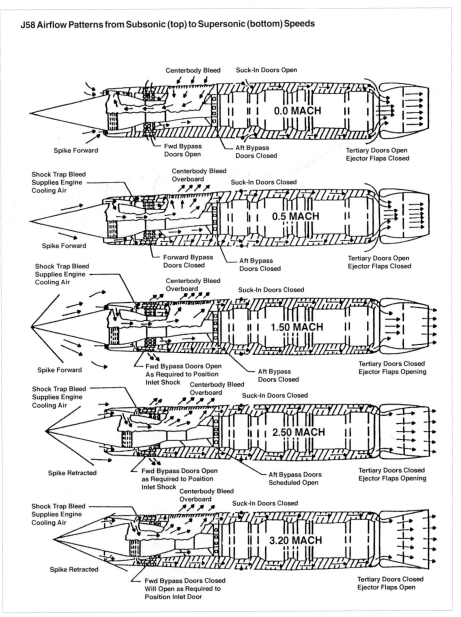

Top: **J58 intake bypass illustration showing spike position and airflow at supersonic speeds.** Pratt & Whitney via Jim Goodall collection

Right: **Series of drawings illustrating the airflow and shock wave processes through the intake and J58 engine from subsonic velocities (top) through 3.0 Mach (bottom).** Pratt & Whitney via Jim Goodall collection

ailerons. There were no leading-edge flaps or slats.

Pitch control was limited to 24° trailing edge up and 11° trailing edge down. This provided good pitch control throughout the aircraft's flight envelope and positive nosewheel lift-off during take-off at all flight loadings.

Roll control was limited to plus or minus 24° included angle below 0.5 Mach and plus or minus 14° above 0.5 Mach. This provided excellent roll control during landing and take-off and throughout the flight envelope, while avoiding problems at higher Mach numbers.

The all-moving vertical tail surfaces provided the necessary control power for an engine failure on take-off or at cruise Mach number, and excellent crosswind landing capability. Comparable to the roll control, the all-movable vertical tails were limited to 20° below 0.5 Mach and 110° above 0.5 Mach.

The irreversible control system was hydraulically powered by two independent systems. Pilot commands through the control stick or rudder pedals were transmitted to the hydraulic actuators through a dual cable system. No power boost was used between the cockpit and the hydraulic actuators. Tension regulators were utilized to eliminate cable slack over the large temperature range and to account for fuselage deformation during a normal flight. To minimize cable expansion with temperature, the cables were made of *Elgiloy*, the material patented by the Elgin watch company for use as watch springs.

The SR-71 was the first aircraft to be equipped with a digital flight control system. This occurred when its earlier analog system was replaced during the early 1980s with the DAFICS (digital automatic flight and inlet control system). The DAFICS consisted of the stability augmentation system (SAS), the autopilot, the Mach trim system, pitch control, and the inlet control system.

In addition to providing improved aircraft control, the DAFICS generated better responses to environmental changes, which allowed the engine/inlet system to operate at maximum efficiency. Aircraft control consequently was improved as well.

Miscellaneous SR-71 Propulsion, Structural, and Reference Items:

(1) Over 93% of the aircraft structure and skin surface were titanium.

(2) All air-conditioning lines were aluminum.

(3) All hydraulic lines were stainless steel.

(4) The wing had pre-formed longitudinal corrugations to ensure wing expansion in the streamwise direction.

(5) The outboard portion of the wing's leading edge had conical camber to move the load inboard and aft.

(6) The aircraft was essentially a flying fuel tank carrying over 80,000 lb. of fuel. Fuel was carried principally in five fuselage tanks and the wing tanks. The wing tanks were used in climb; that was due to the high ratio of surface to volume for thermodynamic reasons. Fuel sequencing was automatic and provided c.g. control.

(7) The fuselage increased in length by 2 in. during cruise.

(8) The leading edges of the outer wing panels were cambered down approximately 3° and the ailerons were set 3° up for neutral position. This configuration better accounted for upwash around the nacelle and provided a more optimum span-wise loading distribution across the entire wing.

(9) Over the course of the J58 production run, spanning 15-plus years, Pratt & Whitney produced a total of 175 of the J58 turbo-ramjet engines.

(10) The prototype J-58, referred to as the "XD" engine, carried serial numbers 1 thru 11. The next advance in the J58 family tree was the "FX" model and Pratt & Whitney produced eleven complete engines carrying serial numbers, 110 through 120. The very first operational J58s were the "YJs", with their distinctive 24-karat gold-plated hydraulic lines. These engines powered the first A-12s and YF-12s. The serial number sequence for the "YJ" series engines ran from 201 thru 254. The final model that powered the launch M/D-21, all of the operational A-12s, later flights of the YF-12A, and from the very first flight, the SR-71, was the Model "K". The Model "K" J58 was produced in the largest numbers (99) with serial numbers running from 301 thru 399.

(11) Prior to the availability of the J58, the early A-12s, and for its entire operational life, the "Titanium Goose" (the one-off training version of the A-12, 60-6927, Article 124), flew with the Pratt & Whitney model J75-P19WSS conventional turbojet engine, which in turn was a modified U-2C/D J75-P13.

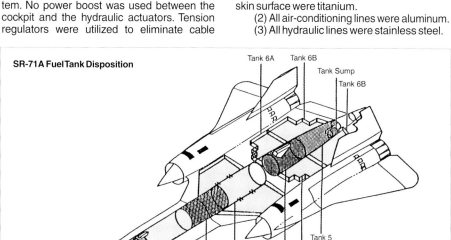

SR-71A Fuel Tank Disposition

Tank 6A
Tank 6B
Tank Sump
Tank 6B
Tank 5
Tank 6A
Tank 4
Tank 3
Tank 2
Tank 1
Tank 1A

Top: **SR-71A fuel tank positions are concentrated in the fuselage and the inboard wing panels.**
Jim Goodall collection

Left bottom: **SR-71A engine nacelle with intake spike extended forward in the subsonic flight position.**
Jay Miller

Aircraft Histories, Chronologies, Dispositions, Personnel, etc.

Aircraft Specifications, Performance, and Individual Histories:

A-12:
Specifications and Performance:
Construction: Titanium (Beta-120/Ti-13V-11Cr-3A1) monocoque with some super-high-temperature plastics
Length: 102 feet 3 inches
Wingspan: 55 feet 7 inches
Wing Area: 1,795 square feet
Height: 18 feet 6 inches
Landing Weight: 52,000 pounds
Maximum Gross Take-off Weight: 117,000 pounds
Maximum Speed: 3.20 Mach above 75,000 feet
Operational Ceiling: above 90,000 feet
Maximum Unrefueled Range: 3,400 nautical miles
Armament: none
Powerplant Data: 2 Pratt & Whitney J75 with 17,000 pounds thrust on first 5 aircraft during flight testing; updated to: (in production) 2 P&W J58 (JT11D-20A) high-bypass-ratio turbojets with 20,500 pounds thrust (dry) and 31,500 pounds thrust (afterburner); later Model "K" engines generated 34,500 pounds thrust in afterburner.

Individual Aircraft Histories:
A-12 60-6924/Article 121 – ff April 26, 1962; pilot was Lou Schalk; 322 flts totaling 418:12 hrs. This aircraft was a dedicated flight-test article and spent its entire career at Groom Lake/Area 51. First flight with J58 in left nacelle, J-75 in right nacelle was October 5, 1962. First flight powered by two J58s was January 15, 1963. First sustained 3.0 Mach flight took place on February 3, 1963, piloted by Jim Eastham. Currently displayed at Blackbird Air Park, Palmdale, CA.

A-12 60-6925/Article 122 – ff June 26, 1962 (arrived at Groom Lake/Area 51); pilot was Lou Schalk; 161 flts totaling 177:52 hrs. Used for RCS testing. Spent the first five months on a pole at Groom Lake/Area 51 before being removed on November 2, 1962. First flight took place in late December 1962 powered by two J75s. Modified to SR-71 standards in late 1966. Currently displayed aboard the carrier USS *Intrepid*, Manhattan, New York.

A-12 60-6926/Article 123 – ff October ?, 1962; pilot was Lou Schalk; 79 flts totaling 135:20 hrs. CIA pilot, Ken Collins lost Article 123 due to problems with the static pitot system near Wendover, Utah; pilot survived. At the time of the accident it was stated that an F-105D had crashed with a nuclear weapon onboard.

A-12B 60-6927/Article 124 – ff January 22, 1963; pilot was Lou Schalk; 614 flts totaling 1076:25 hrs. The only trainer A-12, Article 124 was nicknamed the "Titanium Goose". This

was the only "Blackbird" "Kelly" Johnson ever flew in. As of this writing, the A-12B remains in storage at the Lockheed Martin *Skunk Works*, Plant 10, AF Plant 42, Palmdale, CA.

A-12 60-6928/Article 125 – ff January ?, 1963; pilot was Bill Park; 105 flts totaling 169:15 hrs. Lost on take-off at Groom Lake/Area 51 on December 28, 1965, as a result of improper SAS wiring. CIA pilot Mele Vojvodich ejected and survived.

A-12 60-6929/Article 126 – ff March ?, 1963?; pilot was Bill Park; 268 flts totaling 409:55 hrs. Lost near Calleinte, Nevada. Accident was blamed on a faulty fuel gage and loss of power. CIA pilot Walt Ray was at speed and altitude when the A-12 ran out of fuel. Ray ejected from the aircraft but failed to separate from his ejection seat and was killed.

A-12 60-6930/Article 127 – ff March ?, 1963?; pilot is unknown; 258 flts totaling 499:10 hrs. One of only three operational *Black Shield* A-12s. *Operation Skylark* (Cuban overflights) prepped February 26, 1965. Currently displayed at the Space & Rocket Museum, Huntsville, AL.

A-12 60-6931/Article 128 – ff June ?, 1963?; pilot is unknown; 232 flts totaling 453:00 hrs. First CIA A-12 to go sustained 3.0 Mach on March 25, 1965. Involved in *Operation Scotch Mist* wet weather testing at McCoy AFB, Florida during November of 1965. *Operation Skylark* (Cuban overflights) prepped February 26, 1965. Currently displayed at the Minnesota Air Guard Museum, St. Paul, MN.

A-12 60-6932/Article 129 – ff September ?, 1963? Pilot was Bob Gilliland; 268 flts totaling 409:55 hrs. Lost in South China Sea off Philippine Islands while conducting a functional check flight. CIA pilot Jack Weeks and the A-12 disappeared. No trace was ever found of pilot or aircraft. One of only three operational *Black Shield* A-12s deployed. First (*Silver Javelin*) sustained 3.0 Mach flight on January 27, 1965 (1:15 hrs at or above 3.10 Mach). Dedicated flight-test aircraft for envelope expansion before being turned over to the CIA.

A-12 60-6933/Article 130 – ff December ? 1963?; pilot was Lou Schalk; 217 flts totaling 406:20 hrs. Currently mounted on a three-point pylon at the entrance to the San Diego Aerospace Museum, San Diego, CA.

A-12 60-6937/Article 131 – ff February 19, 1964; pilot was Jim Eastham; 177 flts totaling 342:45 hrs. Loaned for short-term flight test and was used to test a variety of ECM developments and airborne side-looking radar. First A-12 deployed to Kadena AB, Okinawa under *Operation Black Shield*. Flew the first of twenty-nine A-12 missions over North Vietnam on May 31, 1967; the pilot was Mele Vojvodich. Agency pilot, Frank Murray, flew three passes over North Korea in support of *AGER-2*, USS *Pueblo*. This aircraft flew the last *Black Shield* mission on May 8, 1968; the pilot was Jack Layton. One of only three operational *Black*

Shield A-12s deployed. Became last A-12 to fly on June 21, 1968; the pilot was Frank Murray. The flight served to deliver the aircraft from Groom Lake/Area 51, Nevada, to Palmdale, California. Currently displayed at the Southern Museum of Flight, Birmingham, AL.

A-12 60-6938/Article 132 – ff March 4, 1964; the pilot was Bill Park; 197 flts for a total of 369:55 hrs. *Operation Skylark* (Cuban over-flights) prepped on February 26, 1965. Currently displayed in Mobile, AL.

A-12 60-6939/Article 133 – ff March 18, 1964; the pilot was Bill Park; 10 flts totaling 8:19 hrs. Bill Park piloted this aircraft to 96,250 ft. During the ascent, the engines over-temp'd and the hydraulic system failed when an attempt was made to lower the landing gear at 2.40 Mach. The hydraulic system failed completely during approach to landing at Groom Lake/Area 51. Park successfully ejected from the aircraft at an altitude of some 250 ft.

M-21 60-6940/Article 134 – ff December 22, 1964; pilot was Bill Park; 80 flts totaling 123:55 hrs. Pathfinder aircraft for *Tagboard*. Never launched a D-21 and flew photo chase on the last flight of M-21 60-6941/Article 135. Currently displayed at the Museum of Flight, Seattle, WA.

M-21 60-6941/Article 135 – ff May ?, 1965; pilot was Bill Park; 95 flts totaling 152:46 hrs. On July 30, 1966, this aircraft was lost 200 miles west of Pt. Mugu, California, while launching a D-21 drone. It appeared to suffer an asymmetrical un-start, forcing the drone back into the M-21. This caused the aircraft to break up at the 715 joint at a speed of 3.3 Mach at 81,000 feet. Lockheed test pilot Bill Park and launch control officer, Ray Torrick ejected safely. Torrick suffered a broken arm as he ejected and was unable to access his one-man life raft once he landing in the Pacific Ocean. His suit filled with water and he drowned. Bill Park was rescued without incident. This crash led to a decision to terminate the M-21/D-21 program.

A-12 Production:
   13 (60-6924 to '33, 60-6937 to '39)
M-21 Production:
   2 (60-6940 thru 60-6941)

A-12 Experience Record:

First Flight	April 26, 1962
Total flights	2,670
Total fight hours	4,438:00
Total flights at 3.0 Mach	900
Total fight hours at 3.0 Mach	571:06
Longest flight at 3.0 Mach	3:50 hours
Longest 3.2 Mach flight on a single flight	3:30 hours
Longest single flight duration	7:40 hours
Max. speed	3.29 Mach
Max. altitude	92,500 ft.

J-58 Engines:

Total engine flights	9,412
Total engine hours	19,738
Total flights at 3.0 Mach	4,294
Total engine flight hours at 3.0 Mach	2,690
Total Mach 3.0 ground test hours	6,497
Total 150 hours Qualification tests	6

INS:

Total flights	1,616
Total operating hours	3,715
Total operating time	45,739 hours

SAS – Auto Pilot:

Total flights	2,669
Total flight hours	4,437
Total operating hours	42,850

Cameras:

	Type I	Type IV
Total fights	262	67
Total flight operating hours	194	37
Total flights above 3.0 Mach	159	47
Total hours at 3.0 Mach	94	32

Operational Pilots (6):

Average pilot experience	15 years
Average total flight time (all aircraft)	4,110 hours
Time (hours) in the A-12 (least/avg/most)	144/413/483
Time in project	1.72 years
Average A-12 flights	257

Life Support:

Total suit flights (1129th SAS)	1,751

EWS:

Total flight tests	110

Detachment:

Activated	October 1, 1960
Time in training as a unit	60 months*
Average time in project (personnel)	46/50 months

*Detachment 1, 1129th SAS began training as a unit coincident with the delivery of the first trainer A-12B, 61-6927, during January of 1963. Prior to that it had been supporting the LAC flight-test effort.

Oxcart A-12 Aircraft Inventory:

Operational aircraft	6
Two-seat trainer aircraft	1
Flight-test aircraft	1

A-12 Missions:

1129th Special Activity Squadron - Det 1
Kadena Air Base, Okinawa

Date	Mission No.
May 31, 1967	BSX001
June 10, 1967	BSX003
July 13, 1967	BX6708
July 19, 1967	BX6709
July 20, 1967	BX6710
August 21, 1967	BX6716
August 31, 1967	BX6718
September 16, 1967	BX6722
September 17, 1967	BX6723
October 4, 1967	BX6725
October 6, 1967	BX6727
October 15, 1967	BX6728
October 18, 1967	BX6729
October 28, 1967	BX6732
October 29, 1967	BX6733
October 30, 1967	BX6734
December 8, 1967	BX6737
December 10, 1967	BX6738
December 15, 1967	BX6739
December 16, 1967	BX6740
January 4, 1968	BX6842
January 5, 1968	BX6843-North Korea – USS *Pueblo*
January 26, 1968	BX6847
February 16, 1968	BX6851
February 19, 1968	BX6853
March 8, 1968	BX6856
May 6, 1968	BX6858 – Last A-12 mission flown out of Kadena AB, Okinawa

A-12 Chronology:

12/24/57 – First J58 engine run.
03/21/58 – First mention of *Archangel* in "Kelly" Johnson's diary.
12/??/58 – CIA requests funding for a 3.0 Mach reconnaissance aircraft.
08/29/59 – Lockheed and Convair each propose a plan for a 3.0 Mach reconnaissance aircraft.
09/14/59 – CIA awards first *Archangel* research contract to Lockheed.
01/26/60 – CIA orders twelve A-12 aircraft.
02/??/60 – Lockheed begins the search for 24 pilots for the A-12.
05/01/60 – Francis Gary Powers is shot down in a U-2 over the Soviet Union.
02/26/62 – First A-12 leaves *Skunk Works* in Burbank, CA, for Groom Lake by truck.
04/26/62 – First flight of the prototype A-12, 924/121, with Lockheed test pilot Lou Schalk.
04/30/62 – First "official" flight of A-12, 924/121, with Lockheed test pilot Lou Schalk.
05/02/62 – A-12 goes supersonic for first time during second test flight.
07/30/62 – J58 completes pre-flight testing.
10/05/62 – A-12 flies with J75 (in left nacelle) and J58 (in right nacelle) engines.
01/15/63 – A-12 first flight with two J58 engines.
05/24/63 – First A-12 crashes (#06926) near Wendover, UT.
07/20/63 – First A-12 flight over 3.0 Mach.
11/??/63 – A-12 reaches design speed and altitude.
02/03/64 – A-12 cruises at 3.20 Mach and 83,000 feet for 10 minutes.
06/??/64 – Final A-12 (#06939) delivered to Groom Lake/Area 51.
01/27/65 – A-12 flown for 1 hour and 40 minutes above 3.1 Mach for a distance of 3,000 miles.
12/28/66 – Decision is made to conclude A-12 operations by June 1, 1968.
05/22/67 – First A-12 (#06937) flown to Kadena AB by CIA pilot Mele Vojvodich.
05/29/67 – *Black Shield* unit declared operational at Kadena AB.
05/31/67 – First A-12, 06937/131, operational mission over North Vietnam lasted 3 hours, 39 minutes.
11/03/67 – A-12 and SR-71 conduct a reconnaissance fly-off. Results were questionable.
01/23/68 – First A-12 overflight of North Korea during *Pueblo* incident with CIA pilot Frank Murray.
05/08/68 – Last A-12 operational mission flown.
06/05/68 – Last A-12 (#06932) to crash, lost in the South China Sea.
06/21/68 – Last A-12 flight from Area 51 to Palmdale, CA piloted by Frank Murray

YF-12A:

Specifications and Performance:

Construction: Titanium (Beta-120/Ti-13V-11Cr-3A1) monocoque with some super-high-temperature plastics
Length: 101 feet 8 inches
Wingspan: 55 feet 7 inches
Wing Area: 1,795 square feet
Height: 18 feet 6 inches
Landing Weight: 68,000 pounds
Maximum Gross Take-off Weight: 124,000 pounds
Maximum Speed: 3.20 Mach above 75,000 feet
Operational Ceiling: above 90,000 feet
Maximum Unrefueled Range: 3,000 nautical miles
Armament: 3 x Hughes GAR-9/AIM-47A air-to-air radar-guided missiles (4.0 Mach)
Powerplant Data: 2 x P&W J58 (JT11D-20A) high-bypass-ratio turbojets with 20,500 pounds thrust (dry), 31,500 pounds thrust with afterburner.

Individual Aircraft Histories:

YF-12A 60-6934/Article 1001 – ff August 7, 1963; pilot was Jim Eastham; lost on August 14, 1966 (some sources say July 14, 1966), at Edwards AFB, CA. Seriously damaged during landing. The rear half of this aircraft was mated to the front half of the SR-71 static test article to create the SR-71C, 64-17981.

YF-12A 60-6935/Article 1002 – ff November 23, 1963; pilot was Lou Schalk; total number of flights is unknown, though the aircraft logged 524.7 hrs; assigned to NASA where it made its first flight in civilian guise on December 11, 1969. This aircraft is the sole surviving YF-12A. Stored from 1967 to December of 1969. On December 11, 1969, this aircraft was loaned to the NASA as a test aircraft where it eventually logged a total of 145 flights. On November 7, 1979, this aircraft was flown to the US Air Force Museum at Wright-Patterson AFB, Ohio, for permanent display. Flight crew during the delivery flight to Wright-Patterson AFB was Col. Jim Sullivan and Col. Richard Uppstrom.

YF-12A 60-6936/Article 1003 – ff March 13, 1964; pilot was Bob Gilliland; total number of flights is unknown, but the aircraft logged a total of 439.8 hrs; first flight under the auspices of the NASA was March 3, 1979; last flight under the auspices of the NASA was June 24, 1971. This aircraft was used to set several absolute (for class) speed and altitude records on May 1, 1965. The US Air Force team of pilots was led by Col. Robert L. "Silver Fox" Stephens, the first military pilot to fly the YF-12A. Non-fatal crash at Edwards AFB on June 24, 1971.

YF-12 Production:
3 (60-6934 thru 60-6936)

YF-12 Chronology
12/24/57 – First J58 engine run.
07/30/62 – J58 completes pre-flight testing.
10/??/62 – Letter of intent for $1 million for YF-12 delivered to Lockheed.
08/07/63 – First flight of YF-12 (60-6934) with Lockheed test pilot James Eastham.
02/29/64 – President Johnson announces existence of "A-11" (actually the YF-12).
04/16/64 – First XAIM-47 ejected from YF-12 in flight.
03/18/65 – First firing of YAIM-47 from YF-12A.
05/01/65 – Two YF-12A (60-6934 & 60-6936) set speed and altitude records.
09/28/65 – GAR-9 fired from YF-12A at 3.20 Mach at 75,000 feet.
01/05/68 – Skunk Works receives official notice closing down YF-12 operations.
02/05/68 – Lockheed ordered to destroy A-12, YF-12, and SR-71 tooling.
12/11/69 – NASA's first YF-12 (#06935) flight.
11/07/79 – Last YF-12A (#06935) flown to the Air Force Museum at Wright-Patterson AFB

D-21/B:
Specifications and Performance:
Construction: Titanium (Beta-120/Ti-13V-11Cr-3A1) monocoque with some super-high-temperature plastics
Length: 42 feet 10 inches
Wingspan: 19 feet 1/4 inch
Wing Area: ?
Height: 7 feet 1/4 inch
Empty Weight: ?
Maximum Gross Take-off Weight: 11,000 pounds
Maximum Speed: Mach 3.35 at 80,000 to 95,000 feet
Operational Ceiling: 100,000 feet
Maximum Unrefueled Range: 3,400 nm
Armament: None
Powerplant Data: Marquardt RJ43-MA20S-4 ramjet rated at 1,500 pounds thrust at cruising altitude and speed
D-21 Production: 38 (Build nos. 501 thru 538)

Individual Aircraft Histories
(c/o Tony Landis files):
D-21 #501: Modified to D-21B standard. B-52H accidental drop on 09/28/67, no mission flown.
D-21 #502: Modified to D-21B standard. Disposition is unknown but it is thought to be on display at Beale AFB, CA.
D-21 #503: Launched from M-21 (60-6941) on March 5, 1966; flew 150 n. miles. M-21 crew was Bill Park and Keith Beswick.
D-21 #504: Launched from M-21 (60-6941) on July 30, 1966. Drone collided with M-21, both aircraft destroyed. Lockheed Crew was Bill Park and Ray Torick. Torick was killed but Park survived. Ended the M-21 program.
D-21 #505: Launched from M-21 (60-6941) on June 16, 1966; flew 1,550 n. miles. Crew was Park/Beswick.
D-21 #506: Launched from M-21 (60-6941) on April 27, 1966; flew 1,120 n. miles. Crew was Park/Torick.

D-21B #507: Launched from B-52H on November 6, 1967; flew 134 n. miles.
D-21B #508: Launched from B-52H on January 19, 1968; flew 280 n. miles.
D-21B #509: Launched from B-52H on December 2, 1967; flew 1,430 n. miles.
D-21B #510: Displayed at the Seattle Museum of Flight mated to M-21, 60-6940.
D-21B #511: Launched from B-52H on April 30, 1968; flew 150 n. miles.
D-21B #512: Launched from B-52H on June 16, 1968; flew 2,850 n. miles; no camera carried.
D-21B #513: Allocated to NASA and now stored at Edwards AFB, CA.
D-21B #514: Launched from B-52H on July 1, 1968; flew 80 n. miles.
D-21B #515: Launched from B-52H on December 15, 1968; flew 2,953 n. miles; hatch with camera recovered, photos of fair quality.
D-21B #516: Launched from B-52H on August 28, 1968; flew 78 n. miles.
D-21B #517: Launched from B-52H on November 9, 1969; first operational mission, hatch and camera not recovered.
D-21B #518: Launched from B-52H on February 11, 1969; flew 161 n. miles.
D-21B #519: Launched from B-52H on May 10, 1969; flew 2,972 n. miles, hatch and camera recovered.
D-21B #520: Launched from B-52H on July 10, 1969; .flew 2,937 n. miles; hatch and camera recovered; good photos.
D-21B #521: Launched from B-52H on February 20, 1970; flew 2,969 n. miles, hatch and camera recovered; good photos.
D-21B #522: Stored at Davis-Monthan AFB, AZ, at AMARC as of October 10, 2000.
D-21B #523: Launched from B-52H on December 16, 1970; flew 2,448 n. miles on second operational mission of D-21 program; hatch and camera not recovered.
D-21B #524: Displayed at the US Air Force Museum, Wright-Patterson AFB, OH.
D-21B #525: NASA owned. On loan to Blackbird Airpark, Palmdale, CA.
D-21B #526: Launched from B-52H on March 4, 1971; flew 2,935 n. miles; third operational mission of D-21 program; hatch and camera not recovered
D-21B #527: Launched from B-52H on March 20, 1971; flew 2,935 n. miles; fourth and last operational mission of D-21 program; hatch and camera not recovered.
D-21B #528: In storage at the US Air Force Museum pending move to Univ. of Michigan.
D-21B #529: Allocated to the NASA/ stored at Edwards AFB, CA.
D-21B #530: On display at Davis-Monthan AFB, AZ.
D-21B #531: Stored at Davis-Monthan AFB, AZ, at AMARC.
D-21B #532: Stored at Davis-Monthan AFB, AZ, at AMARC.
D-21B #533: On display at the Pima Air Museum, Tucson, AZ.
D-21B #534: Stored at Davis-Monthan AFB, AZ, at AMARC.
D-21B #535: Deaccessioned and returned to Defense Resource Management Organization (DRMO).
D-21B #536: Stored at Davis-Monthan AFB, AZ, at AMARC.
D-21B #537: Allocated to the NASA and stored at Edwards AFB, CA.
D-21B #538: Displayed at the Museum of Aviation at Robbins AFB, GA.

Boeing B-52H/D-21 Launch Aircraft:
B-52H: 60-0036 is currently operational with the 419th FLTS at Edwards AFB, CA. It is nicknamed *Tagboard Flyer*.
B-52H: 61-0021 is currently operational with the 93rd Bomb Squadron, Barksdale AFB, LA. It is nicknamed *Iron Eagle*.

SR-71:
Construction: Primarily titanium (Beta-120/Ti-13V-11Cr-3A1)
Length: 107 feet 5 inches
Wingspan: 55 feet 7 inches
Wing Area: 1,795 square feet
Height: 16 feet 6 inches
Landing Weight: 68,000 pounds
Maximum Gross Take-off Weight: 140,000 pounds
Maximum Speed: 3.20 Mach above 80,000 feet; 3.30 Mach (tactical limit)
Operational Ceiling: over 85,000 feet
Maximum Unrefueled Range: 3,200 nautical miles
Armament: None
Powerplant Data: 2 x Pratt & Whitney J58 (JT11D-20B) high-bypass-ratio turbojets rated at 34,000 pounds thrust each
SR-71 Production:
SR-71A – 29 (61-7950 to 61-7955, 61-7958 to 61-7980)
SR-71B – 2 (61-7956 thru 61-7957)
SR-71C – 1 (61-7981)
21 of the 32 SR-71s still exist.

Miscellaneous Systems:
Communication – HF, VHF, and dual UHF transceivers; IFF transponder; intercom between cockpits, cockpits and ground crew, and cockpits and applicably-configured tankers.

Digital Automatic Flight and Inlet Control System (DAFICS) – Included air data system (ADS), automatic pitch warning system (APW), automatic flight control system (AFCS), and air inlet control system (AICS). ADS supplies Mach, attitude and other air data functions to cockpit instruments and other DAFICS systems. APW provides pitch-up warning or control. AFCS controls flight control surfaces (elevons and rudders), and includes three-axis stabilization, autopilot and auto-navigation using steering inputs from astro-inertial navigation system (ANS). AICS controls engine air inlet surfaces (spikes and forward bypass doors).

Drag chute – Pilot-actuated 40-ft. chute augments main gear brakes for landing.

Egress – Includes ballistically jettisonable canopies and upward-rocket-propelled Lockheed-developed ejection seats useable from zero speed, zero altitude to limits of flight envelope. Ejection seat was activated by a seat-mounted D-ring. It included a high-temperature rocket catapult that resulted in an impulse of approximately 2,000 pound-seconds and a separation velocity of 49 feet per second. The average peak acceleration of the catapult at 70° F. was on the order of 15 g's, with a rate of onset of about 170 g's per second. The seat used a ballistically deployed drogue chute that provided rapid, controlled deceleration and stability, and aided in seat-man separation. The drogue chute was stowed in the headrest and attached to the seat through a four-element bridle. The seat was designed to descend to 15,000 feet when deployment of the main chute was achieved by a drogue gun which assured dependable, predictable, non-fouling, and rapid chute deployment. Other features included a dual pyrotechnic system which provided for rapid system timing, single mode of operation, and high reliability; retractable foot stirrups with dual-fired cable cutters; high energy rotary seat-man separator (butt snapper); and a power wind inertial reel with dual strap cutter.

The SR-1 ejection seat (which included connection points for the David Clark S-1030C pressure suit vent line) was not much different from the Stanley-designed and Lockheed-built C-2, used in the very early A-12 and SR-71 series and later modified into the SR-2 seat. The SR-1 seat removed the leg guards and arm restraint nets which were used on the C-2.

The seat, with the mandatory David C. Clark S-1031C pressure suit, was the highest altitude and airspeed rated seat in the Air Force inventory. Even though the seats were rated for high speed, they were not High Dynamic Pressure seats. High dynamic pressure (high-Q) was a function of air density as well as speed. The SR-71 flew at high altitudes where the air pressure was significantly lower, reducing the dynamic pressure. The SR-71 flying at 2000 mph at near 80,000 ft. was actually experiencing wind force more equivalent to 400 knots equivalent air speed (KEAS).

Electrical – AC busses were powered by two 60 KVa generators. DC busses were powered from two, 200-amp transformer rectifiers. Either generator and either transformer rectifier could carry full AC and DC electrical loads. AC and DC busses were prioritized. A static inverter and a dual battery supplied emergency AC and DC power, when needed.

Environmental System – Powered by dual, redundant, heat-exchanger/cooling-turbine systems. The environmental control system (ECS) provided the following:
(1) Crew compartment cooling and pressurization air.
(2) Flight-essential equipment cooling air (electrical load center equipment and bay [E-bay] environment; communications equipment and bay environment [R-bay]; and astro-inertial navigation system and bay environment [A/C bay]).
(3) Mission equipment cooling air and bay environment.
(4) Canopy seal pressurization air.
(5) Windshield anti-icing air.

Flight Suit – As the SR-71 program was coming in in 1968, the Air Force was using the silver David Clark model S-901J pressure suit. In 1977, the original S-901J suits were replaced with the next-generation S-1030 series suits and by the mid-1980s, the final configuration suit, the S-1031C, was issued to the SR-71 community.

The David Clark Co. S-1031C was produced in twelve sizes. It utilized state-of-the-art fabric materials and hardware. Its four layers consisted of:
(1) An outer coverall of Dacron (a form of Terylene) which was durable, tear and fire resistant, and colored "old gold".
(2) A restraint joint layer held the suit together through restraint lines and acted as a pressure boundary.
(3) A "bladder" layer which performed a function similar to that of an inner tube in a tire and was made of polyurethane.
(4) A final inner scuff layer of lightweight Dacron protected the bladder layer from scuffing against other clothing and the urine collection device (UCD).
(5) Long cotton underwear.

Exceptional comfort and mobility were achieved through an integrated torso harness which removed weight from the pilot's back; a seat cushion that provided total buttock and thigh support; an adjustable kidney pad; and independent differential motion of dual shoulder straps.

Flight Controls – Flight control surfaces (left and right inboard and outboard elevons and all-moving rudders) were hydraulically positioned by commands from the DAFICS or by hydraulically boosted manual inputs from pilot's stick and rudder pedals.

Fuel – There were five fuselage tanks, 16 boost pumps and various manifolds. Also included was a heat sink system that used fuel to cool environmental system air, hydraulic system oil, and some engine components. Fuel tank sequencing (fuel usage from tanks) and fuel aft transfer were automatic and part of automatic c.g. control system. Pilot could manually select fuel tanks and could also control c.g. by forward or aft transfer of fuel between tanks.

Hydraulic Systems – Consisted of four independent, engine-driven, redundant systems. Two systems powered the flight control surfaces. The other two systems powered the movable inlet surfaces, landing gear, brakes, nose wheel steering, and the air refueling door.

Inlet – Engine air inlet surfaces (spikes and air bypass doors) were hydraulically positioned. Spikes and forward bypass doors were controlled by commands from DAFICS or by inputs from pilot's manual controls. Aft bypass doors were manually controlled by the pilot.

Liquid Nitrogen – Three systems (to provide aircraft with long-range capability) converted liquid nitrogen to gaseous nitrogen to inert and pressurized fuel tanks and ancillary equipment during flight.

Liquid Oxygen – Three systems (two for normal oxygen supply, one for emergency) converted liquid oxygen to gaseous oxygen for flight crew breathing.

Navigation – Included ILS (TACAN), UHF direction finding, UHF ranging (with comparably-equipped stations), inertial navigation system (INS), astro-inertial navigation system (ANS), ASARS in-flight radar display and map displays (in each cockpit). Engineering for GPS installation had been accomplished at the time of program termination.

Aircraft temperature at ambient air conditions (standard day: 0.4 psia and -70° F.) 750° F.

Cooling – Aircraft was partially cooled (approximately 52° F.) by radiation as a result of the black external paint. Fuel mass was used as a heat sink and a coolant for the environmental air and hydraulic oil. Cockpits, bays, and compartments were insulated and air-conditioned. Crew pressure suits are provided with ventilation air.

Temperature Effects:

Aircraft Structure – 93% titanium; balance consisted of high-temperature composites plus some corrosion-resistant steel and nickel alloys.

Electrical System – High-temperature wire and connectors were used in hot areas.

Fuel – JP-7; low-aromatic, high-flash-point fuel. Fuel tanks were nitrogen inerted. Tubing was insulated in hot areas.

Landing Gear and Tires – The tricycle landing gear consisted of two non-standard three-wheel mains and a conventional steerable twin-wheel nose unit. The mains retracted inward toward the fuselage centerline into gear wells that were cooled by the fuel tanks. Nitrogen gas was used for inflation to minimize oxidation of the oil.

This was the worlds first all-titanium landing gear; it used Teflon glass bearings. The main gear tires were manufactured by B. F. Goodrich and were impregnated with aluminum powder to help reflect the airframe heat generated thermodynamically at cruising speed. Inflation pressure was 425 psi. using inert nitrogen gas. The tires were 22 ply rating with 3 ply tread with nylon. The rating was 20,000 lb. load per wheel. Tire cost was approximately $2,300 for each and in operation, the tires were good for about 15 take-offs and landings.

Turn-around Time – Turn-around involved many variables, including: servicing, maintenance, possible aircraft reconfiguration, mission planning, and other factors. Historically, two aircraft each were successfully flown on daily 8-hour operational missions for three consecutive days running. The 16-hour turn-around time, adequate for that operation, could be reduced if minimal servicing was required for the next flight and maintenance and other factors were not significant.

Reconnaissance Capability – The coverage of the SR-71A's standard reconnaissance system package was day/night, all-weather, large area synoptic. The aircraft provided a stable platform that could be precisely and automatically directed along preplanned, but alterable flight paths by steering commands to the autopilot from the astro-inertial navigation systems (ANS). The pilot's instrumentation also permitted accurate manual control.

Mission systems were installed as modular kits and were tailored for specific missions. Sensor systems consisted of:
(1) An advanced synthetic aperture radar system (ASARS-I) for high-resolution radar imagery. This was a high-resolution radar imaging system. The system viewed terrain to the left or right of the aircraft's ground track, at selected ranges. The airborne system produced digital data representative of radar-imaged target areas. It also provided a real-time radar cockpit display. Ground-based processing equipment produced high-resolution radar imagery from airborne-collected digital data. The data link system had the capability to downlink ASARS data when flight paths permitted, as well as record that data in the DCRsi recorder, a functional part of the data link system (which see).

The antenna assembly/motion-sensing unit, transmitter, receiver, and related equipment were installed in a specially configured detachable nose. A computer and a data handler were installed in an equipment bay. The in-flight processsor and display unit were installed in the RSO's instrument panel.

Search, acquisition (navigation data update) and two high-resolution spotlight modes were available. The search mode was initiated and controlled automatically by the ANS navigation system or manually by the RSO. Acquisition and spotlight modes were initiated and controlled automatically only. In search and spotlight modes, the imaged area was perpendicular to the ground track, or it could be squinted forward or aft up to 30°. In the acquisition mode, the imaged area for a navigation fixpoint was 37° forward of perpendicular. The system could be operated in turns.

Terrain coverage in straight and level flight from 80,000 ft. included the following:

(a) Search mode – 10 n. mi. swath, positioned 20 to 100 n. mi. to left or right of ground track.

(b) Spotlight modes – Large spot, a square of approximately 1 n. mi. on a side; small spot, a rectangle approximately 1 n. mi. by 1/3 n. mi. Spot could be positioned from 20 to 85 n. mi. to side of ground track.

(c) Along-track terrain coverage – Limited by capacity of DCRsi recorder.

(2) An electromagnetic reconnaissance system (EMR) for gathering precise characteristics and locations of ELINT (electronic Intelligence/emitter) signals. This unit was a computerized broad-band electronic intelligence (ELINT) signal collection system. During system operation it continuously scanned a broad portion of radar spectrum to the left and right of the aircraft flight path. Characteristics of all received radar signals were digitized. Also, characteristics of special preprogrammed signals, when received, were reproduced in analog form as well as digitized. EMR digital and analog ELINT data were supplied to the data link system. That system had the capability to downlink ELINT data when flight paths permitted, as well as record that data in the DCRsi recorder, a functional part of the data link system. The EMR system was manually placed in operation by the RSO. The computer-controlled system operated automatically in straight and level flight and in turns.

The EMR was located in the equipment bays (T-bay and S-bay) and consisted of left and right multi-antenna, signal-collection and analysis units. Signal acquisition extended to the horizon, depending on the received signal strength. Signal collection and processing permitted the accurate determination of emitter locations. The aircraft's presence sometimes brought up emitters that otherwise would have remained silent. Along-track terrain coverage was limited only by the capacity of the DCRsi recorder.

(3) An optical bar camera (OBC) for high-resolution panoramic photography. In operation, this unit took photographs while scanning from left to right across the aircraft ground track. Camera operation was automatic. Camera turn-on/turn-off and operating mode were controlled manually by the RSO.

The camera was installed in a specially configured detachable nose. It had three selectable modes providing vertical exposures, with two different along-track exposure-overlap coverages, and stereo photography. The camera could be operated in turns.

Terrain coverage in straight and level flight at 80,000 ft. was:

(a) For each photograph taken, 2 n. mi. along ground track by 36 n. mi. to each side of ground track. (The side distance increased during banks or turns.)

(b) Along-track terrain coverage was determined by film supply and operating mode. Approximately 2,952 n. mi. could be photographed with 10,500 ft. of film and a 10% exposure overlap; 1,476 n. mi. could be photographed with 10,500 ft. of film and a 55% overlap (and in stereo).

(4) A technical objective camera (TEOC) for very-high-resolution photography of specific target areas or objects. In operation, this camera took photographs at angles from 0° (along aircraft vertical) to 45° to the side. Camera operation was automatic. Camera turn-on/turn-off, operating mode, and pointing angle were controlled automatically by the ANS navigation system or manually by the

RSO. Left and right equipment-bay-configured cameras provided coverage to the left and to the right of the aircraft ground track.

The TEOC could be mounted left, right, or as a pair in the Q-bay and/or P-bay as required for a specific mission. Three selectable aiming modes provided different exposure-overlap coverages in along-track and cross-track directions. The camera could be operated in turns.

Terrain coverage in straight and level flight at 80,000 ft. included:

(a) For each photograph – at 0° pointing angle, a 2.4 n. mi. sq. area, centered on ground track. At 45° pointing angle, a 5 x 6 n. mi. diamond-shaped area, centered 14 n. mi. to side of ground track. Distance and area of coverage to the side could be increased in banks and turns.

(b) Along-track terrain coverage – determined by film supply and pointing angle. Approximately 1,428 n. miles with 1,500 ft. film supply and 0° pointing angle.

Due to the modular option which involved the installation of several different nose configurations, either ASARS or an OBC could be installed depending on the mission requirements.

Defense Systems (DEF) – These were designed to provide the SR-71A with ground-to-air and air-to-air countermeasures against a broad spectrum of missile systems.

Data Link System – The data link system accepted digital inputs from the ASARS-I and digital and analog ELINT inputs from the EMR. ASARS-I and/or ELINT data was recorded and, when flight path permitted, downlined in near-real-time, recorded for later playback and downlink, or recorded for later playback and ground download.

The system included a down-looking antenna and various electronic components for ground station uplink connection and data transmission. A digital cassette recorder system (DCRsi), consisting of an electronics unit and a tape transport unit, provided for recording and playback of ASARS-I and ELINT data. The antenna was located below the C-bay with data link system electronic components located in the C-bay and DCRsi components located in the L-bay.

There were three modes of operation for the data link system: record and near-real-time downlink data to ground station; record data then downlink at a later time; and record data only.

The DCRsi recorded only when data was being received. Capacity for recording ASARS-I and/or ELINT data was approximately 1 hour total. This was the equivalent of about 2,000 n. mi. of along-track coverage.

Mission Recorder System – This served to collect and record specific flight and sensor activity data during the course of each mission, together with the functioning of aircraft and mission systems.

Forward Operating Location Requirements – Most military air bases were capable of accommodating the SR-71. For short periods it could be based at any facility that had an adequate runway. However, for longer-term operations, the following specifications were outlined for an FOL:

Runway length – 9,200 ft. or longer
Runway/taxiway strength – 400 lb. in.2 min.
Hangar size – 80 ft. wide x 120 ft. long min.
Shop facilities – approx. 20,000 ft.2
Mission equipment maintenance – as required.
Sensor data ground processing – dedicated trailers and equipment were available for most systems.

Electrical power – 1.2 GVA, 440 volt, 60 Hz, 3-phase for two aircraft, ground support equipment, and shop facilities
Engine oil – Fed. Spec. 0-T-634, Type I or 0-T-236
Fuel – JP-7 (PWA 535)
Gaseous nitrogen – MIL-P-27401C, Type I
Hydraulic oil – MIL-H-27601A
Liquid nitrogen – MIL-P-27401C, Type II
Liquid oxygen – MIL-O-27210, Type II
Tri-ethyl borane (TEB) – PWA 525
Ground support equipment – as required (see T.M. SR-71-2-1)

Paint – the aircraft's black paint, sometimes referred to as "iron ball" and optimized to help reduce the aircraft's radar return, reduced wing temperatures by about 35° F.

All tools and materials in contact with aircraft – had to be cadmium- and halogen-free to prevent titanium stress corrosion.

Individual Aircraft Histories:
SR-71A 61-7950/Article 2001 – production start was October 10, 1963; rollout took place on August 25, 1964; ff December 22, 1964; pilot was Bob Gilliland; ? flts totaling ? hrs. Last flight was on January 10, 1967, at Edwards AFB, CA. During anti-skid braking tests, the tires exploded and a fire ensued which destroyed the aircraft. Lockheed Test Pilot Art Peterson survived.

SR-71A 61-7951/Article 2002 – production start was December 6, 1963; rollout took place on October 20, 1964; ff March 5, 1965; pilot was Bob Gilliland and RSO was Jim Zwayer; last flight was December 22, 1978: ? flts totaling 796.7 hrs. Was delivered to NASA during the spring of 1971; ff at NASA was July 16, 1971; pilot was Merv Evenson and RSO was Charles McNeer; at Air Force request it was assigned a fictitious serial number, 60-6937 and the designation YF-12C. Currently on display at Pima Air Museum, Tucson, AZ.

SR-71A 61-7952/Article 2003 – production start was January 27, 1964; rollout took place on December 8, 1964; ff March 24, 1965; pilot was ?; ? flts totaling 79.47 hrs. Lost on January 25, 1966, near Tucumcari, NM. While in a 60° bank at 3.17 Mach and 80,000 ft, the right engine suffered an un-start. Aircraft disintegrated. Lockheed RSO Jim Zwayer was killed in the bailout; Lockheed Test Pilot Bill Weaver survived even though he never ejected; the aircraft disintegrated around him.

SR-71A 61-7953/Article 2004 – production start, January 27, 1964; rollout, December 8, 1964; ff June 4, 1965 with Weaver/Andre as crew; ? flts totaling 290.2 hrs; On December 18, 1969, near Shoshone, CA, an in-flight explosion led to USAF pilot Lt. Col. Joe Rogers and RSO Lt. Col. Garry Heidelbaugh to eject. Both survived. No explanation for the explosion was ever found.

SR-71A 61-7954/Article 2005 – production start, April 8, 1964; rollout took place on February 15, 1965; ff July 20, 1965 with Weaver/Andre as crew; ? flts totaling ? hrs; last flight was April 11, 1969, at Edwards AFB, CA. While doing maximum weight take-off tests, the left main gear tires blew causing a fire which engulfed the entire aircraft. USAF pilot Lt. Col. Bill Skliar and RSO Maj. Noel Warner escaped.

SR-71A 61-7955/Article 2006 – production start was April 8, 1964; rollout took place on March 24, 1965; ff was August 17, 1965; ? flts totaling 1,993.7 hrs; last flight was January 24, 1985. Aircraft was assigned to flight test for its entire operational career flying primarily out of Lockheed's flight-test facility, Air Force Plant 42. Site 2, Palmdale, CA. Currently on display at Edwards AFB, CA.

SR-71B 61-7956/Article 2007 – production start was June 18, 1964; rollout took place on May 20, 1965; ff was November 18, 1965; crew as Gilliland/Belgeau; ? flts totaling 3,760 hrs before being turned over to the NASA; last flight was ??/??/98. Had 93 NASA flights. This aircraft was the first SR-71 to be delivered to the US Air Force at Beale AFB, CA on January 7, 1966. Currently on display at Kennedy AFS, Cape Canaveral, FL.

SR-71B 61-7957/Article 2008 – production start was August 28, 1964; rollout took place on June 21, 1965; ff was December 10, 1965; crew as Gilliland/Eastham; ? flts totaling ? hrs; last flight was January 11, 1968. Crashed on approach to Beale AFB when instructor pilot Lt. Col. Robert G. Sowers and his "student" Capt. David E. Fruehauf were forced to eject about seven miles from Beale after loss of control. Aircraft had suffered a double generator failure followed by a double flameout (caused by fuel cavitation). It impacted upside down.

SR-71A 61-7958/Article 2009 – production start was October 1, 1964; rollout took place on July 22, 1965; ff December 15, 1965; crew was Weaver/Andre; ? flts totaling 2,288.9 hrs; last flight was February 23, 1990. During July of 1976, this aircraft was used to set the world's absolute speed record of 2,193 mph and the 1,000 km closed-course record of 2,092 mph. Both records stand as of this writing. Was flown from Beale AFB, CA, to Robins AFB, GA, for delivery to the Museum of Aviation on February 23, 1990.

SR-71A/*Big Tail* 61-7959/Article 2010 – production start was November 3, 1966; rollout took place on August 19, 1965; ff January 19, 1966; crew was Weaver/Andre; ? flts totaling 866.1 hrs. First flight of *Big Tail* conversion was December 3, 1975; last flight was October 29, 1976. Currently on display at the Air Force Armament Museum, Eglin AFB, Ft. Walton Beach, FL.

SR-71A 61-7960/Article 2011 – production start was December 8, 1964; rollout took place on September 20, 1965; ff February 9, 1966; crew was Andre/Weaver; ? flts totaling 1,669.6 hrs; last flight February 27, 1990. Currently displayed at Castle AFB, CA.

SR-71A 61-7961/Article 2012 – production start, January 13, 1965; rollout took place on October 29, 1965; ff April 13, 1966; crew was Weaver/Andre; ? flts totaling 1,601.0 hrs; last flight February 2, 1977. Moved to the Kansas Cosmosphere and Space Center, Hutchinson, KS, during 1992.

SR-71A 61-7962/Article 2013 – production start was February 15, 1965; rollout took place on November 17, 1965; ff April 29, 1966; crew was Weaver/Belgan; ? flts totaling 2,835.9 hrs; last flight February 14, 1990. Aircraft was one of the reserve SR-71s that Congress mandated during FY89. Stored at the Lockheed SR-71 overhaul facility, Site 2, AF Plant 42, Palmdale, CA. During 2001 it was moved to the Imperial War Museum, Duxford, England, UK.

SR-71A 61-7963/Article 2014 – production start was March 16, 1965; rollout took place on December 16, 1965; ff June 9, 1966; crew was Weaver/Belgan; ? flts totaling 1,604.4 hrs; last flight was October 28, 1976. Aircraft is currently residing near the control tower at Beale AFB alongside a D-21B.

SR-71A 61-7964/Article 2015 – production start was April 14, 1965; rollout took place on January 19, 1966; ff May 11, 1966; crew was Weaver/Belgan; ? flts totaling 3,373.1 hrs; last flight March 20, 1990. Flown to Offutt AFB, Omaha, Nebraska, and moved to the Strategic Air Museum, Bellevue, NB. The museum has since relocated off of Interstate Highway 80, near Ashland, NB.

SR-71A 61-7965/Article 2016 – production start was May 13, 1965; rollout took place on February 17, 1966; ff June 10, 1966; crew was Weaver/Moeller; last flight October 25, 1967. The aircraft suffered an INS (Inertial Navigation System) failure while on a night flight. Capt. Roy St. Martin and his RSO, Capt. John Carnochan, ejected safely. The aircraft crashed near Lovelock, NV. This was the second SR-71 lost by USAF.

SR-71A 61-7966/Article 2017 – production start was June 14, 1965; rollout took place on March 21, 1966; ff July 1, 1966; crew was Gilliland/Belgan; ? flts totaling 64.4 hrs; last flight April 13, 1967. Crashed near Las Vegas, NM after Capt. Earle Boone and his RSO, Capt. Richard Sheffield, ejected safely. First SR-71A loss by USAF.

SR-71A 61-7967/2018 – production start was July 14, 1965; rollout took place on April 18, 1966; ff August 3, 1966; crew was Weaver/Andre; ? flts totaling 2,636.8 hrs; Had 9 NASA flights; last flight was February 14, 1990, when the aircraft was flown from Beale AFB, to Site 2, AF Plant 42, Palmdale, CA, for long-term storage and possible reactivation. First flight after reactivation and refurbishment took place on August 28, 1995. Then served with USAF, Det 2, Edwards AFB, CA. With the formal cancellation of the SR-71 reactivation program, the aircraft was relocated to Barksdale, AFB, LA, in 2002 for permanent display.

SR-71A 61-7968/Article 2019 – production start was August 15, 1965; rollout took place on May 17, 1966; ff October 10, 1966; crew was Weaver/Andre; ? flts totaling 2,279.0 hrs; last flight February 12, 1990. Served as a dedicated reserve aircraft until the final program cancellation. On September 21, 1999, was prepared for move to the Virginia Aviation Museum, Richmond, VA. Used to set endurance record for SR-71s on April 26, 1971. Maj. Thomas B. Estes and Maj. Dewain C. Vick flew the aircraft over 15,000 miles in 10 hrs. 30 min. Awards for this flight included the 1971 Mackay Trophy for the "most meritorious flight of the year" and the 1972 Harmon Trophy for the "most outstanding international achievement in the art/science of aeronautics".

SR-71A 61-7969/Article 2020 – production start was September 13, 1965; rollout took place on June 16, 1966; ff October 18, 1966; crew was Weaver/Belgan; ? flts totaling ? hrs.; last flight was May 10, 1970 near Korat Royal Thai Air Force Base (RTAFB), Thailand, when aircraft entered a storm and lost power in both engines.

SR-71A 61-7970/Article 2021 – production start was October 12, 1965; rollout took place on July 18, 1966; ff October 12, 1966; Weaver/Belgan; ? flts totaling 545.3 hrs; last flight was June 17, 1970, near El Paso, TX. Collision with tanker followed refueling.

SR-71A 61-7971/Article 2022 – production start was November 10, 1965; rollout took place on August 16, 1966; ff November 17, 1966; crew was Weaver/Moeller; ? flts totaling 3,512.4 hrs; last flight was 1998; on loan to NASA where it completed 9 flights (10 if turn-over flight counted, though it did not have a NASA crew). Transferred back to Air Force upon reactivation and was assigned to Det 2, Edwards AFB, CA. First flight after reactivation was on April 26, 1995. Fly-by SR-71 at Beale Air Fest '97, flown by Lt. Col. Gil Luloff. Transferred permanently to NASA. With the canceling of the Air Force program, moved to the Del Smith/Evergreen Museum, McMinnville, OR.

SR-71A 61-7972/Article 2023 – production start was December 13, 1965; rollout took place on September 15, 1966; ff December 12, 1966; crew was Weaver/Belgan; ? flts totaling 2,801.1 hrs; last flight March 6, 1990. Set record for speed over a recognized course – Los Angeles to east coast (coast to coast, 2,086 mi); time was 1 hour 7 min. 53.69 sec. with an average speed of 2,124.5 mph. The crew on the record run was Lt. Col. Ed Yielding and Lt. Col. Joseph T. Vida. Currently displayed by the Smithsonian's NASM, Washington, DC.

SR-71A 61-7973/Article 2024 – production start was January 14, 1966; rollout took place on October 17, 1966; ff February 6, 1967; crew was Weaver/Greenamyer; ? flts totaling 1,729.9 hrs; last flight was July 21, 1987. Currently on display at Blackbird Air Park, Palmdale, CA.

SR-71A 61-7974/Article 2025 – production start was February 14, 1966; rollout took place on November 14, 1966; ff February 16, 1967; crew was Weaver/Belgan; ? flts totaling ? hours; last flight was April 21, 1989. Aircraft crashed near the Philippines in the South China Sea.

SR-71A 61-7975/Article 2026 – production start was March 15, 1966; rollout took place on December 15, 1966; ff April 13, 1967; crew was Greenamyer/Belgan; ? flts totaling 2,854 hrs; last flight was February 28, 1990. Currently on display at March Air Force Reserve Base, Riverside, CA.

SR-71A 61-7976/Article 2027 – production start was April 13, 1966; rollout took place on January 18, 1967; ff May 13, 1967; crew was Gilliland/Belgan; ? flts totaling 2,985.7 hrs; last flight was March 27, 1990. On March 21, 1968, this aircraft flew the first operational mission from Kadena AB over Vietnam. Final flight from Beale AFB, CA, to the Air Force Museum, Wright-Patterson AFB, OH.

SR-71A 61-7977/Article 2028 – production start was May 12, 1966; rollout took place on February 15, 1967; ff June 6, 1967; crew was Gilliland/Greenamyer; aircraft destroyed on last flight October 10, 1968, from Beale AFB, CA.

SR-71A 61-7978/Article 2029 – production start was June 13, 1966; rollout took place on March 20, 1967; ff July 5, 1967; crew was Weaver/Belgan; last flight was July 20, 1972. Aircraft was lost at Kadena AB, Okinawa attempting to land with a severe crosswind.

SR-71A 61-7979/Article 2030 – production start was July 13, 1966; rollout took place on April 17, 1967; ff August 10, 1967; crew was Greenamyer/Belgan; ? flts totaling 3,321.7 hrs; last flight was March 6, 1990. Currently on display at Lackland AFB, TX.

SR-71A 61-7980/Article 2031 – production start was August 11, 1966; rollout took place on May 16, 1967; ff September 25, 1967; crew was Gilliland/Belgan; ? flts totaling 2,255.6 hrs; last flight before being reassigned to NASA was February 15, 1990. Assigned to and flown by NASA as #844. 56 NASA flights. With the grounding of all SR-71s and the end of all operations both at NASA and Air Force, last flight of NASA SR-71A, 980/844, was October 9, 1999. Aircraft to be parked in front of the NASA Dryden Flight Research Center on permanent display.

SR-71C 61-7981/Article 2000 – built from front end of SR-71 static test article and the aft end of YF-12 934; ff March 14, 1969; crew was Gilliland/Belgeau; ? flts totaling 556.4 hrs; last flight was April 11, 1976. The "Bastard" as the SR-71C was called, was moved to the museum at Hill AFB, UT, via an Air Force Reserve C-5A during September of 1990.

Cat. I Tests utilized 61-7950, 61-7951, and 61-7952
Cat. II Tests utilized 61-7953, 61-7954, and 61-7955
SR-71 Cat. I flight testing ran from December 22, 1964 thru 1967
SR-71 Cat. II flight testing ran from July 1, 1965 thru '67

SR-71 Chronology:

12/24/57 – First J58 engine run.
05/01/60 – Francis Gary Powers is shot down in a U-2 over the Soviet Union.
06/13/62 – SR-71 mock-up reviewed by Air Force.
07/30/62 – J58 completes pre-flight testing.
12/28/62 – Lockheed signs contract to build six SR-71 aircraft.
07/25/64 – President Johnson makes public announcement of SR-71.
10/29/64 – SR-71 prototype, 61-7950, delivered to Palmdale, CA.
12/07/64 – Beale AFB, CA, announced as base for SR-71.
12/22/64 – First flight of the SR-71 with Lockheed test pilot Bob Gilliland at AF Plant #42.
08/30/65 – Link-built SR-71 flight simulator loaded at night aboard an Air Force C-130E, 63-7893, under extreme secrecy. The flight to Beale AFB, CA, stopped at Bunker Hill AFB, IN, to refuel and then proceeded directly to Beale AFB, CA.
07/02/67 – Jim Watkins and Dave Dempster fly first international sortie in SR-71A, 61-7972, when the INS fails on a training mission and they accidentally fly into Mexican air space.
11/03/67 – A-12 and SR-71 conduct a reconnaissance fly-off. Results were questionable.
02/05/68 – Lockheed ordered to destroy A-12, YF-12, and SR-71 tooling.
03/08/68 – First SR-71A, 61-7978, arrives at Kadena AB (OL 8), Okinawa, to replace A-12s.
03/21/68 – First SR-71, 61-7976, operational mission flown from Kadena AB over Vietnam.
05/29/68 – CMSGT Bill Gormick begins the tie-cutting tradition of *Habu* crews neck-ties.
12/03/75 – First flight of SR-71A, 61-7959, in *Big Tail* configuration.
04/20/76 – TDY operations started at RAF Mildenhall, UK in SR-71A, 61-7972.
07/27-28/76 – SR-71A sets speed and altitude records (altitude in horizontal flight: 85,068.997 ft. and speed over a straight course: 2,193.167 mph).
08/??/80 – Honeywell starts conversion of AFICS to DAFICS.
01/15/82 – SR-71B, 61-7956, flies its 1,000th sortie.

11/22/89 – Air Force SR-71 program officially terminated.
01/21/90 – Last SR-71, 61-7962, leaves Kadena AB, Okinawa.
01/26/90 – SR-71 is decommissioned at Beale AFB, CA.
03/06/90 – Last flight of SR-71A, 61-7972, and the aircraft sets four world speed records.
07/25/91 – SR-71B, 61-7956/NASA 831, officially delivered to NASA Dryden Flight Research Center.
10/??/91 – Marta Bohn-Meyer becomes first female SR-71 crew-member.
09/28/94 – Congress votes to allocate $100 million for reactivation of three SR-71s.
04/26/95 – First reactivated SR-71A, 61-7971, makes its first flight after restoration by Lockheed.
06/28/95 – First reactivated SR-71 returns to Air Force at Det 2.
08/28/95 – Second reactivated SR-71A, 61-7967, makes first flight after restoration by Lockheed.
10/09/99 – The very last flight of the SR-71, 61-7980/NASA 844.

"BLACKBIRD" CREW DATA
(as of January 1990)

Total Flight Hours	53,490
Total 3+ Mach Time	11,675
Total Sorties	17,300
Total Operational Sorties	3,551
Total Operational Hours	11,008
Total Air Refuelings	25,862
Total Crew Members	284 (includes NASA and USAF Crews checked out in aircraft)

Cumulative Hours by Crews:

300 Hours	163
600 Hours	69
900 Hours	18
1,000 Hours	8
1,392.7 Hours	1

RECORDS: Speed and Altitude Records

May 1, 1965
YF-12A, 60-6936/1003
Absolute Altitude: 80,257.86 ft (24,390 m)
Absolute Speed Over a Straight Course: 2,070.101 mph
Absolute Speed Over a 500 km Closed Course: 1,688.889 mph
Absolute Speed Over a 1,000 km Closed Course: 1,643.041 mph

September 1, 1974
SR-71A 61-7972/2023
New York to London (Speed Over a Recognized Course): Distance: 3,490 miles. Time: 1 hr 54 min 56.4 secs.
Crew: Maj. James V. Sullivan, Pilot with Maj. Noel F. Widdifield, Reconnaissance Systems Operator

September 13, 1974
SR-71A 61-7972/2023
London to Los Angeles (Speed Over a Recognized Course): Distance: 5,645 miles. Time: 3 hrs 47 min 35.8 secs. SR-71A, 61-7972
Crew: Capt. Harold B. (Buck) Adams, Pilot, with Maj. Williams C. Machorek, Reconnaissance Systems Operator

July 27-28, 1976
SR-71A 61-7958
Altitude in Horizontal Flight: 85,068.997 ft (25,929.031 m) SR-71A.
World Absolute and World Class Altitude Record for Horizontal Flight – 85,068 ft, surpassing the previous record of 80,257 ft set by a Lockheed YF-12A during June 1965.
Crew: Capt. Robert C. Helt, Pilot and Major Larry A. Elliott, RSO.
Speed Over a Straight Course (15-25 km): 2,193.167 mph SR-71A. World Absolute and World Class Speed Record over a 15/25 km Straight Course - 2,193.167 mph, surpassing the previous record set by a Lockheed YF-12A during June 1965.
Crew: Capt. Eldon W. Joersz, Pilot and Major George T. Morgan Jr., RSO
Speed Over a Closed Course (1000 km): 2,092.294 mph SR-71A. World Absolute Closed Circuit Speed Record over a 1,000 km Course (The SR-71 is a Class C-1 Group III jet engine aircraft, same as the MiG-25) - 2,116 mph, surpassing the previous Absolute Speed Record of 1,853 mph and the World Class Speed Record of 1,815 mph set by a MiG-25 during October of 1967.
Crew: Maj. Adolphus H. Bledsoe, Jr., Pilot and Maj. John T. Fuller, RSO

March 6, 1990
SR-71A #61-7972/2023
Los Angeles to East Coast of USA (Speed Over a Recognized Course): Coast to Coast Distance: 2,086 miles. Time: 1 hr 07 min 53.69 secs. Average Speed: 2,124.5 mph
Los Angeles To Washington, DC: Distance: 1,998 miles. Time: 1 hr 04 min 19.89 secs. Average Speed: 2,144.83 mph
St Louis to Cincinnati: Distance: 311.44 miles. Time: 8 min. 31.97 secs. Average Speed: 2,189.94 mph
Kansas City to Washington, DC: Distance: 942.08 miles. Time: 25 min 58.53 secs. Average Speed: 2,176.08 mph
Crew for the four records: Ed Yielding and J.T. Vida

New York to London
1 hr 54 min 56.4 sec
London to Los Angeles
3 hrs 47 min 35.8 sec
West Coast to East Coast USA
1 hr 7 min 53.6 sec
Los Angeles To Washington, DC
1 hr 4 min 19.8 sec
St Louis To Cincinnati
8 min 31.9 sec
Kansas City to Washington, DC
25 min 58.5 sec

Operational Sorties Flown	3,551
Total Sorties Flown	17,300
Flight Hours (Operation)	11,008
Flight Hours (Total)	53,490
Mach 3 Time (Operation)	2,752
Mach 3 Time (Total)	11,675
Crew Members to Mach 3 Speed	284
VIPs to Mach 3 Speed	105
Total Persons to Mach 3 Speed	385

LOSSES:

A-12 60-6926/ Article 123
May 24, 1963

A-12, Article 123, was the second A-12 to fly but the first to crash. CIA pilot Ken Collins was flying an inertial navigation system test mission. After entering clouds, frozen water fouled the pitot-static boom and prevented correct information from reaching the standby flight instruments and the triple display indicator (TDI). The aircraft subsequently entered a stall and control was lost completely followed by the onset of an inverted flat spin. The pilot, Ken Collins ejected safely. The crash occurred near Wendover, UT. The wreckage was recovered in two days and persons at the scene were identified and requested to sign secrecy agreements. A cover story for the press described the accident as involving an F-105D that was carrying a nuclear weapon.

A-12 60-6939/ Article 133
July 9, 1964

A-12, Article 133, was lost on approach to Groom Lake/Area 51, following a 3.3 Mach-plus check flight. On approach, the flight controls locked up and Lockheed test pilot Bill Park was forced to eject at an altitude of 200 feet while at a bank angle of 45°. Park survived. The official report read:

"Aircraft No. 133 [S/N#939] was making its final approach to the runway when at altitude of 500 feet and airspeed of 200 knots it began a smooth steady roll to the left. Lockheed test pilot Bill Park could not overcome the roll. At about a 45 degree bank angle and 200 foot altitude he ejected. As he swung down to the vertical in the parachute his feet touched the ground, for what must have been one of the narrower escapes in the perilous history of test piloting. The primary cause of the accident was that the servos for the right outboard roll and pitch control froze."

SR-71A 61-7952/ Article 2003
January 25, 1966

Aircraft disintegrated during a high-speed, high-altitude test flight when it developed an engine un-start. The flight was to research and improve high Mach cruise performance by reducing trim drag. The un-start occurred during a turn at a speed in excess of 3.17 Mach and a bank angle of 60°. The nose pitched up and the aircraft broke apart at station 720. Lockheed pilot Bill Weaver was thrown clear (his ejection seat never left the plane). Weaver blacked out during the accident but recovered and landed on the ground safely. Tragically, his Reconnaissance System Officer (RSO), Jim Zwayer did not survive the high-G bailout. It is believed he died instantly from a broken neck before he ever became separated from the aircraft. His parachute opened normally and his body landed about a mile from Weaver's landing position. The accident occurred near Las Vegas, NM. The actual crash scene was the Mitchell Ranch.

M/D-21 60-6941
July 30, 1966

The second M-21 built and the only one to launch a D-21 reconnaissance drone. During the fourth launch of a D-21 the drone pitched down and struck the M-21 at the 715 splice, breaking it in half. Pilot Bill Park and Launch Control Officer (LCO) Ray Torrick stayed with the plane a short time before ejecting over the Pacific Ocean. Both crew members made safe ejections from the stricken aircraft, but Ray

Torrick suffered a broken arm during the ejection and, once he was in the water, was unable to get into his one-man life raft. Running out of oxygen, he opened his helmet visor. His suit quickly filled with water and he drowned. This terrible personal and professional loss resulted in "Kelly" Johnson's decision to cancel the M-21/D-21 program.

YF-12A 60-6934/ Article 1001
August 14, 1966

This aircraft, the first YF-12A built, was seriously damaged as a result of internal systems overheating during a landing accident at Edwards AFB. The rear half was later used to build the SR-71C (61-7981/2000) which flew for the first time on March 14 1969. The airframe remained intact but the damage to internal systems was beyond repair. The pilot, Colonel Vern Henderson and the FCO, Capt. Jim Cooney, suffered no injuries.

A-12 60-6928/ Article 125
January 5, 1967

Occurred during a training sortie flown from Groom Lake/Area 51, NV. Walter L. Ray, an employee of the CIA, joined Lockheed as a civilian pilot on November 7, 1962. During 60-6928's final flight, Ray did not receive a full fuel load from the tanker due to a second aircraft (chase plane) requiring fuel. He determined that he had sufficient fuel to return to Groom Lake/Area 51. He declared an emergency but the aircraft ran out of fuel at speed and altitude near Calienti, NV. The official accident report attributed the crash to a malfunctioning fuel quantity gauge. However, in his radio transmission prior to ejecting Ray stated "I have a loss of fuel and I do not know where it is going; I think I can make it (Groom Lake/Area 51)". Ray was forced to eject. Unfortunately the ejection seat separation sequence (which should have occurred at 16,000 feet) did not work as planned and Ray was killed on impact with the ground...still strapped to his seat

SR-71A 61-7950/ Article 2001
January 10, 1967

The prototype SR-71 was lost at Edwards AFB during an anti-skid braking system evaluation. The main landing gear tires blew and the resulting fire spread to the rest of the aircraft. Lockheed test pilot Art Peterson survived.

SR-71A 61-7966/ Article 2017
April 13, 1967

Lost during a night-time training flight after the aircraft entered a subsonic, high-speed stall. Pilot Capt. Earle M. Boone and RSO Capt. Richard E. (Butch) Sheffield ejected safely. The incident occurred 8 n. mi. SE of Las Vegas, NM. Sheffield estimates that 61-7966 had less than 50 hours of flight time at the time of the crash.

SR-71A 61-7965/ Article 2016
October 25, 1967

During a night flight, the inertial navigation system (INS) platform failed, leading to erroneous attitude information being displayed in the cockpit. There were no warnings to alert pilot Captain Roy L. St. Martin and RSO Captain John F. Carnochan of a problem. In total darkness, in a steep dive and with no external visual references available, the crew had little alternative but to leave the aircraft. They both ejected safely. The accident occurred near Lovelock, NV.

A-12 60-6929
December 28, 1967

Lost seconds into a Functional Check Flight (FCF) from Groom Lake/Area 51, NV. Piloted by CIA pilot Mele Vojvodich. The post-accident investigation revealed the stability augmentation system (SAS) had been incorrectly wired. The pilot was unable to control the aircraft and 100 feet above the runway he ejected safely. Vojvodich did not separate from the ejection seat and hit the ice covered lake at slight glancing angle. He survived with minor injuries.

SR-71B 61-7957/ Article 2008
January 11, 1968

The second SR-71B crashed on approach to Beale when instructor pilot Lt. Col. Robert G. Sowers and his "student" Capt. David E. Fruehauf were forced to eject. The plane had suffered a double generator failure over central Montana. All alternate landing sites were ruled out due to inclement weather. Their long straight-in approach to Beale AFB was without generators and the normal 10° nose up for landing resulted in fuel cavitation due to lack of electrical power to the boost pumps. Both engines failed. The crew ejected at 3,000 feet and only 7 miles from the end of the Beale AFB runway. Both IP and student pilot survived.

A-12 60-6932/ Article 129
June 5, 1968

This A-12 was lost over the South China Sea. CIA pilot Jack Weeks was flying what was to be one of the last crew proficiency flights from the 1129th SAS overseas A-12 base at Kadena AB, Okinawa. Weeks was to fly a Functional Check Flight (FCF) due to an engine change. He was last heard from 520 miles east of Manila, The Philippines. The loss was attributed to a catastrophic engine failure. There was no indication from *Birdwatcher* that Weeks tried to eject, nor was there any radio communication to indicate a problem with the A-12.

The functional check flight was due to replacement of the right engine. Taxi and take-off were uneventful, as evidenced by the reception of the required *Birdwatcher* "Code A" transmission and the lack of any HF transmissions from the pilot. Refueling, 20 minutes after take-off, was normal. At tanker disconnect, the A-12 had been airborne 33 minutes. The tanker crew observed the A-12 climbing on course in a normal manner. This was the last visual sighting of the aircraft. No further communications were received until 19 minutes later when a *Birdwatcher* transmission indicated right engine EGT was in excess of 860° C. Seven seconds later, *Birdwatcher* indicated the right engine fuel flow was less than 7,500 pounds per hour and repeated that EGT exceeded 860° C. Eight seconds later, *Birdwatcher* indicated that the A-12 was below 68,500 feet, and repeated the two previous warnings. This was the final transmission.

Several attempts were made to contact Weeks via HF-SSB, UHF, and *Birdwatcher*, but without success. Operation of recording and monitoring facilities at the home base continued until the time that the aircraft's fuel would have been exhausted, but no further transmissions were received. The aircraft was declared missing some 500 nautical miles east of the Philippines and 600 nautical miles south of Okinawa. The accident report declared that "No wreckage of aircraft number 129 (60-6932) was ever recovered. It is presumed totally destroyed at sea."

SR-71A 61-7977/ Article 2028
October 10, 1968

This SR-71A ended its career in flames by skidding 1,000 feet off the end of Runway 14 at Beale AFB on October 10, 1968. The take-off was aborted when the left brake and wheel assembly failed with pieces of titanium puncturing the wing fuel tanks. Without brakes and a relatively ineffective deployed drag chute, 61-7977, by now on fire, careened off the end of the runway. Maj. James A. Kogler, the RSO, ejected and was slightly injured. The pilot, Maj. Gabriel Kardong, elected to stay with the aircraft and survived. The front cockpit section of this aircraft is now on display in the Museum of Flight in Seattle, WA.

SR-71A 61-7954/ Article 2005
April 11, 1969

During maximum take-off weight testing at Edwards AFB, CA, the left main tires blew just at rotation. Shrapnel from the titanium wheel fragments ruptured the fuel tanks and started a fire that engulfed the aircraft. The pilot, Lt. Col. Bill Skliar and his RSO Major Noel Warner managed to escape uninjured.

SR-71A 61-7953/ Article 2004
December 18, 1969

Whilst climbing and accelerating after an in-flight refueling, a severe nose pitch-up occurred with the nose oscillating from side to side violently. This occurred even though the pilot, Joe Rogers, had the stick full forward. An irrecoverable high-speed stall followed and Rogers (who was Director of the Test Force) and RSO Lt. Col. Gary Heidelbaugh, ejected safely. Although the exact cause of this accident was never determined, it was postulated that an obstruction in the pitot static system could have caused a delay in data to the stability augmentation system (SAS) and this may have been a factor in this accident. The incident and the loss of the aircraft occurred near the southern end of Death Valley close to Shoshone, CA.

SR-71A 61-7969/ Article 2020
May 10, 1970

During an operational mission from Kadena AB, Okinawa, requiring penetration of North Vietnamese airspace, Maj. William E. Lawson, the pilot, initiated a normal full power climb. Stretching before him was a solid bank of cloud containing heavy thunderstorm activity which reached above 45,000 ft. Heavy with fuel, the aircraft was unable to maintain a high rate of climb and as it entered the turbulence both engines flamed out. The rpm dropped to a level too low for engine restart. Lawson and RSO, Maj. Gilbert Martinez ejected safely after the aircraft stalled. The crew was rescued near U Tapao, Thailand. The aircraft crashed near Korat RTAFB, Thailand.

SR-71A 61-7970/ Article 2021
June 17, 1970

Shortly after taking on 35,000 lb. of JP-7 fuel, the pilot encountered clear air turbulence (CAT) and the nose of 61-7970 pitched up, breaking the KC-135Q tanker's flying boom and subsequently hitting the bottom of the tanker. The pilot, Lt. Col. "Buddy" L. Brown and his RSO Maj. Mortimer Jarvis, ejected safely although both of Brown's legs were broken. The SR-71 crashed 20 miles east of El Paso, TX. The KC-135Q flew back to Beale AFB with a damaged vertical stabilizer and refueling boom and made an uneventful landing.

YF-12A 60-6936/ Article 1003
June 24, 1971

The third YF-12A built was lost at Edwards AFB on its sixty-third flight following an inflight fire caused by a fractured fuel line. High winds prevented an emergency landing and as a result, the pilot, Lt. Col. Ronald J. (Jack) Layton and systems operator (SO) William A. Curtis ejected just to the north of Rogers Dry Lake. Both crew members survived.

SR-71A 61-7978/ Article 2029
July 20, 1972

Nicknamed *Rapid Rabbit*, this SR-71A was written-off during the rollout phase of an extreme crosswind landing at Kadena AB, Okinawa. The pilot, Capt. Dennis K. Bush deployed the drag chute to combat the crosswind situation and slow the plane. A go-around was initiated and the chute was jettisoned when it became obvious that the rollout would not be successful. On the next landing attempt, the aircraft touched down slightly "hot". Unfortunately, there was now no drag chute to reduce the aircraft's speed. The pilot was unable to keep the aircraft on the runway. The landing gear hit a concrete barrier. During rollout, the aircraft suffered significant damage. Bush and the RSO, Capt. James W. Fagg escaped without injury. 61-17978 was buried at Kadena; however, some parts – including the rudders – later were used on other SR-71s.

SR-71A 61-7974/ Article 2025
April 21, 1989

Nicknamed *Ichi-Ban*, this aircraft was lost over the South China Sea and thus became the last of the *Blackbird* family to crash. Pilot Lt. Col. Dan House, flying at 3.0 Mach-plus, stated the left engine seized (engine compressor bearing froze causing disintegration) prior to the crash. Shrapnel from the engine hit the right-side hydraulic lines, causing loss of control. The pilot descended to 10,000 ft. and 400 kts before he and RSO Blair Bozek ejected. Both descended safely some 200 yards off the coast of Luzon Island in the Philippines. They were able to broadcast their position before abandoning their aircraft and were immediately rescued by native fisherman.

PERSONNEL:
The following is a list of all Lockheed *Skunk Works* personnel known to have been involved with A-12 development and flight testing (they are arranged, as closely as possible, by hierarchy):

Skunk Works:

C.L. "Kelly" Johnson	Vice President
Dick Boehme	Assistant
Dick Adair	Finance
Henry Combs	Structures Engr. Mgr.
Dave Robertson	Mech. Sys. Engr. Mgr.
Ed Martin	Elect. Sys. Engr. Mgr.
Dick Fuller	Aero. Engr. Mgr.
Ben Rich	Thermal/Propulsion Engineer Manager
L.D. McDonald	RCS Manager.
Mel George	Chem./Matls Engr.
John Ramsey	Material and Supply
Art Veirick	Shop Manager
Dick Greer	Asst. Shop Manager.
? Baker	Quality Manager
Art Bradley	Prog. Manager D-21
Ed Martin	Systems Engr. Mgr.
Dan Zuck	Cockpit/Ejection Seat
Sam Vose	Fuel System
Vic Sorenson	Mixer and Mechanical Flight Controls

Doug Cone	Air-conditioning
Rupe Trinadad	Hydraulics
Sam Murphy	Electrical
Bob Rapp	Hydraulic Actuators
Elmer Gath	Engine Installation Interface
Barney Switzer	Missile Ejector
Pete Law	Thermal Dynamics
John "Bert" McMaster	Aerodynamics
Henry Combs	Structural Design
Lorne Cass	Structural Loads
Ray McHenry	Structural Stress
Pete Garin (?)	Structural Test Engr.
Bob Murphy	Flutter Analysis
Bob O'Connell	Flutter Analysis
Fred Neuremburg	Flutter Analysis
Mel George	Chemical Analysis
Tom Haramis	Materials Analysis
Leon Gavette	Ground Handling Equip. and Transport Trailer
Jack Prosser	Tooling

Contractor Specialists:
Honeywell (Midwest Engineering)

John Larson	Flight Control
Ed Bolenbaugh	Air Data Systems
Fritz Schenk	Aerodynamics
Jim Murray	Flight Control Analysis
Howard Coble	Inertial Navigation

Pratt and Whitney (American Can Co.)

George Armbruster
Bob Skinner
Bob Ermish
Brud Swallow

Garrett-Air Research

Bill McCormick	Inlet Dynamics Analytical
Tom Cleary	Inlet Control Systems Engineer
Larry McKinley	Inlet Control Systems Engineer

Groom Lake/Area 51 Group

Larry Bohanan	Lockheed Flight Test Manager
Lou Schalk	First Pilot
Bill Park	Chase Pilot
Glen Fulkerson	Flight Test Engr. Mgr.
Dorsey Kammerer	Shop Manager
Jerry Carney	Asst. Shop Manager
Fritz Frye	Crew Chief Ship 121
Ward Klages	Machine Shop Supervisor
Gene Reynolds	Quality Control and Inspection Engineer Lead
Don Ritzke	Instrumentation Engineer Lead
Ralph Smead	Supply/Material Supervisor
Jim Godber	Electrical Supervisor
Red Harvey	Hangar Clerk
Don Heard	Instrumentation
Ted Young	Instrumentation
Harvey Smith	Instrumentation
Chuck Phiefer	Instrumentation
Elmer Rice	Parachute Rigger/Pilot's Equip.
Ralph Wiggins	Parachute Rigger/Pilot's Equip.
Glen Fisher	Flight Test Engineer
Keith Beswick	Flight Test Engineer
John Wallis	Flight Test Engineer
Jerry Gerrard	F-104 Crew Chief
Joe Gully	Photographer
Chuck Zarini	Inspection
Sam Holman	Mech. Supervisor

Barney Prim	Mechanic	Tom Bolich		*Fort Robertson Operations*	
Mike Tracey	Mechanic	Jim Conway		Dave Robertson	Engineering Chief
Nic Nicholson	*Constellation* Pilot	Pappy Solheim		Fritz Frye	Chief Mechanic
Bob Brewer	*Constellation* Pilot	Dave Kindell		Barney Prim	Mechanic
Dick Dallas	*Constellation* Pilot	Norb Alber		Mike Tracey	Mechanic
Billy Robinson	DC-3 Pilot	Dave Adrian		Tom Stevensen	Electrical Foreman
Warren Grossklaus	*Constellation* Flt. Engr.	Dave Butterworth		Grant Pelphrey	Electrician
Joe Rampone	*Constellation* Flt. Engr.	John Lee		Don Ritzke	Instrumentation Engr.
Billie Robinson	DC-3 Pilot and Crew Chief			Ted Young	Instrumentation Engr.

Groom Lake/Area 51 Air Force

Col. Robert Holbury	Commander
Col. Doug Nelson	Project Officer
Capt. Don Donahue	F-101
Lt. Col. Jack Thornton	Tanker Specialist
Sgt. Harry Martin	Fuel
Sgt. Clem Byzewski	Flight Operations
Sgt. George Lewis	Supply
Sgt. Robert Armentrout	Supply

Brud Swallow — P&W Technical Rep.
Bob Ermer — P&W Technical Rep.
John Bjostad — Honeywell
Bill Fox — Honeywell
Hank Kleeberg — Honeywell
Bill Harkins — Honeywell
? Campbell — Hamilton Standard

Chuck Phiefer — Instrumentation Engr.

Honeywell
Bill Fox — Flight Control Simulation
Ray Pesola — Flight Control Simulation
Jim Murray — Flight Control Simulation

Groom Lake/Area 51 CIA Security
Charlie White — Manager
Bill Canti — Assistant Manager

Agency Reps at Site
Norm Nelson
Jim Reichert (?)

SR-71 Accidents:

SR-71A, 61-7964, following gear collapse at Beale AFB, California.
US Air Force via Mike Relja collection

SR-71A, 61-7967, following overrun at Beale AFB, California.
US Air Force via Jim Goodall collection

SR-71A, 61-7974, nicknamed *Ichi Ban*, following retrieval from Pacific after engine failure.
Steve Myatt

SR-71A, 61-7977, forward fuselage awaiting disposal at Lockheed's Palmdale, California facility.
Jim Goodall

SR-71A, 61-7977, following wheel and tire failure during take-off from Beale AFB, California.
Appeal Democrat via Jim Goodall collection

SR-71A, 61-7978, nicknamed *Rapid Rabbit*, following cross wind landing at Kadena AB, Okinawa.
US Air Force via Jim Goodall collection

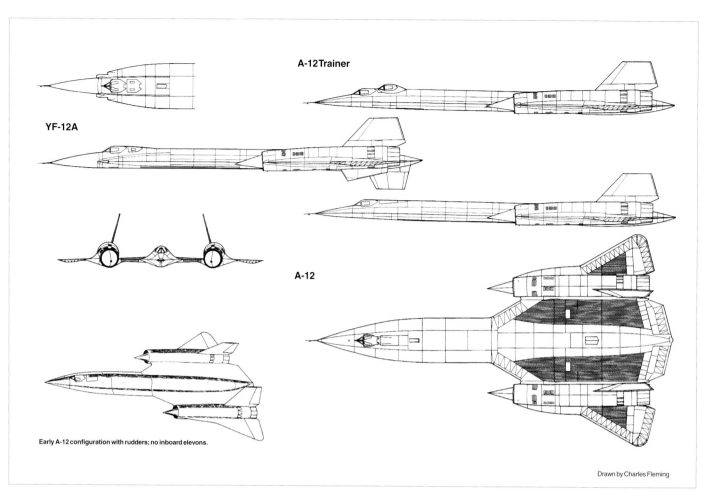

A-12 Trainer

YF-12A

A-12

Early A-12 configuration with rudders; no inboard elevons.

Drawn by Charles Fleming

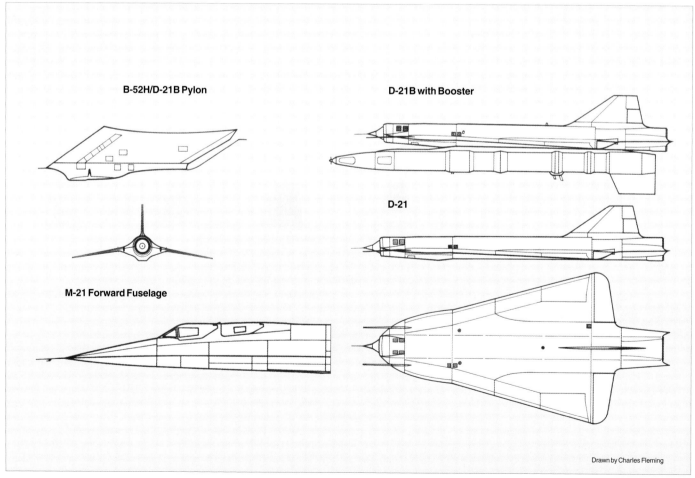

B-52H/D-21B Pylon

D-21B with Booster

D-21

M-21 Forward Fuselage

Drawn by Charles Fleming

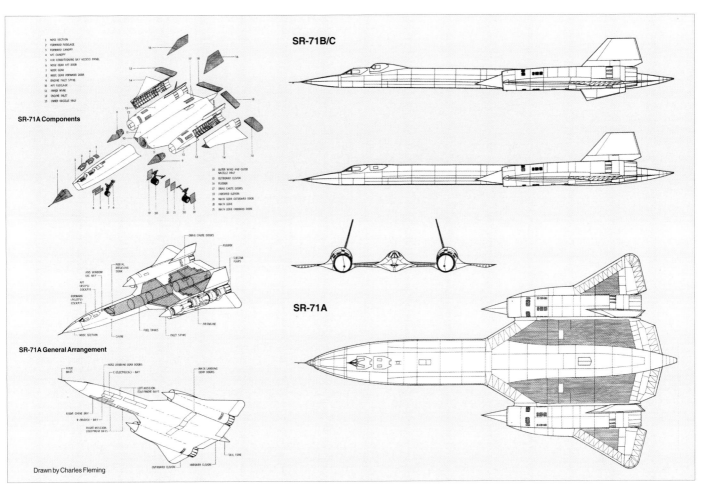

SR-71A Components

SR-71A General Arrangement

SR-71B/C

SR-71A

Drawn by Charles Fleming

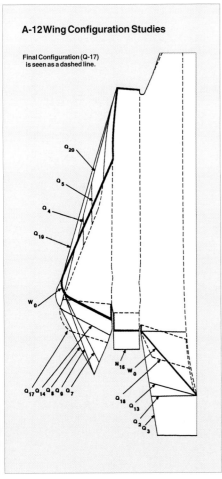

A-12 Wing Configuration Studies

Final Configuration (Q-17)
is seen as a dashed line.

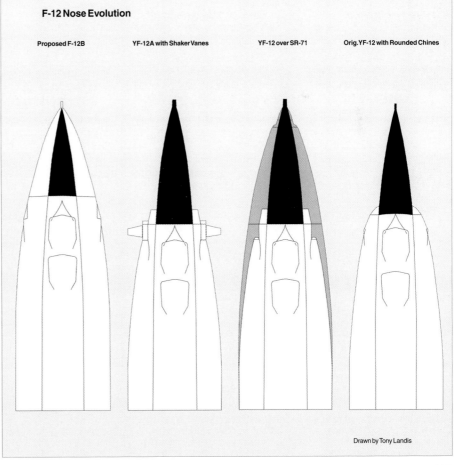

F-12 Nose Evolution

Proposed F-12B   YF-12A with Shaker Vanes   YF-12 over SR-71   Orig. YF-12 with Rounded Chines

Drawn by Tony Landis

US AIR FORCE
The New Century

Bob Archer

Covers current active duty flying wings and autonomous groups, with full details of formation and changes of designation, home stations, aircraft types, years assigned, and a history of each unit with its emblem in colour.

Almost 50 aircraft types currently in service or planned for the USAF are detailed including development, unit assignments, serial batches and an explanation of the role of each variant. Bases are examined, and a list of current tail codes is presented.

Softback, 280 x 216mm, 176 pages
190 colour photos, 127 unit emblems
1 85780 102 4 **£18.95/US $29.95**

THE X-PLANES X-1 to X-45
New, totally revised third edition

Jay Miller

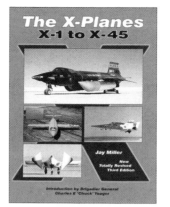

This new, totally revised and updated version of 'The X-Planes' contains a detailed and authoritative account of every single X-designated aircraft. There is considerable new, and newly-declassified information on all X-Planes.

Each aircraft is described fully with coverage of history, specifications, propulsion systems and disposition. Included are rare cockpit illustrations. Each X-Plane is also illustrated by a detailed multi-view drawing.

Hardback, 280 x 216mm, 440 pages
c980 photographs including colour,
approximately 250 drawings
1 85780 109 1 **£39.95/US $59.95**

VIETNAM AIR LOSSES
USAF, Navy and Marine Corps Fixed-Wing
Aircraft Losses in SE Asia 1961-1973

Chris Hobson

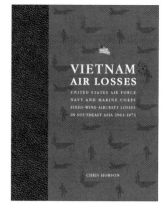

A most thorough review of all the fixed wing losses suffered over a twelve year period. The information is basically a chronological recording of each aircraft loss including information on unit, personnel, location and cause of loss. Information is also provided on the background or future career of some of the aircrew involved.

There are extensive orders of battle, plus an index of personnel, as well as statistics of the war, list of abbreviations, glossary of codenames and bibliography.

Softback, 280 x 215 mm, 288 pages
113 b/w photographs
1 85780 115 6 **£19.95/US $29.95**

Aerofax
MIKOYAN-GUREVICH MiG-15

Yefim Gordon

In this Aerofax, compiled from a wealth of first-hand Russian sources, there is a comprehensive history of every evolution of the Soviet Union's swept-wing fighter and its service. Notably in this volume, there are tables listing intricate details of many individual aircraft, a concept which would have been unthinkable in any publications only a few years ago.

There is extensive and detailed photo coverage, again from Russian sources, almost all of which is previously unseen.

Softback, 280 x 215 mm, 160 pages
214 b/w and 21 colour photographs,
7pp col sideviews, 18pp b/w drawings
1 85780 105 9 **£17.95/US $29.95**

Aerofax
YAKOVLEV Yak-25/26/27/28
Yakovlev's Tactical Twinjets

Yefim Gordon

During the 1950s and 1960s the Soviet design bureau Yakovlev was responsible for a series of swept-wing twin-engined jet combat aircraft, known in the west under various names including *Firebar*, *Flashlight*, *Mandrake*, *Mangrove*, *Brewer* and *Maestro*.

All the various models are covered in this Aerofax – as usual with a mass of new information, detail and illustrations from original Russian sources.

Softback, 280 x 215 mm, 128 pages
202 b/w and 41 colour photographs,
plus drawings and 21 colour side-views
1 85780 125 3 **£17.99/US $27.95**

Aerofax
BOEING KC-135
More Than Just a Tanker

Robert S Hoskins III

This book, written by a former USAF RC-135 crew commander, follows the development and service use of this globe-trotting aircraft and its many and varied tasks. Every variant, and sub-variant is charted, the histories of each and every aircraft are to be found within; details of the hundreds of units, past and present, that have flown the Stratotanker are given. This profusely illustrated work will interest those who have flown and serviced them as well as the historian and enthusiast community.

Softback, 280 x 216 mm, 224 pages
210 b/w and 46 colour photos
1 85780 069 9 **£24.95/US $39.95**

Aerofax
CONVAIR B-58 HUSTLER
The World's First Supersonic Bomber

Jay Miller

Instantly recognisable with its delta wing and 'coke bottle' area-ruled fuselage the B-58 was put into production for the US Air Force in the 1950s.

First published, in 1985, this is a revised edition, which takes a retrospective in-depth look at this significant aircraft, from design studies, through its development and comparatively short service life, to and beyond retire-ment. It includes yet more amazing material and 80 new illustrations, bringing the story up to date.

Softback, 280 x 216 mm, 152 pages
462 b/w, 15 colour, 100 line illusts.
1 85780 058 3 **£16.95/US $27.95**

A-12, F-12, D-21, M-21, SR-71

A-12, 60-6924, Article 121, during fuel dump tests.
Lockheed Martin via Tony Landis collection

A-12, 60-6925, Article 122, during in-flight refueling trials from KC-135A.
Lockheed Martin via Tony Landis collection

A-12, 60-6925, Article 122, taking on fuel from KC-135A.
Lockheed Martin via Tony Landis collection

A-12, 60-6926, Article 123, over the Sudan Crater, Nevada Test Site, Nevada.
Lockheed Martin via Tony Landis collection

Two views of A-12, 60-6931, Article 128, in *Black Shield* markings at the Minnesota Air Guard Museum, St. Paul, Minnesota. Both Jim Goodall

Unidentified A-12, prior to departure from Groom Lake/Area 51, probably during 1964.
Lockheed Martin via Tony Landis collection

YF-12A, 60-6934, Article 1001, during a test flight over Groom Lake/Area 51, prior to public disclosure by President Johnson.
Lockheed Martin via Tony Landis collection

YF-12A, 60-6934, Article 1001, during a test flight over Groom Lake/Area 51.
Lockheed Martin via Tony Landis collection

YF-12A, 60-6934, Article 1001, during flight test over the Nellis Range, Nevada.
Lockheed Martin via Tony Landis collection

YF-12A, 60-6934, Article 1001, in overall black scheme used throughout most of its later operational career.
Lockheed Martin via Tony Landis collection

YF-12A, 60-6936, Article 1003, with Hughes AIM-47A air-to-air radar-guided missile.
Lockheed Martin via Jim Goodall collection

YF-12A, 60-6936, Article 1003, over Mojave Desert, California during test flight. Lockheed Martin via Jim Goodall collection

MD-21, 60-6940, Article 134, during first D-21 captive test flight on December 22, 1964. Lockheed Martin via Jim Goodall collection

Mating of the first D-21 on M-21, 60-6940, Article 134, at Groom Lake/Area 51 during December of 1964.
Lockheed Martin via Jim Goodall collection

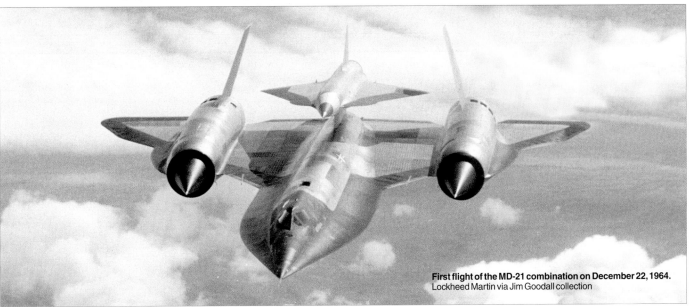

First flight of the MD-21 combination on December 22, 1964.
Lockheed Martin via Jim Goodall collection

MD-21, 60-6941, Article 135, departing from Groom Lake/Area 51.
Lockheed Martin via Jim Goodall collection

A-12 trainer, nicknamed the *Titanium Goose*, 60-6927, Article 124, departing from Groom Lake/Area 51. Lockheed Martin via Jim Goodall collection

A-12 trainer, nicknamed the *Titanium Goose*, 60-6927, Article 124, during training flight over the Nellis Test Range. Lockheed Martin via Tony Landis collection

SR-71A, 61-7950, Article 2001, at the beginning of its flight-test program from Lockheed's Palmdale, California facility. Lockheed Martin via Tony Landis collection

Last four SR-71s on the Building 309/310 production line.
Lockheed Martin via Tony Landis collection

NASA SR-71A, 61-7980/NASA 844, rolling out following landing at Edwards AFB. NASA via Tony Landis collection

SR-71A, 61-7972, in flight following major Lockheed overhaul.
Lockheed Martin via Tony Landis collection

SR-71A, 61-7968, with *Dolby* tail art.
Lockheed Martin via Jim Goodall collection

SR-71A, 61-7961, just south of Folsom Lake, California. Lockheed Martin via Jim Goodall collection

SR-71A, 61-7963, taking on fuel over the Sierra Nevada foothills, California. Ben Bowles via Jim Goodall collection

SR-71A, 61-7964, landing at Beale AFB, California. US Air Force via Jim Goodall collection

SR-71A, 61-7975, leaving dedicated hangar at Beale AFB, California. US Air Force via Jim Goodall collection

SR-71A, 61-7968, in flight over southern California.
Lockheed Martin via Jay Miller collection

Eleven SR-71s on the Beale AFB ramp at the end of the operational program during January of 1990. Lockheed Martin

Double exposure (both engines cannot be started at the same time) of NASA SR-71B, 61-7956/NASA 831, during TEB start. Tony Landis

NASA SR-71A, 61-7980/NASA 844. Tony Landis

The two reactivated SR-71As, 61-7967 and 61-7971 at Lockheed's Palmdale, California facility following upgrades. Lockheed Martin

SR-71A, 61-7961, in standard operational configuration. US Air Force via Jim Goodall

Two views of SR-71A, 61-7959, *Big Tail* with optical bar camera in tail. Both Art Haynes collection

SR-71B, 61-7956, over northern California.
Lockheed Martin via Jim Goodall collection

SR-71B, 61-7957, departing Beale AFB, California.
Lockheed Martin via Tony Landis collection

SR-71B, 61-7956/NASA 831, departing Edwards AFB, California. NASA/Jim Ross

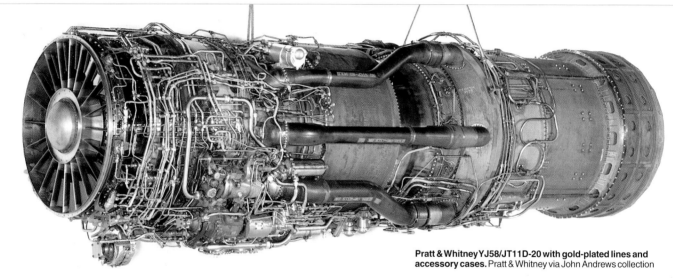

Pratt & Whitney YJ58/JT11D-20 with gold-plated lines and accessory cases. Pratt & Whitney via John Andrews collection

Pratt & Whitney Model "K" J58/JT11D-20 in full afterburner at Pratt & Whitney's West Palm Beach, Florida, test facility. Pratt & Whitney via John Andrews collection